AMERICA'S
UNDECLARED WAR

Also by Daniel Lazare

THE FROZEN REPUBLIC:
How the Constitution Is Paralyzing Democracy

AMERICA'S UNDECLARED WAR

What's Killing Our Cities and How We Can Stop It

D A N I E L   L A Z A R E

Harcourt, Inc.

New York   San Diego   London

Requests for permission to make copies of any part of the work should be mailed to the following address: Permissions Department, Harcourt, Inc., 6277 Sea Harbor Drive, Orlando, Florida 32887-6777.

www.harcourt.com

Library of Congress Cataloging-in-Publication Data
Lazare, Daniel.
America's undeclared war: what's killing our cities and how we can stop it /
Daniel Lazare—1st ed.
p. cm.
Includes bibliographical references and index.
ISBN 0-15-100552-4
1. Suburbs—United States. 2. Suburbs—Economics aspects—United States.
3. Inner cities—United States. I. Title.
HT352.U6 L39 2001
307.76'0973—dc21   00-050567

Designed by Susan Shankin
Text set in Galliard
Printed in the United States of America
First edition

K J I H G F E D C B A

FOR SOPHIE, WHO MUCH PREFERS J. K. ROWLING

CONTENTS

INTRODUCTION: AMERICA THE PARADOXICAL

It is my conjecture that the fundamental
mechanism for social evolution in general is to be
found in the automatic inability not to learn.
JURGEN HABERMAS, *LEGITIMATION CRISIS*

AMERICA IS in the grips of a long-running urban crisis—although *how* long-running most Americans have no idea. Since the late 1970s, the media have been filled with a lot of bubbly talk about an urban renaissance supposedly underway, about skyscrapers, condos, and boutiques springing up in formerly deserted downtowns, about slums like New York's Lower East Side suddenly turning pricey and fashionable, about real-estate prices rising with all the velocity of a fin de siècle Internet IPO. Remarkably, some of it is even true. When film director Martin Scorsese shot his classic psycho-thriller *Taxi Driver* in the early 1970s, he had no trouble achieving just the right urban-noir look. New York City's streets were so gritty, so rancid, so suffused with violence that he had to do little more than point his camera and shoot. But when he recently made

Bringing Out the Dead, a bleak look at the life of an all-night emergency medical technician, he had to have his crew scatter prop garbage about the streets in order to get anywhere near the same effect.[1] In the ensuing twenty-five years or so, even Hell's Kitchen had grown spiffy and upbeat.

This is quite a change. Nonetheless, success stories like these should not be allowed to obscure the broader picture. Impressive as it may be, New York's revival remains not only heavily Manhattan-centric, but centered on the two-thirds of Manhattan that lies south of Columbia University on the West Side and Ninety-sixth Street on the East. Otherwise immense stretches of Harlem and Central Brooklyn remain empty and windblown, while if the South Bronx has risen at all from the depths of the 1970s, it is not immediately apparent to the casual observer. In regional metropolitan centers such as Atlanta, Houston, and Cleveland, the contrast is in some ways even starker. In between the glitzy, Manhattan-style business and hotel districts and equally splashy suburbs lie block after block of depopulated slums. While financial services and a few other business categories continue to gravitate downtown, the dominant trend is in the other direction, i.e., toward the sprawling, low-tax suburbs. Not surprisingly, a study by the Department of Housing and Urban Development of some seventy-seven metropolitan regions between 1990 and 1993 found that 97 percent of new businesses and 87 percent of new jobs were being created not in the cities but in the great hyper-sprawl beyond.[2] This is why inner-city residents often have to travel hours in order to reach their fast-food or cleaning jobs out amid the malls, office parks, and "planned unit developments."[3] Instead of springing up where they are needed, jobs are being created where they are not.

The outflow of jobs and business is evident not only in aging industrial cities with their racial problems and crime, but even in leafy, middle-class towns that journalists invariably describe as looking like something out of a Norman Rockwell painting (meaning that the people in them are white). The affluent small town of Fairfield, Connecticut, for instance, doesn't have a crack house in sight. Yet the owner of a local pizzeria not long ago was bemoaning the loss of customers who once jammed his counter from noon until the early evening. "When I opened here twenty-three years ago, it was alive and really kicking," recalled Mike Jordanopoulos. "People filled the streets and sidewalks all the time." Now, with a dozen storefronts having fallen vacant in less than a year, he added that he is lucky if he gets a full crowd just for lunch. "Not too many days go by that I don't hear about another business in serious trouble down here or about to go out."[4]

Similar complaints can be heard in Latin America, portions of Europe, and other areas of the globe that have adopted America as their development model. All are seeing a net transfer of economic activity from the cities to the malls and shopping centers that are springing up with astonishing rapidity in the great beyond. If this were the result of hard times, it might be understandable. But from the beginning it has been the result of good economic times, at least as such things are measured. The more the economy booms, the more development surges out beyond the city line. The more it surges, the more the affluent consumers feel it is in their interest to travel in their minivans and SUVs out to where the taxes are low and the parking ample. Urban centers are left high and dry as a consequence. Where a few of the larger ones are able to carve out specialized roles for themselves as financial and entertainment centers, those that have not achieved a certain critical mass fall by the wayside.

Any number of explanations have been offered up for this long-term decline. Various urban experts have criticized city governments for incompetence or corruption, for being too tough on business or too weak, for failing to opt for creative solutions such as downtown pedestrian zones or failing to tear up those same pedestrian zones when they turned out to attract mainly homeless people and truants. Yet, a century ago, when big-city politicians were far more corrupt and incompetent than they are now, the great problem besetting urban America was not a dearth of people and jobs, but an overabundance. Cities were so crowded, so dense with workers and jobs, so crackling with energy and conflict, that they seemed ready to explode. Rather than spending their days trying to figure out how to lure more people downtown, reformers, social workers, and other agents of moral uplift spent their days trying to figure out how to persuade the teeming masses to desert their overcrowded slums for the supposedly healthier life out beyond the city gates. Yet the slum dwellers refused to go. They were so attached to the shops, the pushcart vendors, and the crowded streets that reformers like Jacob Riis felt they had to all but pry them loose with a crowbar. Today, the problem is the opposite: how to lure middle-class suburbanites downtown when their every instinct draws them to the office park or mall.

Clearly, what we are dealing with here is something a bit more basic than the errors or misjudgments of this or that petty politician. What is at issue, rather, is a trend that has persisted through the better part of the twentieth century and looks likely to continue at least into the early part of the twenty-first. The trend is not the result of "policy making," as such things are understood in Washington, but something far deeper. In a sense, it is the result of America itself, not the land and people but the political structure of which they are a part. The United States is not just a spot on the map. Rather, it is a system of customs, laws, and principles governing the individual, society, the economy, and the state. If American cities are in such poor shape, it is because something in the American structure has turned profoundly hostile. Where America produced bigger and bigger cities in the nineteenth century almost against its will, it has spent much of the twentieth knocking them down like tenpins. Any attempt to understand why necessarily means burrowing into the inner works of America's most basic political institutions. Coming to grips with American de-urbanization means coming to grips with America itself, which, as any number of political analysts have discovered over the years, is no easy task.

Many people helped with this project whom I would like to acknowledge. Charles Komanoff, one of the country's most creative thinkers in the field of transportation, energy, and urban economics, has been a continuous source of advice and encouragement. Francis C. Moon, J. C. Ford Professor of mechanical and aerospace engineering at Cornell and a leading expert on magnetic-levitation transportation, was generous with his time and assistance. Doug Henwood has provided ample quantities of economic insight. My agent, Tina Bennett, was extremely helpful in getting this project off the ground, while my editor, Walt Bode, was, as usual, tireless in whipping it into shape. Anne Bass has been wonderfully supportive and encouraging, something for which I am truly thankful. Two institutions to which I feel especially grateful are the New York Public Library and Columbia University. For both these institutions, I am simply one anonymous figure among many scribbling notes in the reading room or prowling the stacks. Yet for any writer or researcher, institutions like these are treasures beyond rubies. The historian Barbara Tuchman reports that King Charles V of France was known as Charles le Sage, or the Wise, because in 1373 he owned a library of over a thousand works.[5] Yet these two library systems have millions of volumes each. As information retrieval systems, they far outclass the Internet. They are examples of the cultural and intellectual riches that only a modern city can offer.

· · · · · · · · · · · · ·

A final note: Before writing these last few words, I left my apartment on the Upper West Side for a few moments to pick up some groceries. I exited my front door, strolled half a block to a fruit-and-vegetable stand, selected some onions from an open bin, and handed them to the lady behind the counter. Then I went back home. As urban experiences go, it was utterly forgettable. I didn't linger before any shop windows, didn't pause to enjoy the fresh air, and didn't exchange neighborly words with passersby in the street. I didn't do any of the things that the Jane Jacobs school of urbanology says city dwellers are supposed to do in order to strengthen the urban fabric. I simply paid my money and left.

But then, I didn't do what so many other Americans routinely do in running such a simple errand. I didn't strap myself into a three-thousand-pound vehicle and generate clouds of pollution as I traveled down some hideous commercial strip. I didn't turn on the radio so I could be bombarded by muffler-shop commercials and screaming DJs. I didn't pull into some trash-strewn parking lot belonging to an oversize supermarket. I didn't engage in a state-licensed activity, thereby subjecting myself to a higher level of oversight by the police. I didn't do any of these things, because I didn't have to. Instead, I was free to set out on my own two feet and walk. Amid all the endless self-congratulation over our glorious Constitution and peerless Bill of Rights, it is an example of the sort of urban freedom that Americans have let slip away. Perhaps in the coming years we can begin to win it back.

New York City

21 December 2000

1

THE CITY,
THE INDIVIDUAL,
AND THE NATION

*You know, this country got started by people who
wanted a good letting-alone from government.*

BILL CLINTON

*They [the Americans] keep telling us how
successful their system is. Then they remind us not
to stray too far from our hotel at night.*

EUROPEAN OFFICIAL AT AN INTERNATIONAL
ECONOMICS CONFERENCE IN DOWNTOWN DENVER

AMERICANS TEND to view the past through the lenses of the present.
Because things are the way they are, they assume history unfolded in
order to make them that way. If the United States is a free country, then
the story of America must be one of freedom struggling to break through
to the surface. If America enshrines limited government, then the story
must be one of a people struggling to break free of kings, bishops, and
federal bureaucrats so as to live where they please and how they please,

without "big gummint" telling them otherwise. If America is antiurban, as anyone can attest who has surveyed its shopping malls, subdivisions, and sea-to-sea parking lots, then its story must be one of a people struggling to break away from crowded cities so as to live in glorious isolation in their own homes, on their own turf, with as much space between them and their neighbors as America's ample geography would permit.

Politicians encourage this sort of thinking because it reinforces faith in the status quo and because, by manipulating the past, they figure they can control the present and keep themselves in power. But American history is far richer and more contradictory than this sort of simpleminded teleology would suggest. Freedom did not merely unfold in America. Rather, it evolved, transforming itself both in shape and meaning and at times threatening to turn itself inside out. At various times and among various people, it meant the freedom to enslave or the freedom of slaves to rise in revolt, the freedom to organize unions or the freedom to break them. Despite Bill Clinton's celebration of limited government, the idea that the overriding goal in America was to give ordinary people "a good letting-alone" would have come as an utter surprise to a New England Puritan, a nineteenth-century abolitionist, or a turn-of-the-century labor radical.

As for antiurbanism, although it might appear from the current layout of American society that the overriding goal has always been to put as much distance between oneself and one's neighbors as possible, this is also far from the case. The first English settlers who set foot in North America reacted in various ways to the great empty continent stretching out before them. Some did indeed see it as an opportunity to melt into the wilderness so that "no man should live where he can hear his neighbor's dog bark."[1] But others saw it as an opportunity not to escape society but to join forces with their fellow colonists so as to build a new kind of society, one that would in fact be more tightly knit and communal than what they had left behind.

America's love-hate relationship with the city is no simple matter. Rather, it is a function of its complicated social and intellectual development. The three great waves of English settlement in the seventeenth century reflected the full range of attitudes vis-à-vis society, the community, and the individual. At one extreme were the Puritans, who for the most part were urban to begin with—tradesmen, shopkeepers, and other middling sorts, from London and the smaller cities. They were a people stamped with the city not only in terms of how they lived and worked but how they worshiped and thought.[2] They conceived of Christianity not as a faith of lonely believers wandering in the desert but as a highly social religion revolving around the congregation and community, terms that in Puritan theology were more or less interchangeable. To quote Edmund S. Morgan, the great scholar of New England Puritanism, they came to the New World "not merely to save their souls but to establish a 'visible' kingdom of God, a society where a smooth, honest, civil life would prevail in family, church, and state."[3] This social vision shaped the pattern of development from the outset. The Puritan authorities did everything in their power to discourage stragglers and loners, and colonists were required to settle in compact settlements centering on the church. In 1635, a Massachusetts law ordered that "no dwelling house shall be built above half a mile from the meeting house in any new plantation . . . without leave from the Court, except mill houses and farm houses [of] such as have dwelling houses in some town."[4] In 1639, the Fundamental Orders of Connecticut stipulated that the governor must "be alwayes a member of some approved congregation" and that only freemen who have "beene admitted Inhabitants by the major part of the Towne wherein they live" would have the right to vote.[5] As in ancient Greece, politics were inseparable from the polis.

The Puritan town, moreover, was not just a unit of local government as Americans now understand the term, but something a good deal more powerful. The community regulated all aspects of daily life, no matter how private. The farming community of Springfield, Massachusetts, for instance, passed a series of laws in 1649 regulating whom residents could sell their property to, whom they could allow to live in their homes, and how much they could pay their hired hands. Residents were required to attend the annual town meeting or pay a two-shilling fine and, due to a local shortage, were forbidden to export lumber to neighboring communities.[6] In Boston, the town fathers had a say in everything from taxation, welfare, and the local militia to wages and prices, grazing rights, and land distribution. The system was a direct continuation of the medieval English parish in which the local churchwarden or constable had set the rules for local parishioners right down to the hours when they could play cards or host banquets.[7]

The community was sovereign. Extreme attitudes like these made for an extreme form of urban geography, especially in Boston where settlers squeezed themselves onto a narrow spit of land known as the Shawmut Peninsula. Although the Boston Common suggests an ideal of spaciousness and design, the development pattern couldn't have been more intensive. Despite the vast landscape stretching before them, the first Bostonians built their homes so that they squeezed up against one another like hungry diners at a buffet. Rather than laying them out in some regular fashion, they allowed their streets to grow organically out of narrow footpaths wandering this way and that. At a time when broad avenues were the urban ideal back home in England, a group of royal commissioners complained about the Bostonians in 1665: "Their houses are generally wooden, their streets crooked, with little decency and no uniformity."[8] It was not a city built for troops to parade through, for courtiers to strut about in their finery, or for other displays of social status or political power. Rather, it was a dense jumble that merchants, artisans, laborers, and nearby farmers created for their own needs and purposes.

Much of this pattern of urban development had to do with history and timing. The Massachusetts Bay Colony was settled in the 1630s, a decade prior to the dramatic events back home in England when the Puritans' coreligionists would overthrow the monarchy, chop off the head of King Charles I, and establish a short-lived English republic under Oliver Cromwell. The Puritans were holy warriors, never happier than when they were girding for battle or wrestling with their souls. But because the "commonwealthmen" of Massachusetts had emigrated prior to the great confrontation with Charles I, they were left frozen in a state of perpetual readiness for the showdown that never came—always prepared, always morally engaged. They instinctively formed themselves into close-knit communities in which stolid burghers could stand shoulder to shoulder against the armies of the king.

In the Middle Atlantic region, the pattern unfolded somewhat differently. New Amsterdam was as jumbled and dense as any seventeenth-century Dutch town. But for reasons that were also historical, Philadelphia was laid out along contrary lines. Rather than a product of the great buildup to the confrontation with Charles I, the Quaker migration of the 1680s was the result of the great letdown that followed. Originally a militant revolutionary sect, the Quakers renounced violence after the collapse in 1660 of the Cromwellian republic, made their peace with the newly restored monarchy of Charles II, and turned away from politics altogether.[9] From the extreme left of English politics, they gravitated more and more to the right. William Penn's plans for a garden city on the banks of the Delaware, consequently, reflected all the conservatism of the Restoration, its fear of crowds and tumult, its horror of extremism, and its overriding desire for peace, stability, and equilibrium. He conceived of Philadelphia in spacious, horizontal terms as a collection of widely separated homes grouped around public squares connected to one another by broad avenues. "Let every house be placed," he declared, ". . . in the middle of its plat . . . that there may be ground on each side for gardens or orchards, or fields, that it may be a green country town, which will never be burnt, and always be wholesome."[10]

This was the city as genteel showcase rather than a dangerous warren of back-alley slums seething with conspiracy and revolt, a place of brotherly love rather than fratricidal warfare. Yet, ironically, Penn's design didn't stick. At a time when water transport was vastly cheaper than land transport, merchants and tradesmen had an incentive to cluster around the waterfront, their window to the outside world. They bypassed Penn's spacious squares and squeezed their brick row houses as tightly together along the Delaware as if they were back home on the Thames.[11] High-density urban development asserted itself in this portion of the New World whether the leaders liked it or not.

Farther to the south, however, an opposite pattern was taking shape. Here the notion of the New World as an escape from urbanism did pertain. Rather than the confluence of one or two great rivers, the Virginia colony grew up along western reaches of the Chesapeake Bay, where the shore "frayed into a vast dendritic pattern of fine threads," to quote the geographer D. W. Meinig.[12] Rather than concentrating human activity around a single harbor or riverfront—the case with Boston, New Amsterdam, and Philadelphia—this intricate watery network dispersed it among innumerable rivers and inlets. As a result, the region never developed a proper port until the rise of Baltimore nearly a century later. Instead, each plantation functioned as its own miniport as dozens of ships a year sailed virtually to the doorstep to pick up tobacco and drop off goods.

The consequences for Virginia's social and intellectual development were profound. Without a proper port, the colony had nowhere for a city to take shape, no place for merchants, artisans, stevedores, and other urban types to put down roots. An underdeveloped society sprang up around scattered, semiautarchic estates in which freedom and baronial independence were viewed as one and the same thing. "There are no lords," a seventeenth-century French visitor observed of the Virginia planters, "but each is sovereign on his own plantation."[13] Because the ship captains served as the essential conduits in terms of trade and communication with the outside world, Virginia remained economically and politically stunted. Although the planter might be a person of considerable administrative ability, his business skills withered the more he was cut off from commercial society. The result was a vicious cycle in which declining business abilities led to a growing sense of isolation, dependency, and, finally, hostility. The more they lorded over their own private estates, the more the Virginia planters were at odds with the various representatives of the larger money culture with whom they dealt—with the Scottish factors, who advanced them money from one growing season to the next and whom they accused of conspiring to keep them in debt; with London tobacco merchants, whom they accused of driving down tobacco prices; and with New England peddlers, who swarmed over the countryside like flies. "Some of these Banditti anchor near my estate, for the advantage of traffiquing with my slaves," complained one planter to a friend in Massachusetts. ". . . I am now prosecuting one of them whose name is Grant, for this crime, and have evidence sufficient to convict him! I wish you would be so kind as to hang up all your Felons at home, and not send them abroad to discredit their country."[14] Selling was felonious, commerce was thievery, peddlers were swindling upstarts who should be taken out and hung—this was the centuries-old cry of the backwoods nobility about a money culture it found both irritating and incomprehensible.

The city, of course, was where the money culture originated. Although both were English, Virginians and New Englanders represented opposite poles of Anglo-Saxon society—socially, politically, theologically, and intellectually. The New Englanders were Roundheads, supporters of Oliver Cromwell and Parliament, whereas Virginia was dominated by Cavaliers, gallant, longhaired royalists, whose rural way of life in England had been disrupted by the political turmoil of the 1640s and whose one goal in moving to America was to re-create the existence they had known back home. The life they made for themselves in Virginia was militantly agrarian—"solitary and unsociable," as one traveler put it, "confused and dispersed."[15] Where the New England countryside was thickly populated and neatly groomed, Virginia, with its emphasis on extensive rather than intensive cultivation, had a wild, half-deserted look even after a century of colonization. According to Meinig:

It was an unkempt landscape, a disorderly pattern of natural woods and swamps, half-cleared land studded with stumps and skeletons of giant trees, old fields disappearing under a ragged regrowth, with farming confined to a patch of tobacco and few small fields of corn and wheat. . . . It was a form of shifting cultivation, and could only operate where land was cheap and held in large amounts.[16]

In 1662, London officials urged Virginia planters to "build towns upon every River" on the grounds that they would add "very much to their security and in time to their profit, of which they cannot have a better evidence and example than from their neighbors of New England."[17] But such urgings were to no avail—the planters would have none of it. "[N]either the interest nor inclinations of the Virginians induce them to cohabit in towns," a visiting clergyman observed some sixty years later.[18] The few towns that did manage to take root in such thin soil were never more than half-formed. Jamestown was hardly more than a disheveled, overgrown village, while Annapolis and Williamsburg had no more than a few hundred permanent residents each. Smaller communities consisted of a few houses built around a courthouse, prison, pillory, and stocks. It was a layout reflective of "a society that was not only completely rural but was at bottom peculiarly coercive and chaotic: a small elite poised upon a large body of persons in some form of legal servitude—slaves, bondsmen, short-term tenants."[19] It was antiurban because it was coercive and chaotic, and coercive and chaotic because it was antiurban.

Antiurbanism was particularly pronounced in one of Virginia's most famous sons, Thomas Jefferson. As a leader of the struggle against British imperialism and hence against the British-led urban-mercantile culture, Jefferson disliked even the overgrown hamlet of Williamsburg and, as governor in 1780, seized the first opportunity to transfer the state capitol to Richmond, some forty miles to the west.[20] He built his lonely hilltop villa,

Monticello, so that it faced west also—away from civilization, that is, and toward the great empty frontier. As a young man, he had copied out long extracts from the Roman poet Horace celebrating the calm and beauty of pastoral life.[21] In his *Notes on the State of Virginia*, written in 1784, he observed that:

> Those who labour in the earth are the chosen people of God, if ever he had a chosen people, whose breasts he has made his peculiar deposit for substantial and genuine virtue. . . . The mobs of great cities add just so much to the support of pure government, as sores do to the strength of the human body.[22]

Although not as well known, a letter he wrote in 1800 to Dr. Benjamin Rush concerning a yellow fever epidemic in Philadelphia was perhaps even more revealing:

> Providence has in fact so established the order of things that most evils are the means of producing some good. The yellow fever will discourage the growth of great cities in our nation; & I view great cities as pestilential to the morals, the health, and the liberties of man. True, they nourish some of the elegant arts; but the useful ones can thrive elsewhere, and less perfection in others with more health, virtue and freedom would be my choice.[23]

An epidemic was beneficial, in other words, if it served to rid America of the even worse pestilence of urbanization. Since the city was an affront to the new republican order, Jefferson preferred to see city dwellers die of disease so that the republic would be secure.

Proto–Pol Pot sentiments like these are crucial to any understanding of American urban development, for the simple reason that Jefferson succeeded more than any other individual in putting his personal stamp on the new American republic. He wrote the first draft of the Declaration of Independence, the document that served the new nation as a combined birth announcement and mission statement. Although out of the country at the time of the Constitutional Convention in 1787, he made his presence felt via his protégé James Madison, the so-called father of the Constitution. He was an important force behind the movement for a bill of rights (which did little to strengthen civil liberties until the 1920s and much to weaken federal authority) and, with Madison, coauthored the Virginia and Kentucky Resolutions of 1798–99, which argued that the Union was no more than a voluntary interstate compact, a thesis that helped pave the way for the secession crisis of 1860–61. Equally important, the so-called Revolution of 1800 that he helped engineer in getting himself elected to the presidency not only destroyed the Hamiltonians as an electoral force but created a whole new political alignment. Formerly, agrarians and states' rights advocates had been on the defensive. Under the new framework, however, that was no longer the case. Friend and foe alike now equated democracy with rustic independence, while equating urbanization with all those things that homespun patriots despised: snobbery, foppish manners, corruption, financial trickery, and loss of personal independence. This Jeffersonian concept of democracy as something intrinsically antiurban proved astonishingly durable. It would set the tone of American politics right down to the present day.

. . . .

Among other things, this Jeffersonian reconceptualization of democracy accomplished the neat trick of consigning America's very own sansculottes to political oblivion. In France, of course, the sansculottes, as the eighteenth-century urban masses were known, stood for a concept of democracy that was centralized, egalitarian, nationalistic, and statist. They were the most radical element in the French Revolution and, for a time, in the American Revolution as well. These were the people who not only demanded the execution of Louis XVI, but who, on the other side of the Atlantic, taunted British troops in Boston in 1770 and got shot down in return, who threw British tea overboard in 1773, and who were the backbone of the Sons of Liberty and the Committees of Correspondence. But while America's sansculottes seemed for a time to have found leaders in Washington and Hamilton, the election of 1800 left them stranded between two equally unattractive poles: on one hand, the shattered remnants of a Federalist Party that was growing increasingly conservative and elitist and on the other, a newly triumphant Democratic Party that, despite its egalitarian rhetoric, was antiurban, anti-federal, jingoistic, and in league with Southern slave owners. The urban masses needed "internal improvements," as infrastructure was then known—everything from schools, colleges, and technical institutes to roads, canals, and, later, railways—if the urban economy was to grow and develop. But they also needed a federal government that would be liberated from Southern dominance so that the country would be freed to move in an urban-industrial direction. The planters were hostile to commerce, manufacturing, and urban development in general, yet the constitutional settlement of 1787–88 gave them a degree of control over the nation as a whole that was all but unbreakable. Until the advent of the Republican Party in 1856, no major political force was willing to give the urban masses both of what they wanted: infrastructure investment and freedom from Southern control.

A short detour into the mind and methodology of the architect of this antiurban political framework and the resultant Jeffersonian-Hamiltonian schism is thus essential to any understanding of American social development. Despite decades of celebration by liberal and even Communist historians, Jefferson can in no sense be considered a progressive. To the contrary, he was "the great reactionary of the American political tradition," as a conservative journalist recently described him.[24] Despite his professions of loyalty to the people at large, Jefferson was first and foremost a Virginia patriot whose chief loyalty was to the planters of the Old Dominion—which is what made his predicament so painful. The Virginia planters were under growing pressure from any number of directions—from their British creditors, who had lent them money and were pressing for repayment; from London tobacco merchants, who were offering less and less for the colony's sole export commodity while making a hefty profit reexporting Virginia tobacco to the Continent; and from the incipient capitalism of New England and the Middle Atlantic states. A monocultural tobacco economy chained Virginia to a product whose long-term price was trending downward. Yet the obvious solution— economic diversification—was out of the question. Diversification would require the creation of an entrepreneurial class, which in turn would require markets, laborers, sources of capital, and a business culture that was by turns cooperative and competitive—all things that, in the eighteenth century, were synonymous with urbanization. But urbanization also meant the growth of a nonlandowning population that would inevitably prove hostile to the planters and to the slave system on which the planters depended. Businessmen would never be able to reconcile themselves to a system that held land and slaves in higher esteem than other sorts of property, while urban workers, whose interest was in seeing wages rise higher and higher, would never resign themselves to a system that undermined wage growth by virtue of its growing reliance on unpaid, captive labor. As painful as a monocultural tobacco economy might be, therefore, the alternative was worse. Institutionally incapable of changing their ways, the planters' only choice was to stay put and somehow forestall the inevitable.

This was Jefferson's lifelong mission as the Virginia plantocracy's preeminent leader and spokesman. His strategy was bold and daring: to use the new language of political democracy in order to fend off both British imperialists and Northern capitalists. The Declaration of Independence was his opening salvo. It charged George III with various crimes against human rights, popular sovereignty, and the like and even accused him of imposing slavery on a reluctant South, an allegation so absurd on its face that the Continental Congress edited it out of the final draft. Nonetheless, the document proved immensely successful. Despite Samuel Johnson's famous quip—"How is it that we hear the loudest yelps for liberty among the drivers of negroes?"—it threw the British on the defensive, helped rally international support, and provided American *independistas* with a stirring set of principles around which to rally. Once achieved, though, independence brought with it new problems as Virginia found itself in an unexpectedly close union with the infant capitalist economy of the American North, a union that would soon prove no less threatening.

Beginning in 1790–91, therefore, Jefferson turned his guns in the other direction. His strategy was to capitalize on rising international tension between Britain and France by driving a wedge between the Northern merchant class, whose commercial ties were largely with the British, and the Northern masses, whose sympathies were overwhelmingly with the French, their allies in the Revolutionary War and now their fellow republicans. Jefferson made artful use of the rhetoric of *liberté, égalité, fraternité* to rally the people to his side. He and Madison and their supporters painted the struggle between what would eventually be known as Democrats and Federalists as one between radicals and conservatives, supporters of popular rule and its crypto-royalist opponents. The result was the strange spectacle of Southern slave owners hoisting the revolutionary tricolor, singing the Marseillaise, and accusing Hamilton and his fellow Federalists of attempting to strangle popular democracy in the cradle. In France, the sansculottes directed their anger not only at the urban aristocracy but at the landed nobility. They were pushing for a centralized nation-state far stronger than anything Alexander Hamilton could imagine in his wildest fantasies. Yet Jefferson was able to make use of the French Revolution to foster an antistatist, antiurban agenda that served the interests of America's own rural nobility, the Virginia planters.

Jefferson is best understood as a tory-radical, someone who is often astute and penetrating in his analysis of current political problems but whose solution is to turn back the clock to some supposedly better time in the past. Progress according to a tory-radical viewpoint never means advancement but always retreat. Reform from such a perspective is never new and innovative. To the contrary, real reform entails a rejection of all that is new and innovative in favor of returning to some long-lost golden age. Because change is corrupting, reform is a process of purgation in which the muck and grime of the modern world are washed away so as to reveal all that is bright and shining underneath. Legitimacy is established through precedent on the assumption that anything that existed in the past must be morally superior to anything arising out of the corrupt and slimy present.

As a young Virginia attorney barely in his thirties, Jefferson burst onto the national scene in 1774 when he published a pamphlet entitled "A Summary View of the Rights of British America." Although the conclusion was radical—the tract argued for independence at a time when few patriots could bring themselves to utter the word—it was very much a lawyer's brief at a time when the legal profession had never been more conservative. To prove his argument that America had a right to detach itself from the mother country and go off on its own, Jefferson did what any eighteenth-century Anglo-American jurist was trained to do: He went searching for precedent, the older the better. He found one in the primitive Gothic tribes known as the Angles, Saxons, and Jutes who had migrated in the fifth and sixth century from the coast of modern Holland and Germany to what is now called England (i.e., Angle-land).

What was significant about this migration, Jefferson argued, was that the Anglo-Saxons did not take the laws of Germany with them when they set sail across the North Sea. Instead, they jettisoned the old laws and established new legal traditions on English soil that eventually blossomed into what English-speaking patriots on both sides of the Atlantic regarded as Britain's "free and antient" constitution, a mighty oak of liberty that, as Jefferson put it in his pamphlet, has "so long been the glory and protection of that country."[25] The ability to break away and begin anew was thus the most ancient English liberty of all, the liberty on which all others rested. Now that British North Americans were seeking to break away from their mother country and start anew, it should be evident, Jefferson went on, as to who was acting in accord with ancient constitutional principles. American patriots had the law and freedom on their side, while their overlords in London did not.

There are a number of things to be said for this argument. It was ingenious, certainly, and more than a bit cheeky in its attempt to turn British legal principles against British imperial power. But it was also naive, ahistorical, and almost exaggeratedly legalistic. The idea that a modern colonization effort was in any way comparable to a Dark Ages tribal migration was absurd. So was the notion that the British were to be deprived of the fruits of their investment in the New World because of a one-thousand-year-old legal precedent—it was like trying to repeal the Norman Conquest on the grounds that William the Conqueror's claim to the English throne had been legally flawed. But what makes "A Summary View" important is that it represented, in embryo, ideas that would turn out to be enduring American principles.

Generation after generation of Americans would agree with Jefferson that the freedom to break away and start anew was the ur-freedom, the foundation on which all others depended. Initially, Americans understood such ideas in terms of national independence. But once the republic was established, they would construe them in other ways as well. If Virginians felt constrained by membership in a larger American federation, the answer was to break away and form a separate Southern confederacy. If Westerners felt oppressed by Easterners, the answer was to break away and form a separate state or perhaps a separate republic. If, decades later, individuals felt constrained by membership in a large city, the solution was to break away and start a new community out beyond the city gates, one that would more accurately reflect their own middle-class values and aspirations.

Freedom equaled independence: independence of the nation vis-à-vis the empire, of the state vis-à-vis the nation, and even, as Jefferson would argue in his final years, of miniature "ward-republics" vis-à-vis the individual state.[26] If freedom meant the right of ever-smaller units to break away and go off on their own, then any attempt by society to rein them in was by definition tyrannical. A free republic had to somehow accommodate an untrammeled right of independence. It had to provide room for individuals to continually break away and start afresh.

But there was a problem. As even Jefferson conceded, any republic that provided such an unqualified right would become a party to its own dissolution. Allowing such forces free rein meant allowing society to fly apart in a thousand pieces. The solution that Americans came up with was to place both society and the individual under a neutral body of law that would somehow accomplish what the people could not accomplish themselves, i.e., strike that delicate, if not magical, balance needed to hold the republic together while still allowing the individual the leeway that Jefferson believed was the essence of freedom. "We the people" create law, as the Constitution declares in the Preamble. But since society was the enemy, especially political society in the form of a national government, "we the people" had to create a body of basic law that would control society rather than being controlled by it in return. The result was the sacred Constitution, a document that, once the people had called it into being, would permanently limit the power of the people to refashion either society or the law in a way they would like.

Because the purpose of law was to protect the people as individuals from the people in their capacity as a unified, collective mass, the people's social side had to be constrained. For this reason, Jefferson remained deeply divided—perhaps neurotic is the better term—on the question of majority rule. He was all for it when the popular tide was running in his favor, but against it when it was not. As he stated when he assumed the presidency in 1801, "the will of the majority is in all cases to prevail." Yet, less than two decades earlier, in his *Notes on the State of Virginia,* he had declared no less emphatically that "[a]n *electoral despotism* was not the government we fought for, but one which should not only be founded on free principles, but in which the powers of government should be so divided and balanced among several bodies of magistracy, as that no one should transcend their legal limits. . . ."[27] Freedom did not mean the freedom to transcend eternal law. The majority was all-powerful only as long as it remained within certain fixed legal limits meant to safeguard individual rights. The instant it violated those limits, it was not. In the Declaration of Independence, Jefferson had asserted that whenever government failed to protect "Life, Liberty, and the pursuit of Happiness, . . . it is the Right of the People to alter or to abolish it, and to institute new Government"—which suggested that popular sovereignty was greater than custom, tradition, or law. Yet just two years earlier, he had argued that a one-thousand-year-old legal precedent trumped all other considerations, including, presumably, the popular will.

So which guiding principle did Jefferson believe in—popular sovereignty as a force greater than law or law as a force greater than popular sovereignty? Based on his writings, it is apparent that he believed earnestly in both, which is why his final years were so tortured. Once he turned the presidency over to his Virginian fellow planter "Jimmy" Madison in 1809 and retired to Monticello, he let loose with a stream of opinions, predictions, and *pensées* in letters to acquaintances and friends that were increasingly unrealistic, cranky, and reactionary. Because the United States was free, independent, and unconstrained by government, it was invincible—which is why Jefferson blithely predicted at the start of the War of 1812 that the American side would expel the British and annex Canada in one fell swoop.[28] In fact, the war was a disaster: America's minimalist government was no match for the well-oiled British war machine and by the burning of Washington in 1814 had all but collapsed. When calls went up after the war for a stronger nation-state, Jefferson predicted disaster. Federally financed highways and canals, he was convinced, would lead to bankruptcy and ruin. As he put it, "public fortunes are destroyed by public as well as private extravagance. A departure from principle in one instance becomes a precedent for a second; that second for a third; and so on, till the bulk of society is reduced to be mere automatons of misery. . . ."[29] He added in 1822 that federal expansion was a sign of impending tyranny: "I scarcely know myself which is most to be deprecated, consolidation, or dissolution of the [national] state. The horrors of both are beyond the sense of human foresight."[30] A proposal three years later by John Quincy Adams, the first Northerner to occupy the White House in nearly a quarter century, for a program of internal improvements had him all but reaching for his musket. The breakdown had grown so acute, Jefferson declared, that secession was fast becoming the only option. While Virginians would "consider such a rupture as among the greatest calamities which could befall them," he wrote, it was not the worst. "There is yet one greater, submission to a government of unlimited powers"—all this because Adams had proposed, among other things, a federally financed astronomical observatory and a national university.[31]

. . . .

Freedom meant independence from the federal government, from the fast-growing urban society north of the Mason-Dixon Line, and from commerce and industry, which Jefferson also regarded as threatening because it enslaved the individual to the whims and vagaries of the market. Any discussion of Jeffersonian ideology, however, is incomplete without a discussion of its Hamiltonian opposite—and opposite the two men were in nearly every conceivable respect: in their political and economic ideas, in their intellectual methodologies, in their social attitudes, and, above all, in their conception of urban and rural development. Where Jefferson believed in states' rights and local control, Hamilton was a tough-minded nationalist who longed to do to the states what the French republicans had done to the old feudal provinces, which was to break their power by dividing them up into smaller *départements*. Where Jefferson was suspicious of centralized power to the point of paranoia, Hamilton believed in a sovereign nation-state in the fullest sense of the term, one with a complete and total mandate to reach into every last corner of society in order to reshape it in accord with national policy. "[T]he vigor of government is essential to the security of liberty," Hamilton wrote in the opening installment in the Federalist Papers—as un-Virginian a statement as one could imagine.[32] Where Jefferson was an agrarian, Hamilton was a thoroughgoing urbanist. In his 1791 "Report on Manufactures," one of the most remarkable documents ever to emerge out of the U.S. government, he lauded the growth of "large districts, which may be considered as pretty fully peopled and which . . . are thickly interspersed with flourishing and increasing towns." Because such districts "hav[e] fewer attractions to agriculture, than some other parts of the Union, they exhibit a proportionally stronger tendency toward other kinds of industry."[33] Where Jefferson saw America's superabundance of agricultural land as a blessing, Hamilton believed that such abundance could be a drawback if it encouraged Americans to sit back and live off nature's bounty. A *shortage* of land, on the other hand, could be advantageous if it encouraged them to make more productive use of their talents by going into business and manufacturing.

This was also as un-Virginian a statement as one could imagine. Jefferson believed that city dwellers grew up stunted and twisted. New Englanders, he wrote to a fellow Southerner in the 1790s, "are circumscribed within such narrow limits, and their populations so full, that . . . they are marked, like the Jews, with . . . a perversity of character. . . ."[34] Yet Hamilton believed that fullness of population could be a spur to creativity. Where Jefferson believed that cities were threatening to ancient liberties—"the *canaille* of the cities," he wrote in 1813, are dedicated to "the demolition and destruction of everything public and private"[35]—Hamilton believed that, by fostering economic growth, cities expanded the ambit of human experience; if they destroyed ancient liberties, they created new ones in their place. Significantly, right around the time that Jefferson was earnestly hoping that yellow fever would thin out the urban population, Hamilton was among a group of New Yorkers attempting to win state approval for a project to safeguard the city's water supply.[36] One man wanted the city to collapse, while the other wanted to nurture and protect it so that it would grow.

Although at times politically conservative (albeit in a different way from Jefferson and his fellow Virginians), Hamilton was very much a product of the accelerating urban revolution of the eighteenth century, one in which megacities like London and Paris were growing not only in terms of population but in their power and reach over larger society. As a boy clerking for a pair of merchants in St. Croix in the Virgin Islands, Hamilton had been in the thick of the new urban-mercantile culture, corresponding with merchants and ship captains throughout the Atlantic. When he arrived in the thriving port of New York in his midteens to make his fortune, it was clearly a form of a homecoming. Something about the city, its pace and excitement, suited Hamilton, and he would remain a New Yorker to his dying day.

All of which was enough to mark Hamilton in Jefferson's eyes as an alien breed. For all their differences, though, Hamilton burst onto the national stage in a curiously similar fashion. Just a few months after Jefferson published "A Summary View," Hamilton drew attention by dashing off a pamphlet of his own entitled "The Farmer Refuted." A rebuttal of a widely circulated Tory tract, it also sketched out an argument for independence, but one that was utilitarian rather than legalistic. Ultimately, Hamilton wrote, the question facing America was one of political geography. America was big and could only grow bigger as it expanded across the Appalachians. It was rich in land, people, and natural resources and soon would be even more so. The idea that it should remain chained in perpetuity to an island kingdom some three thousand miles away was preposterous. Consequently, whatever the legal ties binding the American colonies to the British throne, they took second seat to the real-life forces driving them apart. Man-made law, Hamilton argued, was subordinate to "the law of nature, and that *supreme law* of every society—*its own happiness.*"[37] If Americans wished to break away from the mother country, it was not because some one-thousand-year-old legal precedent gave them the right but because modern exigencies left them no alternative. Rather than the supremacy of law, Hamilton was arguing the very opposite, i.e., that modern political considerations trumped any concept of legal precedent.

From this one philosophical difference, it might be said, all else about the great Hamiltonian-Jeffersonian rift followed. One of the many curious things about American historians is the way they have uncritically accepted the Jeffersonian myth about Hamiltonian authoritarianism. The idea is a gross oversimplification. Jefferson, as we have seen, believed in the freedom of the individual from society. Rather than the untrammeled rule of the demos, he believed in the eternal, "natural" rights of the solitary human being, which is to say the solitary white male. The advantage to the Southern slaveholder of a system that upheld the authority of individual whites over all other beings was obvious. But if Hamilton did not believe in the sovereignty of the individual over society, neither did he believe in the superiority of society over the individual. Instead, it would not be reading too much into his writings to say he believed in something more sophisticated and more complex, i.e., the notion that the Jefferson dichotomy between society and the individual was a false one and that individual fulfillment was to be achieved through society rather than in opposition to it. Society could only develop by encouraging the growth of the individual, while the individual could develop only by contributing to the growth of society. The fortunes of both were closely intertwined. His own "conservatism" notwithstanding, Hamilton also recognized that the only possible base for a modern republic was the people themselves. However much one might call upon the people to slow down and temper their actions, in the end the decision of whether to go fast or slow was up to the people themselves.[38] Thus, where Jefferson looked to the Constitution and natural law to constrain democracy and channel it in a small-scale, localized direction, Hamilton's vision was more expansive. Since the nation-state was a creation of the people, the people could take it anywhere they wanted to go. Sovereignty did not lie with the states or with township-sized "ward-republics," but with the people as a whole. Despite his hostility to the French Revolution, Hamilton was closer to the Jacobin concept of popular sovereignty, "one and indivisible," than either he or Jefferson realized.[39]

What made this all so confusing, however, was Hamilton's skepticism toward democracy as the word was then defined. At a time when it was understood by friend and foe alike to mean something anarchic and undisciplined, Hamilton, a thoroughgoing statist, was indeed leery. Democracy in America in the late eighteenth century meant opposition to government and the emerging nation-state, whereas Hamilton believed that a stronger central government was what was most needed. As he wrote during the Revolutionary War:

> [T]here are some, who maintain, that trade will regulate itself, and is not to be benefitted by the encouragements, or restraints of government. . . . [T]hey will argue, that there is no need for common directing power. . . . This is one of those wild speculative paradoxes, which have grown in credit among us, contrary to the uniform practice and sense of the most enlightened nations.[40]

Far from reactionary, sentiments like these place Hamilton firmly in the modern democratic tradition, whereas Jefferson's obsessive fear of federal authority establishes him as a forerunner of Newt Gingrich, Tom DeLay, and other such troglodytes of the contemporary American right. When Hamilton famously blurted out, "The people, sir, are a great beast," he was chiefly guilty of a failure to distinguish between Americans as they were and Americans as they could be, between a group of widely scattered coastal communities endlessly suspicious of centralized authority and the well-organized nation-state he was trying to create. The people in their present condition *were* a great beast—primitive, thoughtless, ignorant of their own potential. Rather than flattering Americans, Hamilton wished to spur them on to something better.

Hamilton's urban policies flowed from his ideas about law, politics, and the nation-state. Because he wished to strengthen society, he wished to strengthen the city since that was where society was most concentrated and visible. The city was a place of workshops and stores, of docks, warehouses, and places of exchange—all those things that Jeffersonians viewed with unease but which Hamilton viewed as sources of creativity and growth. This is not to say that Hamilton favored the city *over* the countryside. To the contrary, his "Report on Manufactures" gave agriculture pride of place in the national economy. But it did so for reasons of national security rather than some a priori belief that "those who labour in the earth" are morally superior to those who spend their days in countinghouses or workshops. Rather than Jeffersonian-style subsistence agriculture, Hamilton wished to foster commercial agriculture geared to the urban marketplace. Rather than backwoods barter, he favored a money economy that would generate both tax revenue and capital investment. This was the idea behind the Whiskey Tax in 1791: Because whiskey served as a de facto currency west of the Appalachians, requiring the frontiersman to pay a tax on the whiskey they produced forced them to reenter the money economy. Rather than the Jeffersonian ideal of communal autonomy, he wanted Americans to feel that they were part of a national enterprise that was bigger than they were and hence more important than the particular community in which they lived. As in France, nationalism, urbanism, and economic growth were all aspects of the same phenomenon.

. . . .

The American independence movement, like all national liberation movements to follow, thus brought together mutually contradictory forces—urbanism and agrarianism, capitalist exchange and barter, nationalism and local control—under one roof. The alliance was strictly temporary, and once independence was achieved—indeed, before it was achieved—the various elements began pulling in different directions. Hamiltonianism was triumphant after 1789, but then overreached itself in the late 1790s. After being routed by Jefferson's new Democratic Party in the elections of 1800, it all but disappeared as an electoral force. While some elements of the old Hamiltonian program did manage to creep back in after 1815, the prevailing ideological framework remained fundamentally hostile. Government equaled tyranny, urbanization equaled corruption, while democracy was understood by Jeffersonians and neo-Hamiltonian Whigs alike to mean states' rights and local control. Politicians proved their "democratic" mettle by competing to see who could denounce the federal government most vociferously. As a visiting Englishwoman named Frances Trollope observed in 1832:

> If I mistake not, every debate I listened to in the American Congress was upon one and the same subject, namely, the entire independence of each individual state, with regard to the federal government. . . . [M]an after man [would] start eagerly to his feet to declare that the greatest injury, the basest injustice, the most obnoxious tyranny that could be practised against the state of which he was a member, would be a vote of a few million dollars for the purpose of making their roads or canals. . . .[41]

This was the Jeffersonian terror over the emerging nation-state at its most debilitating. "We the people" had created the federal government, yet now "we the people" were mobilizing to prevent that government from creating anything resembling a unified nation. Fueling the panic was the realization that, rather than slowing, the urban juggernaut, the driving force behind national consolidation, was accelerating. Ironically, Jefferson himself had started things rolling in 1807 when, in a last-ditch effort to keep the United States out of the Napoleonic Wars, he imposed a unilateral embargo on trade with the various European combatants. Jefferson, knowing all too well that war makes the nation as much as the nation makes war, wished to preserve peace so as to forestall the growth of a national military establishment. Yet not only did the embargo fail to keep the peace, but it had two wholly unexpected side effects. It stimulated demand for domestic manufactures, precisely what Jefferson had most wanted to avoid, and, by discouraging shipping, shifted commerce away from the Atlantic seaboard and toward the interior.

Capitalism thus penetrated deeper into the heartland. The steamboat revolution that Robert Fulton unleashed a year later gave inland commerce another boost by slashing the cost of river transport. While this arguably helped strengthen the Jeffersonian camp by expanding trade along the Ohio and Mississippi River complex, controlled by the South via the port of New Orleans, the canal boom that got under way a decade or so later tipped the scales in the other direction. The Erie, completed in 1825, did not reduce traffic on the Mississippi and Ohio, at least not absolutely. But by slashing trans-Appalachian shipping costs by 90 percent or more, it reduced the rivers' relative share of the Ohio Valley's burgeoning output and helped insure that a growing portion would flow to the urban Northeast.[42] Commerce in the American heartland soon began reorienting itself from a north-south to an east-west axis.

The result was a spur to urbanization on both sides of the Appalachian divide. Along the Eastern seaboard, power shifted from a mercantile elite chiefly interested in maritime trade to a rising manufacturing class whose sights were set on continental development. The Ohio Valley found itself increasingly "New Englandized" as contacts with the East expanded. Timothy Dwight, a man of impeccable Puritan heritage who was president of Yale for more than twenty years, noted that the Yankees traveling west via the Erie Canal and Great Lakes included not just farmers but "a proportional number of mechanics, manufacturers, merchants, physicians, and lawyers"—people who, rather than scattering themselves over the landscape, instinctively adhered to the old Puritan pattern of forming themselves into villages and towns.[43] A new urban-industrial culture took advantage of the opening afforded by the Erie Canal to spread itself across America's northern tier.[44]

For Jeffersonians and their Jacksonian successors, the result was a growing crisis in which questions involving slavery, the emerging conflict between national and local democracy, the growth of the cities, and the urbanization of the economy were all coming together in one increasingly explosive package.

2

THE FIRST
URBAN CRISIS

Stadtluft macht frei. *(City air makes one free.)*

MEDIEVAL PROVERB

It is obvious, that in towns, all the things which
conspire against the country gentleman,
combine in favor of the money manager and director.

EDMUND BURKE

FOR JEFFERSONIANS attempting to force the infant U.S. to stick to a narrow path of agrarian political development, the problem they confronted was not only the pace of American urbanization but the nature of
it as well. A city in the eighteenth century could be many things—an
administrative center, a fashion or cultural center, or a center for production and trade. But where major European cities usually managed to combine all three functions in one to some degree or another, the cities that
were taking root in British North America were notably lopsided. They
were underdeveloped as administrative centers for the simple reason that
royal power in the colonies was severely underdeveloped until the 1750s
and 1760s. They were underdeveloped as centers of aristocratic fashion

and consumption for the simple reason that aristocratic fashion was as out of place in the American social environment as a gilded carriage on a narrow Indian trail. And since American culture during this period was nonexistent in any formal sense—"Who, the wide world over, reads an American book?" asked the English clergyman Sydney Smith in 1820—there was no role for the city as cultural showcase either.

But the city as a center for buying, selling, and production—that was another story. From the very beginning, what we hear from travelers concerning the embryonic cities of New England and the Middle Atlantic region is that while the roads were ill paved and the manners rude and unpolished, the air fairly crackled with economic energy. John Drayton, a visitor to colonial Boston, complained that "the streets are crooked and narrow . . . extremely disagreeable, and inconvenient to those who walk them." Yet he couldn't help but be struck by "the industry of its inhabitants: and their attention to business."[1] Indeed, so industrious were the people of Massachusetts Bay that the Puritan divine Increase Mather complained that they were taking things too far by working even on the Sabbath:

> Have not God's Holy Day been profaned in New England? Have not Burdens been carried through the streets on the Sabbath Day? Have not Bakers, Carpenters, and other Tradesmen been employed in Servile Works on the Sabbath Day?[2]

Where the authorities in the Old World complained that the people worked too little, in Puritan New England they complained that they worked too much.

This superindustrious urban model made for a city that was not less crowded as a consequence, but more so. As Lewis Mumford once noted, political power has come to express itself in different urbanological terms

than in earlier periods. In the Middle Ages, both the nobility and bourgeoisie had striven for height in the form of immense castles looming
over the countryside, gothic cathedrals soaring over the cities, or the
famous towers sprouting like asparagus out of small Italian city-states.
Beginning around the fifteenth century, however, the new political force
known as royal absolutism began to distinguish itself by its ability to
extend itself in an entirely new direction: horizontally. A king advertised
his prowess not by building the tallest structure but by carving out the
broadest square amid the urban clutter. Slums had to be cleared so that
the royal palace would be shown to its best advantage. Piazzas had to
be created so that the local potentate could display his person on appro-
priate occasions to the assembled multitudes. Room had to be made for
monuments, parks, or boulevards so that finely arrayed royal horsemen
could parade this way and that. In his great fresco "The Effect of Good
Government on Town and Country," the fourteenth-century Sienese artist
Ambrogio Lorenzetti had depicted the late-medieval urban ideal as one of
concentrated activity: buildings packed together as tightly as sardines,
carpenters hammering overhead, the streets filled with merchants, artisans, peasants bearing goods to market, and so on. Not a royal statue,
boulevard, or parade ground was in sight. The baroque age, by contrast,
demonstrated its prowess by creating urban expanses that were vast, formal, "harmonious," and, above all, empty. If the medieval city was so
crowded as to lead to feelings of claustrophobia, the baroque city, to
quote Mumford, was so vast and open as to lead to the opposite sensation:
agoraphobia.[3]

Ironically, America would not get this kind of horizontal city until
Jefferson got his wish for a national capital, constructed along French
lines in the 1790s. What it got instead were decidedly nonmonumental
cities devoted nearly exclusively to commerce and production, cities that,
because they had no need for "horizontalist" displays of power, were once
again as free to be as tightly packed as they wished. Although the Boston

Common eventually evolved into a park and recreation area, it was originally conceived merely as an economic resource, a continuation of the old English custom of granting every parishioner "equall Right of Commonage in the towne."[4] It was land that was deliberately left untouched so that the rest of the city could crowd together as closely as it wished. If a penny saved was a penny earned (to quote one of Boston's more famous sons, Benjamin Franklin), then every unnecessary footstep that could be avoided was one whose energy could be put to some more profitable end. Shopkeepers and artisans squeezed up against one another in order to be close to customers and suppliers, while merchants packed themselves tightly along the waterfront to be as close as possible to the ships that came in to dock. When that proved too crowded, they drained marshes and built new wharves jutting out into the water in order to create additional urban space. The more tightly the city was laid out, the greater its efficiency as an economic instrument. Urban space existed not for purposes of display but to be used.

· · · · · · · · · · · · ·

Boston, the largest city in Anglophone North America for most of the colonial period, represented this process of early bourgeois urbanization at its most extreme. At least initially, governance was in the hands of Puritan elders and clergymen who, while hardly shy about exercising authority, felt no more need to make a show of their power than to make a show of their person by dressing up in fancy clothes. To the contrary, the Puritan style was modest, somber, and businesslike, as the Puritan urban style would be as well.

The Puritans chose the Shawmut Peninsula, the site of present-day Boston, not only because of its strategic location at the mouth of Boston Harbor, but because it had the advantage of being connected via a narrow land bridge to the mainland. Given the nature of seventeenth-century transportation, this enabled the Puritans to maximize the benefits of both wheeled and waterborne transport. Although John Winthrop, the colony's first governor, called for a "city on a hill" in his famous sermon aboard the *Arbella* as he and his fellow settlers sailed for the New World, the community they initially had in mind was something more along the lines of an English country village. Each family would have its own land to farm, and it was assumed that agriculture would be the mainstay for generations to come. Yet such assumptions soon fell by the wayside when residents realized that they could make more money outfitting new arrivals than by planting wheat and corn. Following a falloff in immigration in the late 1630s, Boston floundered for a bit as it searched for a new means of existence. But it was soon able to reinvent itself as a regional entrepôt of growing importance. Instead of merely receiving ships from England, Bostonians now began sending them out, first to the other English colonies from Maine to the borders of Dutch New Amsterdam, then to the Caribbean, Spain, and other distant points. As Boston's commercial role expanded, its economy began to deepen and diversify and its streets to grow more crowded. Ships had to be built, outfitted, and repaired, which meant work for carpenters, shipwrights, sail makers, blacksmiths, and numerous others. While on shore, crews had to be fed and entertained, which meant business for everyone from brewers and distillers to prostitutes. (By the 1670s, the "Whores of Boston" were famous throughout the colonies.) Intemperate sailors had to be dealt with, which meant work for jailers and other municipal officeholders, not to mention municipal revenue in the form of fines for drunkenness and disorderly conduct. (Pity the poor sailor who had to spend his shore leave among unforgiving Calvinists. . . .) Cattle raising led to an export industry for meat and leather products, which provided jobs for butchers, tanners, glovers, and shoemakers. Coopers kept themselves busy making casks and barrels.[5]

"It hath pleased God so to dispose that o[u]r Towne chiefly consists of Trade, a mart to the countrie through the resort of Artificers of all sorts, and the access of shipping," the town fathers declared in 1648—not the first time that New England Calvinists would confuse profitability with blessedness.[6] Significantly, Boston nurtured this process of primitive capitalist accumulation not by encouraging private property and individual acquisitiveness but by curtailing them. The city laid claim to all land on the Shawmut Peninsula, which it then proceeded to dole out to individual families not on the basis of monetary wealth but according to need and social rank. Although ownership thereafter was nominally in private hands, the political and moral rules concerning how land was to be used were so thick and pervasive as to leave little doubt where real control lay. Puritans were no freer to do with "their" property what they would than they were with their dress. The town fathers imposed wage and price controls to discourage profiteering and imposed sumptuary laws to discourage frivolous expenditures. By "problematizing" consumption, they left Bostonians no alternative but to plow their profits back into business, thereby fueling economic development and urban expansion all the more. Clearly, the connection between capitalist accumulation and private ownership was a good deal more complicated than latter-day free-market economists like to believe.

It is very easy to poke fun at Puritans for talking incessantly of God while driving competitors to the wall. In 1699, an English visitor to Boston noted acidly that:

> The Inhabitants seem very Religious, showing many signs of an inward and Spiritual Grace: But tho' they wear in their Faces the *Innocense of Doves,* you will find them in their dealings, as *Subtile* as *Serpents. Interest* is their *Faith, Money* their *God,* and *Large Possessions* the only Heaven they covet.[7]

Yet such hypocrisy, if that is what it was, was not only inevitable but historically progressive. Like any community, Boston defined itself by distinguishing between insiders and outsiders. In his *Arbella* sermon,

John Winthrop outlined a theory of the Puritan community as virtually an extended family:

> Wee must be knitt in this work as one man, wee must entertaine each other in brotherly affeccion, wee must be willing to abridge our selves of superfluities, for the supply of others necessities, wee must uphold a familiar Commerce together in all meekeness, gentleness, patience and liberallitie, wee must delight in each other, make others Conditions our owne[,] rejoyce together, mourne together, labour, and suffer together.[8]

Rather than a source of competition, commerce was seen as a means of reinforcing social cohesion, of binding the community together rather than driving members at each other's throat. The flip side of this highly developed sense of communal solidarity is that it gave the community a common economic base of operations. By enabling Puritans to pool and develop their resources, both moral and economic, it functioned as a launching pad for more and more vigorous forays into the outside world. The urban corporation of the seventeenth and eighteenth centuries was the direct forerunner of the business corporation of the nineteenth and twentieth.

Unfortunately for the Puritan religious establishment, urbanization and economic expansion gave rise to a force that would ultimately prove its undoing: secularization. As business grew, Bostonians turned their attention from theology to more mundane matters of profit and loss. As urbanization expanded, the Puritan strategy of molding themselves into a separate moral community began to break down. Growth meant diversification. The more widely the city cast its net, the more outsiders it admitted in the form of sailors, non-Puritan traders, and ordinary laborers and craftsmen who no longer bothered to go to church. As church membership declined relative to the total urban population, the Calvinist concept of the congregation-cum-community began to disintegrate. Church and state were no longer one. But because the Puritans had egalitarianism in their bones, the Calvinist concept of a priesthood of all believers gave way to the secular concept of an urban democracy of all citizens. As one upper-class Puritan declared in 1640 in explaining why he planned to stay put in England rather than join his coreligionists in Massachusetts: "No wise man should be so foolish as to live where every man is a master, and masters must not correct their servants."[9] The same John Drayton who complained about the difficulty of walking Boston's streets also complained about the refusal of laborers to make way for a gentleman. "Carts, waggons, drays, trucks, wheelbarrows, and porters are continually obstructing the passage in these streets," yet the people who man them "seem so conscious that all men are equal that they take a pride in shewing their knowledge of this principle upon every occasion."[10] When Massachusetts's royal governor Joseph Dudley ran into a group of carters on Boston's narrow land bridge in the middle of a snowstorm in 1705, he demanded that they move aside so that his carriage could pass. Replied one of the carters: "I am as good flesh and blood as you . . . you may get out of the way." When Dudley exploded in a shower of expletives—"You lie, you dog; you lie, you devill"—one of the workmen answered coolly: "Such words don't become a Christian."[11] No laborer would have dared to answer back in such a manner in England. Yet in the free city of Boston, it was the only way a common laborer knew how to speak.

As Boston grew, it expanded intellectually. In the seventeenth century, a priesthood of all believers had meant a community of theological hairsplitters as congregations broke up and dissenters such as Anne Hutchinson and Roger Williams were expelled. But the decline of religion did not mean the decline of intellect. Rather, it merely placed it on a new footing. As a visitor reported in 1719:

> [A]t Boston the Exchange is surrounded with Booksellers
> Shops, which have a good trade. There are five Printing Presses

in Boston, which are generally full of work, by which it appears,
that Humanity and Knowledge of Letters flourish more here
than in all other English Plantations put together.[12]

Instead of theology, Bostonians now broadened their reading to
include literature and the humanities. If he had been born a generation or
two earlier, Benjamin Franklin might very well have entered the ranks of
the clergy, the only outlet at the time for someone of his intellectual abilities. But, instead, the freer and more open atmosphere of the 1720s and
1730s allowed him to become a printer, writer, and newspaper pub-
lisher—a public intellectual, in other words, writing for a public audience.

The ties that bound Bostonians together were also becoming more
political than religious. Although Congregationalist ministers remained
influential in the community, the days when they could monopolize
political power were fast receding in the distance. Instead, as the political
crisis of the 1760s and 1770s grew more acute, the "black regiment" of
the clergy joined forces with other members of the community as equals
in organizing resistance to the British. Instead of the congregation, it was
now the city that stood shoulder to shoulder—merchants, doctors, and
distillers right down to brawny, thirsty dockworkers and frugal ladies
brewing sassafras tea and spinning homegrown wool in protest against the
import taxes imposed by London.[13]

The severe religious discipline of the seventeenth century thus gave
rise dialectically to the urban freedom of the eighteenth. *Pace* Locke and
Jefferson, freedom was not something that preceded settled society but,
rather, something that settled society produced through the creation of
new urban forms. The city was the crucible in which freedom was reinvented and redefined. As one historian has noted:

Although eighteenth-century America was predominantly a
rural, agricultural society, its . . . commercial cities were the

cutting edge of economic, social, and political change. . . .
The cities predicted the future, even though under one in
twenty colonists lived in them in 1700 or 1735 and even
though they were but overgrown villages compared to the
great urban centers of Europe, the Middle East, and Asia.[14]

This notion of the city as a crucible of freedom echoed the late-
medieval concept of the city as an island of liberty in a sea of feudal
oppression. However, where the medieval peasant was tied to the land due
to any number of feudal obligations, the American yeoman farmer was
not. Outside of the Hudson Valley, where a Dutch-style patroon system of
big landlords and tenant farmers had taken root, the very concept of an
oppressed European-style peasantry was alien. Yet amid this generally high
level of freedom (for white males, that is), the newly emergent American
city was the loftiest peak, a place where cheap newspapers and pamphlets
could be purchased at a time when they were heavily taxed back home in
England, where the best sermons could be heard, where the liveliest
debates could be sampled—a place, in short, where freedom could be
found in its most potent forms.

•••••••••••

The New England model of urban development, moreover, was spreading.
As Philadelphians bypassed William Penn's spacious squares for the jumbled
and lively waterfront, the local economy also began to deepen and diversify much as Boston's had a generation or two earlier. By 1685, just four
years after its founding, Penn was happily writing that the city was home
to a veritable Noah's Ark of New World artisans: carpenters, joiners, bricklayers, masons, plumbers, glaziers, tailors, butchers, and bakers—if Penn
neglected to mention candlestick makers, it was undoubtedly an oversight. These were arts that Jefferson regarded as innately corrupting and
therefore antirepublican. New York, due most likely to a combination of

poor leadership and unsettled political conditions, was somewhat slower getting off the ground. But although its population lagged some 15 percent behind Philadelphia's by the 1740s, the town center was already more thickly populated, a sign of things to come.[15]

The tumultuous events of the 1770s and 1780s had a dramatic, albeit contradictory, effect on American urbanization. Political turmoil and economic dislocation could not help but slow the pace of urban growth. But ratification of the Constitution, despite its agrarian leanings, couldn't help giving urbanization a boost. Even if just one governing institution, i.e., the House, was to be chosen by the people at large, it still meant that elections would have to be held, broadsides printed, and debates conducted, all of which by definition would take place in the cities and towns. The city was where democracy was most visible; therefore to the degree that the Constitution opened the door to democracy, however partially and incompletely, it couldn't help giving the city a new centrality in national political life. The creation of a national government helped speed up the pace of society in a way that struck people at the time as distinctly urban. A livelier political life, a more vigorous economy, and a quickening urban tempo—from an eighteenth-century perspective, these were all very much the same.

There is no better illustration of this process of urban modernization than Washington Irving's great short story "Rip Van Winkle." The tale, of course, concerns a likable ne'er-do-well named Rip who, out hunting one day, stumbles upon a party of ghostly Dutchmen playing ninepins in a mountain glade, drinks a magic potion, and then falls asleep for twenty years. Although precise dates are not given, the encounter seems to take place somewhere in the mid-1770s, allowing Rip to awaken just in time for America's first nationwide partisan political contest, the presidential election of 1796. As Rip makes his way home, the accelerating pace of change is the first thing he notices. His sleepy old hamlet is "larger and more populous. There were rows of houses which he had never seen before, and those which had been his familiar haunts had disappeared."

Instead of the old inn at the center of town, there is now a large, rickety structure dubbed the Union Hotel. Instead of the old tree out front that used to shade him and his cronies on hot summer days, there is now "a tall naked pole" topped by "a flag, one which was a singular assemblage of stars and stripes." The old portrait of the king seems more or less the same, but the inscription beneath it is different. Instead of "George III," it now reads, "General Washington."

Rural somnolence has given way to urban hustle and bustle. "The very character of the people seemed changed," the story continues. "There was a busy, bustling, disputatious tone about it, instead of the accustomed phlegm and drowsy tranquility." Outside the hotel, Rip spies "a lean, bilious-looking fellow, with his pockets full of handbills, . . . haranguing vehemently about rights of citizens—elections—members of congress—liberty—Bunker's Hill—heroes of seventy-six," all of it "a perfect Babylonish jargon to the bewildered Van Winkle." When Rip finds himself at the center of a crowd of suspicious townsfolk, he tries to reassure them by explaining, "I am a poor quiet man, a native of the place, and a loyal subject of the King, God bless him"—exactly the wrong thing to say in an excitable young republic. "A tory!" the crowd shouts in alarm, "a tory! a spy! a refugee! hustle him! away with him!" When Rip reels off a few local names to prove that he is really from those parts, he finds that one after another of his old friends has gone. One is dead, another disappeared in the war, while a third, Van Bummel, the puffed-up local schoolmaster, "went off to the wars too, was a great militia general, and is now in Congress." This, too, is change. Thanks to the revolution, a village pedagogue formerly condemned to view great events from afar has gotten an opportunity to participate in them directly. All of which is too much for poor Rip to handle:

> God knows, I'm not myself—I'm somebody else—that's me
> yonder—no—that's somebody else got into my shoes—I was

myself last night, but I fell asleep on the mountain, and they've changed my gun, and everything's changed, and I'm changed, and I can't tell what's my name, or who I am.

Written in 1820, the same year that Sydney Smith was pronouncing American literature nonexistent, "Rip Van Winkle" was filled with a very nineteenth-century impatience for the slowpoke world of the *ancien régime*. Change, as Washington Irving describes it, was not entirely absent from the world of Rip's youth, but it was exceedingly slow moving. Thereafter, just as Rip was going to sleep, it began to pick up. Institutions crumbled, and entire belief systems were transformed. Instead of a humble subject of the crown, an ordinary fellow like Rip was now expected to declare himself a proud and upright citizen of the republic. Rather than abjuring politics, he was expected to express himself forthrightly on all manner of topics from the rights of man to the doings of Congress. Although Irving was genially skeptical about certain aspects of the new order, he left no doubt that, on balance, change was for the good. With its "lean, bilious-looking" political agitators, the new regime could be irritating and abrasive. But it was also more exciting and alive. If it was busy and disputatious, it was because it was filled with people who, instead of dozing in the sunshine or wandering aimlessly through the woods, now acted, planned, and entered into various schemes and enterprises—all of which was reflected in a stepped-up urban pace.

. . . .

Thanks to the Erie Canal, this urban speedup was spreading itself through the Mohawk Valley to the Great Lakes. In 1800, as Henry Adams was later to write, the outlook for the infant American republic was far from promising. With a population equal to that of Ireland scattered across vast stretches of forest and bog, urbanization, progress, and all else that went with them seemed to be the unlikeliest of prospects. The ties binding

Americans together had been left almost purposely weak, while the regional rivalries pulling them apart were growing stronger and stronger. According to Adams, it seemed just a matter of time before the whole affair dissolved into European-style internecine warfare:

> A thousand miles of desolate and dreary forest, broken here and there by settlements; along the sea-coast a few flourishing towns devoted to commerce; no arts, a provincial literature, a cancerous disease of negro slavery, and differences of political theory fortified within geographical lines,—what could be hoped for such a country? . . .[16]

The famous American spirit of invention, Adams added, was nowhere to be found. At a time when James Watt was arousing excitement throughout Europe with his new steam engine, an American mechanic named John Fitch developed the world's first working steamboat nearly two decades ahead of Robert Fulton. Yet, as Fitch discovered to his despair, Americans couldn't be bothered. Who cared to go about by steam when one could go about by sail? Although the idea for a canal linking the Great Lakes with the Hudson had been floated as early as 1783, it took more than three decades before the New York State legislature could stir itself to vote the necessary credits. Who needed a canal when one could travel along narrow Indian trails by foot? If the pace was slow in New York, moreover, in other parts of the country it was positively languorous. Out in the hinterlands, Adams wrote, foreign travelers complained about "loungers and loafers, idlers of every description, infest[ing] the taverns, and annoy[ing] respectable travelers both native and foreign. . . . [I]n truth," he continued, "less work was done by the average man in 1800 than in aftertimes, for there was actually less work to do." Said one traveler of Kentucky: "Good country this for lazy fellows; they plant corn, turn their pigs into the woods, and in the autumn feed upon corn and pork. They lounge about the rest of the year."[17]

Yet by the time the Marquis de Lafayette made a triumphant return visit to the U.S. in 1824, nearly everything had changed. Lafayette found an America fairly overflowing with industry and bursting with pride over all that it had accomplished. Henry Clay, leader of a new generation of neo-Hamiltonian nationalists, rattled off the achievements: "the forests felled, the cities built, the mountains leveled, the canals cut, the highways constructed, the progress of the arts, the advancement of learning, and the increase in population."[18] Between 1800 and 1810, urban population grew at nearly double the national rate. Thanks to the War of 1812, it then fell back to a level that was merely on par with that of the U.S. as a whole. But beginning in 1820, it shot back up again to better than double the national rate, where it would remain the next half century.[19] Urban population growth between 1810 and 1860 was three times greater than rural, while the U.S. population growth overall was four times greater than that of Europe.[20]

In 1805, a farsighted Pennsylvanian named William Blodget had observed that bringing America's scattered population within reach of efficient transportation would mean "converting the entire country into *one great city.*"[21] Blodget was not speaking literally, of course. America was still a place of woods, fields, and farms and would remain so for generations to come. But as communication and transportation improved, it was clear that a specifically urban culture would spread itself far and wide. This is precisely what began to happen after the War of 1812, a crucial turning point in American development that has not gotten the attention it deserves. Particularly in the North, observers noted that western migration now seemed to take place in stages. First would come an advance guard of subsistence farmers, not much more economically advanced than the Native Americans they replaced (or, to put it more precisely, drove out or exterminated). Then, some years later, a second wave would bring denser, more urban development. New York's Mohawk Valley was a sleepy backwater of scattered farms and villages until the 1820s, when, thanks to the Erie Canal, it found itself suddenly inundated by wave after wave of laborers, entrepreneurs, and other disruptive sorts. In Illinois,

Southern "Butternuts," driven across the Ohio by the expanding cotton empire, had the place pretty much to themselves until the 1830s, when they suddenly found themselves swamped by Yankees coming down from the north by way of the Erie and the Great Lakes. The Butternuts were stunned. The new arrivals were transplanted New Englanders, for the most part, who worshiped at the shrine of industry and progress. As a onetime Illinois governor named Thomas Ford put it, they were a restless, "enterprising" element who "built mills, churches, school-houses, towns, and cities; and made roads and bridges as if by magic." According to one old Butternut, they worked

> jes' fer the fun o' ploughin' en reapin'. . . . Ez fer me, I kin
> shoot en trap all I kin eat, jes' plantin' 'nough corn fer hoecake
> en a leetle fodder, en some taters en turnips en pum'kins . . .
> en I 'low I kin give a traveler hoe-cakes en fried chicken all he
> wants to fill up on.

In return, the Northerners viewed the typical Southerner equally askance as "a long, lean, lank, lazy, and ignorant animal . . . content to squat in a log-cabin with a large family of ill-fed and ill-clothed, idle, ignorant children."[22] The upshot was a prolonged Kulturkampf between Democrats and Whigs over everything from public schools to public works and eventually to slavery. The more the restless, enterprising urban spirit spread itself across the countryside, the more the old Jeffersonian-Hamiltonian conflict flared and widened.

· · · · · · · · · · · ·

This was the first urban crisis, fueled by a growing conflict between urban growth and a generally antiurban constitutional framework. At first glance, it would seem that the urbanization of the early 1800s should have benefited the Whigs who, however gingerly, were carrying forward some semblance of the old Hamiltonian program. Yet, initially, at least, the opposite was the case. As the ranks of urban laborers swelled, class conflict rose. This was not class conflict in the modern, European sense—the *Communist Manifesto,* after all, was still a decade or two away—but something more primitive and anarchic. As Democratic ideology evolved in the face of changing circumstances, it was broadening its social base. Where Jefferson had regarded subsistence farmers as God's chosen people, a new generation of Jacksonian Democrats following in his wake now extended that honor to laborers, tradesmen, and other members of the "productive classes," a deliberately vague category constructed so as to include everyone except the old Federalist elite on the top and slaves and free blacks on the bottom. But, otherwise, the ideological framework remained the same: Egalitarianism was still married to antiurbanism and anticentralism. If, through some political sleight of hand, "the mobs of great cities" no longer detracted from "the support of pure government" but actually contributed to it, it was only because they were at war with the urban economy of which they were a part. Cities were still seen as sources of foppery and corruption, while industry was as suspect as ever because it forced self-employed artisans to surrender their independence and take jobs working for others. Not only did a growing money economy force farmers to grow crops for the local market but, when that was no longer possible, it forced them to give up farming altogether and enter the ranks of urban laborers, where they competed for jobs with free blacks and Irish immigrants.

This was the crowning blow. Jeffersonianism had not made peace with the city; to the contrary, it viewed it more than ever as an affront to white, male, republican pride. The result by the 1830s was the unholiest of alliances among Southern planters, western farmers, and Northern artisans and laborers, one that claimed to stand for egalitarianism and anticapitalism but in fact reflected a growing sense of panic over the strange new world of banks and factories that was robbing farmers, artisans, and planters of their economic autonomy.

This was not inaccurate as far as it went—urban capitalism *was* doing away with the old independence—although it is certainly worth pointing out that the autonomy of the Southern planter depended on the massive violation of the personal autonomy of his captive workforce. Still, slave owners argued that because they shared a common enemy in the Northern manufacturer and businessman, they were in essentially the same boat as the Northern laborer. "When we contend for the undivided profits and proceeds of our labour, do you not see that we stand precisely in the same situation as the labourer of the North?" asked Francis W. Pickens, a spokesman for nationalist-turned-Southern partisan John C. Calhoun. Southern planters, Pickens went on, "are the only class of capitalists, as far as pecuniary interest is concerned, which, as a class, are identified with the labourers of the country."[23]

The consequences could not have been more perverse. With Democratic encouragement, every noxious belief imaginable took hold among the Northern laboring masses—jingoism, nativism, and, most especially, racism. The proper way for Northern workers to show their manly republican pride, it seemed, was to attack capitalists and African Americans with equal vigor. Politics turned into a zero-sum game in which every step forward for plebeian whites had to be accompanied by an equal step backward for blacks. Even as it struck down virtually all voting restrictions affecting white males, for instance, New York's populist "Bucktail" revolt of 1821 raised the bar for free blacks to the point where all but a tiny number of the well-to-do were disenfranchised. Similar "democratic" reform movements resulted in blacks being stricken from the voting rolls in New Jersey in 1807, in Maryland in 1810, in Connecticut in 1811, and in virtually every other state by the 1820s and 1830s with the exception of Massachusetts, New Hampshire, Vermont, and Maine.[24] Because free blacks had routinely voted Federalist since the late eighteenth century, the plebeian white mob viewed them as the enemy. Because Irish immigrants were taking away jobs, the mob viewed them as the enemy also. Because abolitionists had effectively declared war on the Southern plantocracy, the worker's ally in the struggle against urban capitalism, they were the greatest enemy of all. To quote Arthur M. Schlesinger Jr.'s largely pro-Southern account in his Pulitzer Prize–winning 1945 study, *The Age of Jackson:*

> The Jacksonians in the thirties were bitterly critical of abolitionists. The outcry against slavery, they felt, distracted attention from the vital economic questions of Bank and currency, while at the same time it menaced the Southern alliance so necessary for the defense of the reform program.[25]

Yet these "bitterly critical" Jacksonians were responsible for a tidal wave of urban violence in which abolitionists were beaten, ridden out of town on rails, or, as in 1837 in the case of Elijah Lovejoy, murdered. Even in the cities—especially in the cities—U.S. "democracy" seemed to be inherently self-limiting. The more egalitarian it purported to be, the more inegalitarian it became by virtue of its embrace of racism and jingoism.

・・・・・・・・・・・・

This should have boded ill for American democracy and American urbanization alike, yet, ultimately, the very opposite occurred. To the extent that the Constitution of 1787 reflected the agrarian principles of the most important of the Founders, the political system seemed able to tolerate just so much urbanization and no more. Beyond a certain limit, it gave rise to a general perception that there was something intrinsically un-American about large masses of people crowding together in a very small place; something about the American constitutional structure made the very idea seem unnatural and perverse. Since the constitutional structure was unchangeable, therefore, urbanization should have begun leveling off—it should have, that is, but did not. Rather than urbanization yielding ground, it was the Jeffersonian constitutional order that began to give way beginning in the 1840s. Despite the best efforts of the Democrats, the old alliance between Northern laborers and Southern planters began to unravel. Whatever their alarm over the growth of large-scale industry and finance, farmers and laborers could not help noticing how the dramatic growth of the slave system was undermining white Southern farmers who did not own slaves and could not compete with those who did. Economic conditions for this middle segment were plummeting, which could not help but arouse fears among Northern workers and farmers as to what was in store for them as the Southern plantocracy moved to tighten its grip on the federal government. The more slavery threatened to spread into the western territories and to bring the Northern states to heel, the more the U.S. as a whole threatened to devolve into a single great slave republic, with disastrous consequences for the class of free farmers and laborers.

Southern firebrands were growing impatient with the alliance as well. By the 1850s, Jacksonian egalitarianism was giving way to the neo-aristocratic "mudsill" rhetoric of people like James Hammond of South Carolina, who, in a famous speech on the Senate floor, declared:

> In all social systems there must be a class to do the menial duties, to perform the drudgery of life. . . . It constitutes the very mudsill of society. . . . Such a class you must have, or you would not have that other class which leads [to] progress, civilization, and refinement. . . . Your white hireling class of manual laborers or "operatives," as you call them, are essentially slaves. The difference between us, is that our slaves are hired for life and well compensated . . . yours are hired by the day, not cared for, and scantily compensated.[26]

Property that was owned was better cared for than property that was merely rented. The sooner Northern cant about the rights of "free" labor was done away with, therefore, the better for all. As one Georgia newspaper wrote:

> Free Society! we sicken at the name. What is it but a conglom-
> eration of greasy mechanics, filthy operatives, small-fisted
> farmers, and moon-struck theorists? . . . The prevailing class
> one meets with [in the North] is that of mechanics struggling
> to be genteel, and small farmers who do their own drudgery,
> and yet are hardly fit for association with a Southern gentle-
> man's body servant.[27]

The cities, of course, were where "greasy mechanics, filthy operatives, . . . and moon-struck theorists" were to be found in the greatest
numbers. The *Southern Literary Messenger* added in 1860 that
Southerners

> came of that race . . . recognized as Cavaliers . . . directly
> descended from the Norman Barons of William the Conqueror,
> a race distinguished in its earliest history for its warlike and
> fearless character, a race in all times renowned for its gallantry,
> chivalry, honor, gentleness, and intellect.[28]

If ever there was something designed to rouse city-dwelling Puritans
to a fury, this was it. If Southern Cavaliers were moved by "racial" memories of battling on behalf of William the Conqueror, New Englanders were
moved by equally ancient memories of the long Anglo-Saxon struggle to
overthrow "the Norman Yoke" imposed on them in 1066.

Simultaneously, Northern Whigs, heirs of the old Federalists, were
groping toward a new kind of politics. Recognizing that snobbish old
ways would no longer do, they were struggling to learn the new language
of popular democracy, a field in which the skills of a rising Whig star

known as "Honest Abe" Lincoln, the Illinois rail-splitter, were especially useful. Suddenly, every Northern politician, no matter how well off, was desperate to prove that he had been born in a log cabin. Instead of a high-born individual condescending to the masses, the new political ideal was that of an ambitious striver—ambitious for himself and for the nation as a whole. "I am not ashamed to confess that twenty-five years ago I was a hired laborer, mauling rails, at work on a flat-boat—just what might happen to any poor man's son!" declared Lincoln in 1860. Yet "[t]he man who labored for another last year, this year labors for himself, and next year he will hire others to labor for him."[29] Rather than the old Jeffersonian ideal of self-sufficiency and rustic independence, the goal was now to construct a solid majority around a new form of democratic capitalism, one in which a vigorous economy would result in growing opportunities for individual advancement. The idea was to create a base of popular support for both urbanization and industrial growth. Not only did Republican fortunes depend on the success of such a program, but the nation's future did also.

. . . .

A tectonic shift on this scale would not have been possible, however, if a new element had not entered the picture in the form of technology. Although America had long been a society of backyard tinkers, the technological storm that hit the U.S. in the 1840s was of a different order of magnitude, a hurricane of such overwhelming fury that it seemed to bowl over everything in its path.

The railroads, of course, were at the forefront. Very simply, the steam locomotive was the greatest revolution to hit land transportation since the invention of the wheel. While water transport had been repeatedly revolutionized since the Renaissance thanks to the development of oceangoing ships, effective means of navigation, and, most recently, the steamboat, land transport had hardly budged. By the late eighteenth century, even royalty could travel no faster than fourteen miles per hour, and only then with a fresh change of horses every seven miles. In America, due to a paucity of good roads, conditions were even worse. Yet, within half a century, anyone who could afford the price of a railway ticket could travel at speeds three times as great.[30] The nineteenth-century diarist George Templeton Strong could barely contain himself at the spectacle of a nighttime train

> whizzing and rattling and panting, with its fiery furnace gleaming in front, its chimneys vomiting fiery smoke above, and its long train of cars rushing along behind like the body and trail of a gigantic dragon—or the d——l himself—and all darting forward at the rate of twenty miles an hour. Whew![31]

No less importantly, rail revolutionized the *economic* relationship between land and water transport. Since ancient times, the former had been many times more expensive than the latter. The Roman emperor Diocletian, who ruled from A.D. 284–305, calculated the difference at as much as fifty-six to one,[32] a ratio that may have actually increased in subsequent centuries as the Roman highway system crumbled and the empire disintegrated. As late as 1815, it was estimated that it cost as much to ship a ton of goods thirty miles inland from a typical American port as it did to ship it across the Atlantic.[33] Yet the rail revolution stood this age-old relationship on its head by making land transport many times cheaper than water. After plunging better than 90 percent as a consequence of the canal boom of the 1820s and 1830s, overland shipping rates in the United States fell another 75 percent thanks to the even more feverish rail construction of the 1840s.[34] Commerce was suddenly free to detach itself from the harbors, rivers, and canals and head out over dry land.

The urban consequences were nearly incalculable. The railroad was as much a machine for making cities as the new Bessemer converter was a machine for making steel. Wherever one of the new iron horses stopped, passengers would get on and off, goods would be loaded, porters would gather around, as would teamsters with their wagons, vendors with their newspapers and snacks, innkeepers looking for customers, and so on. Virtually overnight, buildings would sprout, land speculators would begin buying up deeds, and towns would seemingly spring up out of nowhere. In 1854, West Urbana was little more than a depot on the Central Illinois line. A year later, it was a thriving town of a hundred or so houses, with three hundred more buildings under construction, including two large hotels, six stores, a large furniture warehouse, a schoolhouse, and a Presbyterian church.[35] Farther downstate, the town of Jonesboro was a county seat, while Anna was the name of the neighborhood around the local train station about a mile and a half away. A few years later, as rail traffic multiplied, the relationship was reversed. Anna was now a thriving small city, while Jonesboro was a mere satellite.[36]

The most spectacular example of all was Chicago, which as late as 1848 was still a modest port at the southern tip of Lake Michigan, with no paved streets, sidewalks, or sewers, not a single mile of railroad track, and a population of fewer than eleven thousand people. Cows grazed a mile from city hall, while, not long before, wolves had been spotted at the intersection of Wabash and Adams. A scant seven years later, it was the railroad capital of the West, with a population of eighty thousand, half of it foreign-born. Between 1850 and 1856, grain shipments in and out of the city sextupled, while the value of manufactured goods produced within its confines rose sixfold as well. Between 1845 and 1856, land values rocketed from two hundred dollars to twenty thousand dollars an acre.[37]

· · · · · · · · · · · ·

The political consequences were nearly incalculable, too. Ever since Lewis and Clark, Americans had been gearing up for the great push through to the Pacific Ocean. Yet while individual settlers might make it over the

Rockies, the idea that the U.S. flag might follow and unite the entire transcontinental expanse under the sway of a single nation-state seemed far-fetched. There was no practical way of binding together such a vast, thinly settled republic. Steamboats were useless west of the Mississippi, horse-drawn wagons were too slow, while sail power around the Horn was only marginally better.[38] By the mid-1840s, though, when the first serious proposal for a transcontinental railroad was floated, it was apparent that rail could make it work by bringing even the Pacific Coast into close and regular contact. Thanks to a growing rail network, Texas was effectively no farther away from Washington than Philadelphia had been a few decades earlier; presumably, California would soon be no farther away than Texas was now. National expansion was following on the heels of technological development. The railroads were multiplying the capabilities of the nation-state.

Simultaneously, the new technology was multiplying the conflict between North and South. Obviously, planters and factory owners both needed labor to propel their systems forward. But as the industrial pace accelerated, factory owners needed labor power of a different kind: not just brute force but labor that was flexible, attentive, and skilled. For this reason, it needed a wage system that would not only permit employers to take on workers and let them go with relative ease but allow them to reward the best workers and winnow out the worst so as to raise the quality of labor overall. Yet the labor-management tools available to slave owners were far too crude to permit anything comparable. Planters could not purchase a worker's labor power alone; instead, they had to purchase the entire worker, lock, stock, and barrel, which was far less efficient. Since a planter was unable to offer a slave the only thing he really desired, which is to say his freedom, the only motivational tool at his disposal was the lash. Because a slave did not even control his own body, he had no incentive to raise himself up—no incentive to save, to develop his skills, to struggle for advancement. Indeed, considering the degree to which he was robbed of the fruits of his own labor, he had every incentive to sabotage the system of which he was a part, by dragging his feet or appearing stupid or all thumbs. Southern productivity lagged farther and farther behind as a consequence. While there is no doubt as to who was the chief victim in all this, it is worth noting that the system was dragging both sides down— the slave by giving him every reason to be lazy and unproductive, and the master by forcing him to behave with ever growing brutality.

The city, meanwhile, was where the free-labor market was most highly developed. Not only was it where workers were to be found in the greatest number, but thanks to the growth of schools, cultural institutions, and the penny press, it was where the best-educated and hence most-productive workers were concentrated. (At more than 95 percent, the adult literacy rate in New England, the most heavily urbanized region of the country, was perhaps the highest in the world.[39]) The city was also the place where competition was at its most intense—not only among workers for the best jobs but, when economic winds were favorable, among employers for the best workers. The dramatic growth of the rail system from the 1840s on served to pump up this urban labor system by continually pouring more workers into the cities and driving competition to new heights.

The city, finally, was where two competing concepts of democracy— labor and capitalist—seemed to overlap, if only briefly. If employers wanted a well-educated workforce, workers did, too, since education was the only way that they could raise themselves up, both singly and collectively. If employers wanted freedom to hire and fire, workers also wanted to be free to change jobs when it was in their interest. As Lincoln declared in 1860, "I like the system which lets a man quit when he wants to, and wish it might prevail everywhere." Of course, workers wanted high wages while bosses wanted low, and if workers wanted the freedom to join one of America's nascent labor unions, employers wanted to be free to bust them. Nonetheless, the lines were still sufficiently ambiguous in the 1840s and 1850s for both workers and employers to join forces against Southern slave owners, who represented by far the greater threat to the freedom of both.

Workers and capitalists wanted something else—a flexible, democratic form of government that would allow them to make the changes necessary to foster continued industrial growth. Not only did the Constitution protect slavery by surrounding it with a series of impenetrable legal barriers but it multiplied the slave power as well. The infamous three-fifths clause, which allowed slaves to be counted as three-fifths of a person for purposes of congressional representation even though they were deprived of the right to vote, gave the South as many as twenty-five extra seats in the House. The principle of equal state representation in the Senate not only allowed Southern states to maintain parity with Northern states, even though the latter were growing more populous with each passing decade, but it also gave the South effective veto power over federal judicial appointments. Thus, an increasingly underdeveloped, underpopulated region was able to dominate the nation as a whole. Given the growing unpopularity of constitutional provisions such as these, the obvious solution would have been to repeal them. But given that Article V required that any amendment be approved by two-thirds of each house plus three-fourths of the states, the slavocracy's position was secure as long as it was able to control anything close to an equal number of states. No matter how much Northerners might fuss and fume, slavery was legally impregnable.

But there was a problem. As the South well realized, parchment barriers were of limited effectiveness in holding back a swelling popular tide. No matter what Northerners might say to the contrary, the South feared that the day was approaching when the North would use its growing numerical preponderance to sweep aside such obstacles by hook or by crook. Although the infant Republican Party tried to paint itself as more Jeffersonian than the Jeffersonians, this was precisely what the party's victory in 1860 represented in Southern eyes. The Constitution of 1787 was still sacred. But regardless of what it actually said, the Republicans were determined to bend it to the will of the democratic majority.

Where Jefferson had tried to lock the U.S. into a permanent agrarian framework in the so-called Revolution of 1800, the "Revolution of 1860," to use the historian James M. McPherson's term,[40] amounted to a great collective effort to do the opposite: to cast off such restraints and propel the nation in an urban-industrial direction. As secession fever spread and Southern senators and congressmen began packing their bags and going home, Republicans used their control of a rump Congress to ram through a host of measures that had long been waiting in the wings: a tariff act to protect domestic industries in 1861, a Homestead Act to solidify the free-labor character of the West in 1862, an act to rebuild the national banking system in 1863, an immigration act to insure a free flow of foreign labor in 1864, and so on. As the historian Charles Beard put it, "All that two generations of Federalists and Whigs had tried to get was won in four short years, and more besides."[41] Authorization to begin work on a trans-continental railroad was also approved in 1862, an especially audacious move at a time when the very fate of the Union was in doubt.

If the events of 1776–89 had been America's Girondist revolution, moderate and decentralized, those of 1860–65 were the Jacobin second act, fierce, radical, and uncompromising. The people had been goaded to a fury and, as a result, were determined to make a clean sweep. As George W. Julian, a leading Radical Republican, declared on the floor of the House in 1862:

> Should both Congress and the courts stand in the way of the nation's life, then "the red lightning of the people's wrath" must consume the recreant men who refuse to exercise the people's will. Our country, united and free, must be saved at whatever hazard or cost; and nothing, not even the Constitution, must be allowed to hold back the uplifted arm of the government in blasting the power of the rebels forever.[42]

The people were sovereign over the Constitution rather than under it. Democracy was superior, rather than subordinate, to the law. As an astute Northern journalist named Sidney George Fisher (whose work, sadly, has been all but forgotten) wrote in a book published the same year:

> The people rule. The country is theirs and they govern it. The Constitution is theirs, and they can and will mould and modify it to suit their wishes. . . . The people see the Government overstep what have generally been considered its constitutional limits every day, and they rejoice.[43]

The results were a victory not only for democracy but for a specifically urban form of democracy, since the city was the place where the masses, the new driving force, were most concentrated and powerful. Fort Sumter was an opportunity for the "commonwealthmen" of New England to have a go at their old enemy, the Cavaliers, both militarily and economically. Boston was the center of the antislavery resistance, while New England was the seedbed of American industry. As an Argentine visitor had remarked in 1847, New England Yankees had carried "to the rest of the Union the . . . moral and intellectual aptitude [and] . . . manual capability which makes an American a walking work shop. . . . The great colonial and rail road enterprises, the banks, and the corporations are founded and developed by them."[44] By 1860, the North had twice the rail density as the South, while Lowell, Massachusetts, had more cotton spindles under operation than the entire Confederacy combined.[45] The war was thus a chance to prove once and for all the superiority of an urban system based on free labor vis-à-vis an agrarian system based on a captive workforce.

The Puritans took as long to put their military machine in working order in the 1860s as they did in England in the 1640s, but once they found their Oliver Cromwell in men like Grant and Sherman, the results were decisive. As John Sherman wrote to his brother William T. in 1865:

> The truth is the close of war with our resources unimpaired gives an elevation, a scope to the ideas of the leading capitalists, far higher than anything ever undertaken in this country before. They talk of millions as confidently as formerly of thousands.[46]

A few years later, George W. Julian told his daughter that what he had fought for in the war was a new system in which "labor would be respectable, our democratic theory of equality would be put into practice, closely associated communities would be established as well as a system of common schools offering to all equal educational opportunities."[47] Equality, free labor, popular education—all depended on "closely associated communities" that were tight, neighborly, and compact. Democracy, urbanism, and economic progress all went hand in hand. With the close of the war, both American capitalism and American urbanization were about to enter a new stage.

3

THE SECOND
URBAN CRISIS

The generation between 1865 and 1895
was already mortgaged to the railways, and no one
knew it better than the generation itself.

HENRY ADAMS

Anything that centralizes the bourgeoisie
is of course advantageous to the workers.

KARL MARX

Even the smallest settlement [in America] denies itself
the character of a village and tends to become a city.
The town rules the whole style of living, even in the country.

CARL JUNG

THE CIVIL WAR was the great turning point in the history of the American city and in the history of American attitudes toward the city. To begin with the most obvious, cities were now bigger. Manhattan's population rose from 814,000 in 1860 to 942,000 in 1870 and then to 1.16 million in 1880, a 43 percent increase. Philadelphia's population rose from 566,000 to 847,000, a 50 percent increase; Brooklyn's more than doubled, from 279,000 to 599,000; while Boston's doubled from 178,000 to 363,000. Chicago, the most meteoric of all, saw its population more than quadruple during the same twenty-year period, going from 112,000 to 503,000. Although urban growth decelerated somewhat in the 1870s due to the agricultural boom out West, urban population still grew 35 percent faster than the nation as a whole. By the 1880s, moreover, it was once again racing ahead at more than double the national rate.[1]

But cities were not only growing quantitatively—their very nature was changing. The urban labor market was consolidating in ways deeply shocking to American sensibilities. In 1860, when the average workshop employed just ten people and only a handful of factories in the entire country employed five hundred or more, workers in a given market had hundreds, sometimes even thousands, of prospective employers to choose from. Forty years later, when more than a thousand companies each employed five hundred or more workers and the giant Baldwin locomotive works employed eight thousand, workers sometimes had only a handful of choices. Many local labor markets were now effectively controlled by a small number of industrial magnates who seemed able to set wages with impunity.[2] Where previously people had believed that it was not in the American nature to bow and scrape and plead for a job, in an age of economic royalism, workers had no choice. They had to take what was offered—and be grateful for it besides.

Prior to 1861, the economy was still comparatively localized. Although a few cities were beginning to specialize, most were forced by the still-limited circulation of commodities to keep on hand a full complement of butchers, bakers, millers, and so on. After the war, with the railroads busily knitting the country into a single integrated market, this was less and less the case. Particularly in the Midwest, entire cities were now dominated by a single industry. Thanks to a couple of New Englanders named

Cadwallader C. Washburn and Charles A. Pillsbury, plus a transplanted Alabamian named George M. Christian, Minneapolis was now emerging as the nation's grain-milling center, while thanks to Gustavus Swift's refrigerated railroad cars, which allowed dressed carcasses to be transported long distances, Chicago was emerging as "hog butcher for the world." By some measures, corporate centralization was actually less advanced in the U.S. than in either Britain or Germany. Yet Americans' unique eighteenth-century Constitution made them hypersensitive to centralization in any form whatsoever, which is why the corporate concentration of the post–Civil War period was more than enough to set their nerves on edge.

The urban population was itself changing. Not only was the new industrial working class increasingly foreign-born, it was born of different foreign stock. Rather than from Germany and the British Isles, new arrivals were pouring in from Southern and Eastern Europe, points on the globe that, from the perspective of the average native-born Protestant, might just as well have been the Dark Continent.[3] Not only did the new immigrants speak in strange tongues, they worshiped strange gods: Most were not even Protestant and many were not even Christian. Because few headed for the countryside, the cities became outposts of immigrant culture. By 1880, 87 percent of Chicago's population was either foreign-born or the children of foreign-born immigrants, as was 84 percent of Milwaukee's and Detroit's, 80 percent of New York's and Cleveland's, and 78 percent of St. Louis's and San Francisco's. Although the U.S. was hardly the only country to see mass immigration during this period, it drew from an exceptionally wide range of sources. Argentina, by comparison, drew two-thirds of its immigrants from just two countries, Italy and Spain. Canada drew three-fourths from the U.S. and Great Britain, while Australia drew almost entirely from the U.K. By 1910, at a time when four million New Yorkers were either immigrants or the children of immigrants—most of them from Ireland, Italy, and Eastern Europe—London's population was still 94 percent English or Welsh.[4]

This, too, was shocking to American sensibilities, yet the process seemed irreversible. No matter what Washington did or did not do, the tide of immigrants continued to swell. Western expansion was supposed to slow urban expansion by drawing off city dwellers to the countryside. Yet the opening of the West meant more subsidies for the railroads in the form of generous land grants, which fueled rail expansion all the more. More people than ever crowded into growing metropolitan centers where more rail lines now terminated. While a tight monetary policy might have been expected to hold down urbanization by tamping down industrial growth, the brutal deflationary wave that began around 1873 proved even more devastating to agriculture. The result was a prolonged rural contraction that forced hundreds of thousands of indebted farmers and ranchers off the land and into the cities, where they now found themselves living in uncomfortable proximity to people from Italy, Poland, and other exotic places.

Changes like these were more than unsettling—they were disorienting and traumatic. For many Americans, it seemed incomprehensible that abstract economic forces could be responsible for anything so sweeping. Someone had to be pulling the strings. There were any number of likely candidates for the role of puppeteer-in-chief: the banks, the railroads, or shadowy international financiers in places like London and Zurich who seemed intent on punishing the United States for failing to go on the gold standard. It wasn't just debt-strapped farmers in Alabama or the Dakotas who thought this way; it was also sophisticated Boston Brahmins such as Henry Adams and his brother Brooks, a sometime historian who not only lambasted the railroads and banks but for good measure vilified the Jews, who he was convinced were at the bottom of it all. Railroads were strangling the cities and monopolists were strangling consumers while bankers were strangling the global economy by "engross[ing] the gold of the world, and then, by legislation, ma[king] it the sole measure of value."[5] When international speculators began a run on the U.S. Treasury in 1893, Brooks did not hesitate in fixing the blame. It was all the fault of those "rotten, unsexed, swindling, lying Jews represented by J. P. Morgan" who have been "manipulating our country for the last four years."[6]

This was nonsense, of course. Rather than being manipulated from afar, the U.S. economy was changing shape on its own. Despite the popular image of a shadowy capitalist cabal that had gotten the country by the throat and would not let go, the real story was richer and more complex. Economic opportunity was contracting for some small producers, most notably debt-strapped farmers and ranchers in the South and the Great Plains. But it was opening up for others. The late nineteenth century was something of a golden age for the urban entrepreneur, everyone from the pushcart vendor to the clothing manufacturer and vaudeville producer. Such elements were well situated to take advantage of urban economies that were expanding not only outwardly but inwardly as they learned how to pack more people, jobs, and services into every cubic inch of urban space. The nickelodeon, the department store, the rise of huge newspaper empires—these were areas in which business was learning to take advantage of rising population densities so as to maximize value.

The late nineteenth and early twentieth century was the age of grandiosity, one in which capitalism was exploring the economies of scale in the form of the big city, the grand hotel, the global empire, and the corporate merger. But it was one in which capitalism was also learning the *diseconomies* of scale. Business was discovering that big industrial systems were vulnerable in ways that had not been anticipated. A strike by a small group of strategically situated workers could close down an entire factory or, in the case of the railroads, shut down an entire district or region. If cities were increasingly proficient at turning out new goods and services, they were also proficient at turning out strange new ideas, unsettling new art forms, and other things not to the propertied classes' liking. Thus, not only was New York's Lower East Side the center of a burgeoning garment industry, but the *New York Times* complained in 1893 that it was also turning out a bumper crop of "hatchet-faced, pimply, sallow-cheeked, rat-eyed" Russian Jews who were drinking deeply of the "pestiferous milk of Nihilism and dynamite throwing."[7] The Reverend Josiah Strong, one of the most famous clergymen of the day, complained in 1885 that the city was producing socialists by the carload:

> When our urban population has been multiplied several fold, and our Cincinnatis have become Chicagos, our Chicagos New Yorks, and our New Yorks Londons; when class antipathies are deepened; when socialistic organizations, armed and drilled, are in every city, and the ignorant and vicious power of crowded populations has fully found itself . . . THEN will come the real test of our institutions. . . .[8]

The city was productive in more ways than one. If urbanization was threatening to Southern agrarians prior to the Civil War, it was now proving no less worrisome to a growing range of bourgeois elements up North: urban reformers worried about the growth of the slums, industrialists and financiers worried about the growth of radicalism, small-town Bible thumpers up in arms over sex and sin, and so on. These were the people who had beaten the South but were now frightened by the new Frankenstein in their midst, a belief made even worse by the sense that all the forces that had made the city could only accelerate. To understand why, it is necessary to know a bit more about railroads and urban growth.

•••••••••••••

Rather than slowing down after the Civil War, the rail boom accelerated. As early as the 1840s, the industry was soaking up more than $200 million in investment capital per decade, more than all the money that had by that point gone into canals, steamboats, and private turnpikes.[9] Yet by the 1870s, the rail sector was soaking up far more, as much as 50 percent of what was by now a much larger pool of American capital.[10] Between 1850 and 1860, railway mileage in the U.S. more than doubled.[11] Between 1865 and 1872, it doubled again, while between 1872 and 1900, it tripled. Prior to 1861, a typical rail company was a small-time operation having no more than a hundred miles of track, with the result that a passenger had to change trains as many as seventeen times in traveling from Chicago to New York.[12] As late as 1871, as many as twenty-three different rail gauges were in use.[13] Thereafter, amid a period of rapid consolidation, gauges were standardized and express interurban service became the order of the day. In place of a slow and balky short-haul system, a national rail network was emerging in which long-range, cross-country travel played a larger and larger role.

Every last aspect of American life would be transformed as a consequence. As Henry Adams observed, the railroads gave rise to an entire constellation of closely related industries and financial institutions: "banks, mines, furnaces, shops, power-houses, technical knowledge, mechanical population, together with a steady remodelling of social and political habits, ideas, and institutions to fit the new scale and suit the new conditions."[14] Not only did the railroads standardize time zones across the U.S., they helped usher in a new age of punctuality. People who had previously told time by the sun now relied on the train whistle and pocket watch. While many gained as a consequence of the new industrial order, many did not. Inland water transport, for example, was the most conspicuous loser. There was simply no way that canals could compete with the iron horse. They dried up in summertime, froze over in winter, while even under the best of circumstances were comparatively slow and expensive. Not content to let nature take its course, however, the powerful New York Central imposed a boycott on the old Erie and forced other rail lines to do likewise; elsewhere, railroads simply bought up canals for the express purpose of shutting them down. The Mississippi, once the heartland's great outlet to the sea, also went into eclipse: The Civil War had hurt business on the lower portion, while the upper half was reduced to little more than an appendage of the burgeoning Midwestern rail network.[15] Riverboat captains who once regarded the river as their own private fief now fairly begged for work. Even the road network suffered. When overland transport was chiefly by wagon or coach, state and local governments had had an incentive to keep roads in decent repair. But with the growth of the railroads, any such incentive disappeared. By the 1890s, the *Nation* was complaining that America's muddy, potholed roads were in the worst shape since the Jamestown colony.[16]

All of which was enough to persuade some that the railroads were wringing the country dry. As a half-dozen rail giants emerged out of the welter of small and midsize firms to take charge of the system and standardize operations from one end of the country to the other, they seemed to be closing down any and all alternatives so that anyone who wanted to travel any significant distance would have to pay tribute. Yet what was remarkable about the railroad merger movement was the degree to which it was driven by weakness rather than strength. As deflation deepened, the chief problem facing the industry was one of excess capacity: too many trains chasing too few customers. Ruthless fare-cutting was the inevitable upshot. Between 1862 and 1882, railroads slashed freight rates a full 66 percent in constant dollars.[17] By 1876, the cost of transporting cattle from Chicago to New York fell to as little as a dollar a carload, while the price of a passenger ticket between Boston and Cleveland declined to just $6.50.[18] Despite the usual populist rhetoric about price-gouging monopolists, the railroad companies that survived the crunch were not the ones that jacked up prices most ruthlessly but those with sufficient financial reserves to drive rates *down* most ruthlessly and still remain on their feet.

Paradoxically, plummeting shipping rates did not make life easier for farmers and other small businessmen, but in some respects made it worse. Cheap rail transport allowed commodities to circulate over a wider area, which meant that cozy regional markets now found themselves inundated by goods from afar. Instead of competing with a rival businessman across the street, small-town producers and retailers now found themselves competing with giant combines in Chicago, Cleveland, and beyond. And this was only the beginning. Thanks to a corresponding rail expansion in Europe and Latin America and the development of ocean-going steamships, commodity markets were becoming internationalized to an unprecedented degree. The transatlantic telegraph cable, laid in 1866, allowed commodity prices to be relayed instantaneously from one side of the world to the other, which meant that grain farmers in the Great Plains now found themselves competing head to head with growers in Argentina and the Ukraine. In the space of two or three generations, the United States had gone from a place of segmented, regional economies to a major player on the international scene.

The psychological impact was profound. When heightened competition destroys someone else's business, it is one thing, but when it blows away one's own business, it is quite another. Moreover, when the competitive winds blow from a country one has never heard of, it is even worse—a gigantic international conspiracy intent on destroying all that is sacred and holy. The result of this unprecedented form of globalization was an immense wave of nativism flowing out of the Midwest and Great Plains beginning in the late 1880s and early 1890s, a flood tide of resentment aimed at everyone from the railroads, Wall Street speculators, and the Rothschilds to the foreign immigrants flowing into U.S. cities.

Although few were inclined to shed a tear for a Jay Gould or a John D. Rockefeller, stepped-up competition was also hard on the robber barons. Despite the emergence of a handful of corporate superpowers like U.S. Steel and Standard Oil around the turn of the century, the number of players in any given field was not shrinking, as complaints about growing monopolization would suggest, but expanding. Instead of gaining market share, the biggest players were losing it. Between 1899 and 1909, when the outcry over monopolization was at its peak, the number of manufacturing firms in the United States rose nearly 30 percent. Of nine areas of manufacturing with a product value of more than $500 million a year, one had 446 companies competing for a piece of the pie, while another had more than 1,000. Standard Oil, the monopoly at which even small children loved to hiss, steadily lost ground after 1899 to wildcatters in the newly discovered oil fields of Texas, Oklahoma, and California. National banks found themselves under assault by a growing number of state lending institutions.[19] Rather than lords of the jungle, corporate giants like these were coming to resemble exhausted stags surrounded by packs of hungry, snarling wolves.

The truth was thus more complicated than most people were inclined to admit. But if Americans tended to exaggerate the degree of *corporate* concentration, they did not exaggerate the degree of *geographic* concentration. There is no doubt that productive capacity was expanding most rapidly in a small number of fast-growing cities—in Minneapolis, for instance; in Chicago; and most spectacularly, in that Babylon of Babylons, New York. Despite feverish talk of plots and conspiracies, there was nothing the least bit mysterious about the process. To the contrary, it was a direct consequence of the economics of nineteenth-century transport, in particular the plummeting cost of long-distance travel. From a railroad's point of view, stopping and starting were expenses to avoid—they took time and soaked up energy. The more competition heated up, the more the railroads were inclined to bypass one-horse towns in favor of the major urban markets where business was increasingly concentrated. Cities like New York, Chicago, and Minneapolis loomed larger and larger as a consequence. By the same token, if cities were not only bigger but more crowded, it was the result of a not-unrelated gap between long- and short-haul costs. If one was falling, the other was shooting through the roof. On disembarking in a city center, a rail passenger ran headlong into a dense thicket of porters, teamsters, carriages, and wagons. Rigs would become tangled, horses would rear and buck, and wagons would overturn—the bigger the city, the denser the snarl. Just as it was once as expensive to transport goods thirty miles inland as it was to ship them across the Atlantic, it was now becoming as expensive to ship them across town as it was to ship them across state. Close physical proximity to a railhead or terminal was growing more and more valuable.

In 1896, an engineering publication declared that the differential between long- and short-haul transport was approaching a thousand to one, an indication of how intense such crowding had become.[20] Yet everything the railroads did to alleviate such conditions only made them worse. The more they cut long-distance rates, the more interurban traffic rose. The more parlor, dining, and sleeping cars they offered in order to win customers from their competitors, the more traffic rose as well, which meant that congestion around depots and terminals continued to thicken. The electric trolley boom that began in the 1880s was supposed to alleviate the problem by facilitating travel within the city, thereby allowing urban development to spread itself over a broader area. Yet by expanding travel between the urban center and the outlying suburbs, the trolley wound up doing the opposite. More people than ever traveled downtown to where streetcar lines now converged as well, adding to the congestion. European cities were able to get around this problem by requiring trolley companies to build concentric ring lines, which made it possible to travel within the city without having to pass through the downtown hub.[21] But such remedies required a high degree of government regulation and sometimes even outright government ownership, both of which were anathema in the United States. Instead, a boom-or-bust cycle prevailed in which each trolley line fought its way into the center of the city to get a slice of the downtown business.

Congestion was more than just an economic problem—it was a political problem. Not only was rail technology herding ever more people and jobs into ever more crowded urban places, it was squeezing in mutually hostile forces: businessmen in search of profits, immigrants in search of work, and displaced farmers who had been forced to move to the city to look for employment and hated their new surroundings all the more for it. The city by the late 1800s was drawing everyone into its vortex, city lovers and city haters, libertarians, libertines, and scandalized bluenoses. The more such forces were forced into close proximity with one another, the more the collective temperature rose. Brooks Adams described the modern industrial metropolis as "our pride and our terror."[22] Henry Adams described it around the turn of the century as a veritable eruption of steam, brick, and stone:

> Power seemed to have outgrown its servitude and to have asserted its freedom. The cylinder had exploded, and thrown great masses of stone and steam against the sky. The city had the air and movement of hysteria, and the citizens were crying, in every accent of anger and alarm, that the new forces must at any cost be brought under control. Prosperity never before imagined, power never yet wielded by man, speed never reached by anything but a meteor, had made the world irritable, nervous, querulous, unreasonable and afraid.[23]

Class was meanwhile the most fundamental source of urban tension. Urban geographers have long noted how class conflict was leading to a spatial reorganization of the urban environment—how the growth of an urban proletariat in the early 1800s, for instance, had caused the middle and upper classes to retreat into more genteel neighborhoods well removed from the noise, tumult, and political disturbances of "the lower orders." The historian Eric Hobsbawm described urban development during this period as

> a gigantic process of class segregation, which pushed the new laboring poor into great morasses of misery outside the centres of government and business and the newly specialized residential areas of the bourgeoisie. The almost universal

European division into a "good" west end and a "poor" east end of large cities developed in this period.[24]

Perhaps the most dramatic spatial reorganization of all occurred in 1852 when Baron Georges Haussmann, the Robert Moses of his day, set about evicting tens of thousands of the laboring poor from central Paris at the behest of Napoleon III, leveling the slums, and cutting a series of broad boulevards through the heart of the medieval city. It was an immense remodeling effort aimed at opening up the city to air and sunlight, while at the same time dispersing a dangerous working-class population to the outskirts and making the metropolis easier to patrol. Nothing comparable took place in the United States in the mid-nineteenth century for a number of reasons: because government in America was not yet capable of such an ambitious undertaking, because the condition of the urban poor was not yet quite as wretched, and because, notwithstanding the urban tumult of the 1830s and 1840s, there was as yet nothing to compare to the events in France of 1789–94 or 1848. Because Americans had less reason to fear, they had less reason to act.

But the Civil War marked the start of a process of convergence. Instead of the artisans and day laborers of the prewar period, something approaching a genuine urban proletariat was beginning to emerge, masses of unskilled and semiskilled workers laboring in larger and larger factories in bigger and bigger cities. Instead of working shoulder to shoulder with their bosses in the hallowed old republican fashion, the American industrial worker of the 1870s and 1880s was far likelier to work for a huge, impersonal corporation commanded by the likes of Henry Clay Frick and Andrew Carnegie, men who seemed to exist on an entirely different plane. Class lines were hardening not only socially, politically, and economically but geographically. The post–Civil War city was as much a walking city as the antebellum city had been. But foot traffic increasingly tended to segment itself into separate and distinct neighborhoods. Entire communities were springing up in the shadows of factories, rail yards, or, in the case of Chicago, slaughterhouses. In addition to workers and their families, they included grocers, saloon keepers, and other tradesmen, plus a smattering of working-class intellectuals: socialists, journalists, sidewalk agitators, and barroom philosophers. Still, it was the factory or rail workers who predominated, not only numerically but politically. It was their relationship to the new set of corporate employers that set the tone for the neighborhood as a whole and shaped its consciousness.

Although the question is controversial among historians, it appears that as steerage rates fell and low-cost rail travel penetrated deep into the European hinterlands, the result was to bring onto market new sources of labor that had previously gone untapped.[25] Thus, the same thing began happening to factory labor in the late nineteenth century that was happening to commodities such as wheat or corn: It was being internationalized. As more and more labor power offered itself for sale, the markets were growing glutted, and prices, which is to say wages, were beginning to drop. "Taking into account differences in the cost of living," summed up one labor historian, "much evidence suggests that less skilled workers in the United States earned little more than their counterparts in Europe."[26] "If we eat, we can't dress," observed an iron-ore miner in the Mesabi Range of northern Minnesota, "and if we dress, we don't eat."[27] This equalization was especially disturbing to American sensibilities because of what would subsequently be known as "American exceptionalism"—the notion that America was different from all other nations, that it was uniquely blessed, and that it was therefore exempt from the usual laws of capitalist development. Yet as unskilled factory workers in the U.S. joined their European counterparts in what was fast becoming a race to the bottom, it was becoming clear that America was not exempt, not exceptional, and that what it was witnessing, in fact, was the same pauperization of labor that socialists on both sides of the Atlantic argued was an inescapable feature of industrial capitalist development.

The post–Civil War urban working-class population differed in yet another respect: It was better organized. Before the war, labor unions had been weak, unstable, and poorly defined. Little effort was made to distinguish between wage earners and independent small producers, whose interests—Jacksonian ideology to the contrary—were often at odds. But beginning in the early 1860s, a new generation of labor organizations began taking shape, organizations that were stronger, better organized, and more thoroughly class-based. The process began during the war itself, which saw no fewer than five major unions get off the ground: the American Miners Association, precursor of the United Mine Workers, in 1861; the Brotherhood of Locomotive Engineers, the Cigar Makers' National Union, and the Iron Moulders' International Union in 1864; and the Bricklayers' and Masons' International Union in 1865. The Knights of Labor, a new kind of organization that attempted to unite all workers under a single umbrella, was organized in Philadelphia in 1869.[28] Indeed, one could argue that unions and corporations were now following parallel lines of development. Both were growing bigger, more centralized, more heavily armored, so to speak, as they prepared themselves for long-term combat.

The Great Rail Strike of 1877 was an important turning point. It was not just the biggest strike ever in the U.S. but quite simply the biggest labor conflict ever to erupt in the industrialized world.[29] It began when Jay Gould and other railroad magnates imposed a 10 percent wage cut—the second in four years—on the four major trunk lines leading from the Midwest to the East. Gould and his colleagues were so confident that workers would accept such cuts without protest that, to quote the historian Samuel Eliot Morison, they were positively "jaunty" in announcing them—which made the response all the more astonishing.[30] Thousands of workers armed with guns, knives, and other weapons rose in revolt. They destroyed bridges, set fire to trains, and tied up two-thirds of the country's seventy-five thousand miles of track. The explosion of working-class outrage immobilized much of the nation's manufacturing base and tied up traffic throughout the Ohio Valley and the Middle Atlantic States. In Pittsburgh alone, strikers destroyed the Pennsylvania Railroad's Union Depot along with thirty-nine other buildings and set fire to more than one hundred locomotives and two thousand railroad cars.[31] Even though state militias retaliated by killing scores of people and injuring hundreds more, militia commanders were uneasy as to where their troops' real loyalty lay. "It is impossible for me to do anything with my company," complained one officer. "Most of them are railroad men, and they will not respond."[32] Previously, noted the historian James Ford Rhodes, most Americans were confident in the belief that America was immune to European-style class warfare such as the Paris Commune. A host of republican institutions, from free public schools and strong churches to cheap land, supposedly rendered such outbreaks impossible.[33] But now references to the "American Commune" were rife.[34] "Optimistic as we are, we cannot fail to know that the increasing proportion of the incapable among us is repeating here the problem of the Old World," wrote the *Atlantic Monthly* a few years later. "[E]very year brings the conditions of American labor into closer likeness to those of the Old World."[35]

Labor relations quieted down for a spell after 1877 but then began heating up again in the mid-1880s. A rail strike led by the Knights of Labor in early 1886 tied up traffic throughout the Southwest, while some 350,000 workers across the country heeded the call a few months later for a one-day general strike in support of the eight-hour day. 1892 saw an epic strike at Andrew Carnegie's Homestead steelworks, in which workers fought a running gun battle with Pinkerton guards on the banks of the Monongahela River. 1894 saw an even more tumultuous uprising, the Pullman Porter Strike. This was arguably the seminal event in American urban politics in the final years of the nineteenth century, not only because it was the biggest and most violent labor eruption to date but because of where it occurred: right in the heart of Chicago, the nerve center of the North American rail network.

. . . .

The Pullman Porter Strike exemplifies the geopolitics of the late-nineteenth-century class struggle. The conflict began not in Chicago itself but in the model company town of Pullman, some fourteen miles to the south. Not only was the Pullman Company on the cutting edge of rail technology—the famous Pullman Palace Sleeping Car, a veritable grand hotel on wheels, was one of the innovations that was making long-distance train travel increasingly popular during this period—but it was on the cutting edge of corporate social thought. Its model town, built in the early 1880s, was an effort at total engineering, a meticulously groomed, all-brick community designed to bring out the best in each worker by reengineering all aspects of his daily existence. Modeled after the Krupp community in Essen, Germany, and Sir Titus Salt's Saltaire, in England, Pullman was built along lines best described as pseudo-pastoral. The community was almost oppressively green, filled with "bright beds of flowers and green velvety stretches of lawn," to quote a company brochure, "shaded with trees and dotted with parks and pretty water vistas and glimpses here and there of artistic sweeps of landscape gardening." It was a community in which "all that is ugly and discordant and demoralizing is eliminated, and all that inspires to self-respect is generously provided."[36] In contrast to the typical mill-town of the day, buildings were widely spaced so as to allow for an abundance of fresh air and sunlight. Unlike Chicago, where a "law of chaos" made "the saloon . . . as welcome as the school house," in the words of a local clergyman, Pullman's goal was order and harmony. Working-class saloons were prohibited, and the one bar in town, located in the main hotel, was deliberately priced out of the reach of the hoi polloi.[37] Prostitution, wide-open in most American cities at this time, was, needless to say, forbidden. So were politics, a favorite urban sport. The aim, to quote one member of the Illinois state labor commission, was "to remove . . . workers from the close quarters of a great city" so "they would be free, so far as it lies in the power of management to keep them free, from [its] many seductive influences." Workers were free, in other words, whether they wanted to be or not. "The citizen is surrounded by constant restraint and restriction, and everything is done for him, nothing by him," said Richard Ely, a Johns Hopkins professor of economics who studied the town intensively. It was a "real spectacle," he wrote, to see a "population of eight thousand souls where not one single person dares speak out openly his opinions about the town in which he lives." Ely summed up Pullman-style total planning as "[t]he establishment of the most absolute power of capital, and the repression of all freedom."[38]

That was in 1884. A decade later, the town blew. The Panic of 1893 led Pullman to cut wages by 25 to 40 percent, which meant that, once rent was deducted for company-owned housing, workers were often left with just pennies with which to buy food and clothing. When workers noticed that the company had simultaneously boosted stock dividends by 16 percent, they demanded a commensurate reduction in rent. The company refused on the grounds that such a reduction would undercut other landlords in the area. When employees elected a grievance committee in an attempt to negotiate, the company laid off three of its members. Eugene V. Debs, leader of the newly organized American Railway Union, called for binding arbitration, but the company refused. When he then ordered his men not to handle Pullman cars, the railroad companies responded with a lockout. By late June, the general strike was on.

"The whole country is in an inflammable condition," Debs had declared a couple of months earlier, and events certainly bore him out. The strike paralyzed rail service throughout the Midwest and the South and as far west as California. Chicago was immobilized, with thirteen of its twenty-three rail lines shut down and the rest severely hobbled. When U.S. Attorney General Richard Olney, a railroad director himself, issued an order sending in federal troops, huge crowds responded by going on a rampage, overturning railroad cars and smashing windows. Three days later, they began putting rail yards to the torch. The night sky glowed red as an estimated two thousand cars went up in flames. "The people were bold, shameless, and eager in their robbery," recounted one eyewitness. "It was pandemonium let loose, the fire leaping for miles and the men and women dancing with frenzy."[39] The *Chicago Tribune* was particularly aghast that women and children had joined in the fray. "The women climb on knolls of ground, on cinder heaps and piles of rock, on every vantage point, to peer over the seething mass of men," it declared in the purple newspaper prose of the day. "And when the blackness of night gives its shadowy protection, the forms that creep about the yards and apply the burning brands are not those of men alone, but of women and children, too—active, eager, wild, and vengeful."[40]

From an urbanological point of view, two things about the conflict stand out. One is the sheer number of rioters, up to twenty-five thousand at a time, according to newspaper reports, some rail workers but others various hangers-on—friends, relatives, neighbors, and anyone else with a reason to hate the railroad bosses.[41] Plainly, crowds of this magnitude would not have been possible if rail yards had not been located cheek by jowl with the centers of working-class population. But another thing that stands out is the railroads' vulnerability to attack. Downtown Chicago was the hub, the spot where the national rail system's various spokes all converged. Yet it was surrounded by a population for whom the railroads were enemy number one. From a strategic point of view, this made no sense whatsoever. Why allow such a hostile population to gain access to such an easy target? It was like allowing hostile Indians into the fort rather than keeping them outside the gate. But the railroads had no choice. The economics of nineteenth-century rail transport dictated that rail lines converge downtown and that rail workers live within walking distance of their jobs. Proximity was unavoidable. The more the railroads bowed to the inevitable, the more vulnerable they became.

This point was not lost on General Nelson A. Miles, the military commander in Chicago, who was reportedly disappointed when higher-ups refused him permission to shoot down strikers on sight.[42] Urbanization leads to crowding, he declared a few weeks after order was restored, and although he didn't specify exactly how, crowding led to class conflict. "For the last few decades the tendency has been to the congregating of the people in larger cities and towns," he wrote, "and a feeling of discontent, unrest, and disaffection has become almost universal; until the feeling between the men who labor and his employer is at present surely not satisfactory." What made matters even worse in Chicago, he went on, was the fact that "the great food producing centre," i.e., the food distribution point for much of the American heartland, was located precisely where the strike was at its strongest. To an old soldier like Miles, the solution was obvious. A way had to be found to move urban workers to a place where they could no longer do any harm: "There has been too much concentration in the cities. More of our people should go out into the country, into the pure air and among the birds, flowers, and green fields, where they may cultivate the ground. . . ."[43] If crowding promoted class conflict, decrowding would defuse it.

"Had it not been for the admirable action of the Federal Government," declared Teddy Roosevelt, "Chicago would have seen a repetition of what occurred during the Paris Commune, while Illinois would have been torn by a fierce social war."[44] The chief problem, a blue-ribbon panel convened by President Cleveland found, was that the strike had broken out in a

> vast metropolis, the center of an activity and growth unprecedented in history, and containing all that this implies. The lawless element are at present augmented by shiftless adventurers and criminals attracted by the [Chicago] Exposition [of 1893]. . . . [There are also] many of a certain class of

objectionable foreigners, who are being precipitated upon us by unrestricted immigration. No more dangerous place for a strike could be chosen.[45]

In a series of articles that he wrote and illustrated for *Harper's Weekly*, the artist Frederic Remington described Chicago as "a seething mass of smelly, stale beer, and bad language" and the strikers themselves a "malodorous crowd of anarchist foreign trash." Describing the departure of federal troops after the strike had been suppressed, he reported that "[a]s the column cleared the city and got into the United States of America proper, it was saluted by the waving of flags and cheers, which was quite a relief after being in the midst of a hostile population for so long."[46] Chicago—Remington made no effort to distinguish between the city and its working-class population—was both physically and politically repellent, a cancerous growth that had to be excised. Because the city gave rise to the crowd and the crowd gave rise to the class war, the industrial metropolis, clearly, was the source of the problem. If the problem of the city could somehow be "solved," the problem of spiraling class conflict would be solved as well.

. . . .

Such reasoning was not limited to the United States but was endemic during this period throughout the industrialized world. The classic expression was Gustave Le Bon's *The Psychology of Crowds*, a volume published in France in 1895, a year after the Pullman strike, which would shape conservative thought well into the twentieth century. Le Bon's thesis, which he somehow managed to pad out to some two hundred pages, was exceedingly simple: Capitalism meant cities, cities meant crowds, and crowds meant destruction and decay. By allowing ordinary citizens to rub shoulders with one another in the streets, the city was making the masses conscious of their own numbers and strength. It was filling their heads with dangerous ideas, while at the same time insuring that the stupidest and most bestial among them would take the lead. Since capitalism could only grow and cities only expand, mob rule was bound to intensify. The result was a vaguely Nietzschean atmosphere of doom and gloom designed to send a shiver of fear down the spine of Le Bon's middle-class readership.

"While all our ancient beliefs are tottering and disappearing, while the old pillars of society are giving way one by one, the power of the crowd is the only force that nothing menaces, and of which the prestige is continually on the increase. The age we are about to enter will in truth be the ERA OF CROWDS."[47] This is a fairly representative sample of Le Bon's overheated prose. If crowding was unstoppable, then all the negative attributes of a mob-dominated society were unstoppable as well, the hysteria, the cowardice, the brutality and irrationality. Individually, people were capable of honor and courage. But whenever they gathered in groups, "the sentiment of responsibility which always controls individuals disappears entirely." Instead, a member of a mob becomes "an automaton who has ceased to be guarded by his will."[48] Le Bon then went on to describe some of the specific characteristics of mob behavior. For instance:

- The crowd is destructive: "Civilizations as yet have only been created and directed by a small intellectual aristocracy, never by crowds. Crowds are only powerful for destruction. Their rule is always tantamount to a barbaric phase."

- The crowd encourages moral and political decay: "In consequence of the purely destructive nature of their power, crowds are like those microbes which hasten the dissolution of enfeebled or dead bodies."

- The crowd is in love with its own ignorance: "The masses have never thirsted after truth. . . . Whoever can supply them with illusions is easily their master; whoever attempts to destroy their illusions is always their victim."

- The crowd is simultaneously violent and cringing: "It is the need not of liberty but of servitude that is always predominant in the rule of crowds. They are so bent on obedience that they instinctively submit to whoever declares himself their master."[49]

Since mob rule was growing, it followed that any politician who could harness the power of the crowd would be tapping into an immense new energy source, one that would place him far ahead of all his rivals. He would become a warrior at the head of an urban horde, an unstoppable conqueror—provided, that is, he was able to master the psychological techniques needed to keep the mob in control. He needed to know when to bully it and when to flatter it, how to build it up to new heights of hysteria, how to fill its head with stuff and nonsense about national destiny and the master race.

Le Bon's book became a major ingredient in the "blood-and-soil" nationalism of the day.[50] Mussolini, who read *The Psychology of Crowds* as a schoolboy, praised it as "one of the books that interested me most," while Hitler paraphrased entire sections in *Mein Kampf* (without attribution, needless to say) and plagiarized certain passages outright. Le Bon was a militarist, racist, and anti-Semite who opposed virtually every significant political reform of his era.[51] But what made him more than a run-of-the-mill reactionary was the way he was both contemptuous of the masses and awed by them. Civilization was giving way to barbarism, which meant that any politician who hoped to stay on top had to change his tactics accordingly. If brute strength was the only language the mob understood, then it followed that brute strength was about to become the predominant idiom. To be successful in the new era, one had to become a brute oneself.

The difference between the antiurbanism of a Jefferson and a Le Bon is one of context. Jefferson's beloved Virginia existed on the edge of the developed world of the late eighteenth century, both geographically and politically. The urban masses may have been troublesome, but they were far from dominating American society, and Jefferson was hopeful nearly to the end that the new United States would be able to keep them marginalized by remaining true to ancient republican principles. Writing from the safety of his country estate, he could afford to be ambiguous as to whether his agrarianism was conservative or radical, democratic or traditionalist. He could be a friend of the common man but an enemy of the broader commonality because the question of one or the other had not yet been starkly posed. Le Bon had no such leeway. Thanks to a century of industrial capitalism, the mob, he believed, was already in control. Schemes aimed at fostering rural expansion at the expense of urban-industrial development were too late. The city's domination of the countryside could only grow, which meant that the mob's grip on society could only tighten:

> Whatsoever fate it may reserve for us, we shall have to submit to it. All reasoning against it is a mere vain war of words. Certainly it is possible that the advent of the power of the masses marks one of the last stages of Western civilization, a complete return to those periods which seem always destined to precede the birth of every new society.[52]

On the other hand, if the world was indeed plunging into a new age of barbarism, then the unstated implication of Le Bon's book was to make the most of it. If the times demanded that the ruling classes behave like Teutonic knights on a rampage, then so be it. That was what they would have to do. The fascism of the interwar years did not spring up out of nowhere. Rather, as the historian Arno J. Mayer has pointed out, the

intellectual foundations were being laid in the two or three decades leading up to the First World War.[53]

• • • • • • • • • • • •

If Chicago was frightening from the point of view of the American middle
and upper classes, meanwhile, another metropolis by the late nineteenth
century was even more so. This, of course, was New York. One reason
had to do with sheer size. By 1890, eight years prior to the consolidation
of the five boroughs, New York's population had reached 2.5 million,
better than double that of Chicago. But another reason had to do with
the kind of urbanization that New York represented. Rather than a railroad hub, New York was an international port, a junction not only
between two worlds, the Old and the New, but between two modes of
mechanized transport: railroads and steamships. Charles H. Cooley, a
leading sociologist of the day, described the results as a transportation
"break," a place where goods were loaded off of one mode, repackaged,
reassembled, or otherwise improved, and then loaded onto another.[54]
By the late nineteenth century, these items consisted of a bewildering variety of tangible and intangible goods, everything from garments and
machinery to theater, opera, and other forms of cultural "content." But
they also consisted of people, a growing volume of immigrants who were
similarly offloaded at Ellis Island, repackaged and reassembled by being
taught a smattering of English, and then turned loose on the job market.
Since a light-industrial economy such as New York's consists predomi-
nately of small shops rather than large factories, it might be argued that
such an economy was less "advanced" than a heavy-industrial one and
therefore less productive of radicalism and class conflict.

But the reality was more complex. If factories were smaller in New
York, the city itself loomed larger. Compared to Chicago, more capital
investment was going into urban infrastructure in the form of lofts, tenements, trolleys, bridges, and subways than into factories alone. The result

was an almost hyper-urban economy in which the city itself figured more and more heavily as an instrument of production. With its crowded streets and tall buildings occupying every last inch of available real estate, New York was a capitalist nerve center par excellence, one constantly on the alert for new markets and new ways of doing business. Sensitive to the slightest shift in fashions, it had to be fast thinking and quick on its feet. This meant, among other things, that it had to have a workforce that was also quick on its feet and state-of-the-art communications and transportation. Around the turn of the century, this implied such high-tech devices as subways, telephones, and the high-speed press. But it also implied an abundance of low-tech but still highly efficient modes of communication: cafés, taverns, delis, and even sidewalks and stoops—venues in which words could be exchanged, gossip traded, and ideas batted back and forth.

This was New York's great strength. Contrary to virtually every observer of the day, New York's enormous population densities—by the 1890s, the Lower East Side was the most crowded residential district in the western world[55]—were an economic asset rather than a liability. The greater the density, the greater the number of face-to-face contacts ("F2F," in contemporary cyber-jargon) per capita, the more quickly information could be relayed, and the better solutions could be formulated to the problems of the day. In *World of Our Fathers,* his best-selling history of the Lower East Side, Irving Howe discussed various possibilities as to why mortality rates in Jewish areas were lower than in equally poor Christian neighborhoods nearby, e.g., lower rates of alcoholism, kosher laws that may have provided a measure of protection against pork-borne diseases, close-knit family life, and perhaps even the famous Jewish reverence for doctors, which may have made them more likely to seek out medical attention.[56] But what Howe neglected to consider was the role of population density. Although crowding may have contributed to the spread of disease, it may also have contributed to its prevention and cure. A sick child would bring any number of people running—family members, boarders, neighbors from across the hall, and so on—all with suggestions of what to do. Some of these ideas were no doubt useless, but others may have been of value. Crowded immigrant neighborhoods made for a vibrant political life, which in turn made possible a high density of mutual-aid societies disseminating information about health and hygiene. Although middle-class reformers viewed slums like the Lower East Side as centers of ignorance, the opposite may actually have been the case. Ease of communication in such a jam-packed environment may have made for a population that was better informed rather than worse.

. . . .

Indeed, the attitude among middle- and upper-class New Yorkers was contradictory. On one hand, they believed that such neighborhoods were ignorant, while on the other, they feared that they were all too well informed about things that they, the genteel classes, did not like. Information and ideas fueled volatility. "The city is the nerve center of our civilization," said Rev. Strong. "It is also the storm center."[57] "There are the same explosive elements beneath the surface of New York as of Paris," declared Charles Loring Brace, founder of the Children's Aid Society.[58] The slum was a Dark Continent, filled with all kinds of dangerous forces that had somehow insinuated themselves into America while no one was looking. Because it was both threatening and unknown, "a cultural offensive" embracing everyone from rural prohibitionists to Anglo-Saxon urban reformers had to be organized to reclaim the slum block by block.[59]

Jacob Riis, the Danish immigrant-turned-newspaperman whose exposé *How the Other Half Lives* ushered in a new era of urban reform, was the seminal figure in this urban *reconquista*. By turns sympathetic and harsh, Riis readily conceded that the battle against the slum necessarily entailed a battle against the slum dweller, the benighted immigrant who felt at home amid "the crowds, the bands, the kosher butcher shops, the fake auction stores, and the synagogues" and, as a consequence, had to be all but dynamited loose from his surroundings.[60] Riis was a self-made man, with all the strengths and weaknesses the term implies. His first years after arriving in New York as a young man in his early twenties were difficult ones. He went hungry, prowled the streets looking for a bed, and finally hit rock bottom in 1874 when his pet dog was clubbed to death outside a police-run lodging house. Driven out into the rain, Riis couldn't have felt more miserable and alone. "[N]ot one was for me," he recalled years later. "It was all over. . . . Nobody cared."[61] Fortunately, he eventually found a job as a newspaper reporter and began his long uphill climb out of poverty. A stint as a police reporter sent him ranging through tenement houses, flophouses, and basement beer halls where few members of the genteel classes dared to go. The result in 1890 was *How the Other Half Lives,* a muckraking classic that made him an overnight sensation. Riis was a powerful prose stylist whose descriptions were so vivid that at times they bordered on the hallucinatory. But what made his book so successful was its depiction of an exotic unknown practically on the middle-class reader's doorstep. For East Side matrons or Wall Street bankers, the scenes that Riis described were all the more exciting by virtue of being only a stroll away.

"It is a dreary truth," Riis wrote in *How the Other Half Lives,* "that those who would fight for the poor must fight the poor to do it."[62] In describing a policeman using his billy club on a drink-addled vagrant, he was highly sympathetic—to the cop, that is, rather than to the victim. Writing about a police raid on a basement beer hall in which some 275 people were rounded up, charged with vagrancy, and sentenced to six months each, Riis described with his usual gusto the tramps cowering like rats, the police flailing about with their truncheons, and so forth. But what he never paused to consider was why the raid was occurring in the first place. What were the tramps guilty of other than drinking stale beer? What had they done wrong? For Riis, the answer was so obvious it didn't have to be put into words: The tramps were guilty of excessive poverty.

A war on poverty meant that its victims would have to be scattered and suppressed.[63]

Riis's tone was sometimes jocular, sometimes condescending. His description of an outdoor market on the Lower East Side was typical of his style:

> One of the shops is a "tobacco bureau," presided over by an unknown saint, done in yellow and red—there isn't a shop, a stand, or an ash-barrel doing duty for a counter, that has not its patron saint—the other is a fish-stand full of slimy, odd-looking creatures, fish that never swam in American waters, or if they did, were never seen on an American fish-stand, and snails. Big, awkward sausage, anything but appetizing, hang in the grocer's doorway. . . . What they are I never had the courage to ask.[64]

So foreign was the Lower East Side that even the fish was alien. Riis has been criticized for his anti-Semitism, and in fact there is much to condemn. He saw Jews as a moneygrubbing people of low moral character. He criticized Lower East Side garment workers for violating the sanctity of the family by taking work home and enlisting their children as helpers, yet never paused to consider the economic conditions that drove them to do so in the first place.

But as repellent as this was, Riis's attitude toward another ethnic group—New York's Chinese—was positively poisonous. Outwardly, he admitted, Chinatown seemed normal enough, filled with ordinary people doing ordinary things. But beneath that calm exterior was a swamp of evil. Seemingly innocuous Chinese laundries were fronts for "white slavery," he declared, telling of one owner who had tried to "inveigl[e] little girls into his laundry to hook them on opium and force them into prostitution." Dozens of houses along Mott and Pell Streets were "literally jammed, from the 'joint' in the cellar to the attic, with these hapless victims of a passion which, once acquired, demands the sacrifice of every instinct of decency to its insatiate desire." While the Italian ghetto on Mulberry Street may have seemed more violent, the Chinese district a short distance away was worse precisely because the moral disease it bred was so well hidden:

> [I]n their very exclusiveness and reserve they are a constant and terrible menace to society. . . . The severest official scrutiny, the harshest repressive measures are justifiable in Chinatown, orderly as it appears on the surface. . . . [T]he poison that proceeds from Mott Street puts mind and body to sleep, to work out its deadly purpose in the corruption of the soul.[65]

Not only was actual physical evidence unnecessary from Riis's point of view, but its very absence was somehow proof that the reality was even worse than middle-class readers could imagine. Chinatown's "inscrutability" gave him license to let his fantasies run wild. Fu Manchu–style opium lords masquerading as innocent laundrymen, harems filled with drugged-out white women, evil seeping out onto the streets like a toxic fog—the more lascivious the fantasy, the better.

Still, the Chinese were a case apart. Otherwise, Riis's reactions to Manhattan's various immigrant neighborhoods were milder, although still disdainful. There were too many children, "bewildering swarms of youngsters that are everywhere or nowhere as the exigency and their quick scent of danger direct." The streets were too crowded: "When the sun shines, the entire population seeks the streets, carrying out its household work, its bargaining, its love-making on street or sidewalk." The voices were too loud, the manners too indiscreet: Mothers in Little Italy "who are not in the streets are hanging half way out the window, shouting at someone below."[66] "Sadly," Riis concluded, New York lacked a Napoleon III of its own "to clean up and make light in dark corners."[67]

On the other hand, if all these jabbering, gesticulating foreigners had stayed on their side of the street, things might not have been so bad. But what gave Riis's tour of the underworld its nightmarish edge was the gnawing fear that they wouldn't stay put, that the poor would overflow their boundaries as conditions grew more and more dire and engulf the whole city:

> Crowding all the lower wards, where ever business leaves a foot of ground unclaimed; strung along both rivers like a ball and chain tied to the foot of every street, and filling up Harlem with their restless, pent-up multitudes, they [the immigrant masses] hold within their clutch the wealth and business of New York, hold them at their mercy in the day of mob-rule and wrath. The bullet-proof shutters, the stacks of hand-grenades, and the Gatling guns of the Sub-Treasury are tacit admission of the fact of the quality of mercy expected. When another generation shall have doubled their census of our city, and to that vast army of workers, held captive by poverty, the very name of home shall be as a bitter mockery, what will the harvest be?[68]

Riis's analysis was not that far from that of a General Miles or Gustave Le Bon. Bourgeois society had been strangely passive in permitting the enemy to slip through the fortifications and take up positions inside. It had allowed the foe to mass within striking distance of the most vital centers of power and wealth. Something therefore had to be done to move an overwhelmingly hostile population away. As a good American imbued with a proper can-do spirit, Riis refused to believe that the problem was insoluble. Rather, he had faith that things could be set right through a program of revived agrarianism in which slum proletarians would be relocated out amid the birds and bees where the moral and political influences were more benign. In 1902, he praised a B'nai B'rith "removal plan" that proposed "nothing less than the draining of the Ghetto" by fostering Jewish agricultural settlements.[69]

On another occasion, Riis told of walking along a country road at sunset and encountering

> a sunburned, bearded man, with an axe on his shoulder, talk-ing earnestly with his boy, a strapping young fellow in overalls. The man walked as one who is tired after a hard day's work, but his back was straight, and he held his head high. . . . This was the Jew of my dream, no longer despised, driven as a beast under impossible burdens, in the Ghetto of men's con-tempt, but free and his own Master. . . . The Jew redeemed to the soil, to his ancient heritage, a prince among his fellows, a man among men.[70]

The path to freedom "must be by way of the soil," Riis added. "There is the real freedom. *There* man's soul can expand. That way lies not only economic independence, but the ethical rehabilitation of man." In a Chautauqua lecture, Riis declared that "God made the country, man made the city," adding that "the man in the garden is yet the ideal. . . . He is the ideal citizen." A few years later, Riis decided to put such Tolstoyan ideas to the test by purchasing a farm in central Massachusetts and returning to the soil himself. He found the going tougher than he had expected. Financially strapped, he agreed to embark on a fund-raising lecture tour, and in April 1914, he collapsed in New Orleans. A month later he was dead.[71]

What Riis failed to notice, of course, was that the ancient republi-can ideal of a nation of yeoman farmers was even less realistic now than when Jefferson had propounded it in the late eighteenth century. The last thing America needed was millions of slum dwellers pouring out into the countryside in hopes of scratching out a living from the dirt. Rather than hordes of amateurs, it needed a smaller number of better-trained farmers able to put agriculture on a more businesslike footing. Riis's error was to see industry and urbanization as eternally joined. Detaching the worker from one, in his view, meant detaching him from the other. Yet modern production was the only way that a society like the United States could develop and grow. Rather than separating city workers from industry, the real trick was to somehow separate industry workers from the city. It was a problem that a few industry leaders were already putting their minds to.

4

THE GATHERING
ASSAULT

The cords of political memory, savagely cut
by the Civil War, were painfully sewn together
in the last quarter of the century. An English
observer in 1912 was "struck by the persistence
of old issues, old ways of looking at things,
old shibboleths, in an age newest of the new."

MERRILL PETERSON

I N   A   S E N S E, the twentieth century can be seen as one long effort at
crowd control. Broadly speaking, three strategies have emerged. One,
that of socialism, rejected Le Bon's characterization of the mob in toto,
arguing that the urban masses were not irrational and destructive but, to
the contrary, potentially more thoughtful and deliberative than the individual bourgeois. The goal was to mobilize the urban proletariat so as to
create an economic and social democracy that would be more rational
than the regime it replaced. The second, that of fascism, accepted the
crowd more or less as Le Bon saw it, which is to say as something irrational, violent, cringing, and servile, the only difference being that where
Le Bon still viewed the mob with a measure of aristocratic disdain, Hitler

and Mussolini embraced it wholeheartedly. They believed that if they could somehow marshal its violence and irrationality, they would be able to create a warrior society that would be hard and authoritarian, one that would act on the basis of instinct rather than intellect. The third strategy, that of twentieth-century liberalism, especially the variant known as American individualism, also accepted Le Bon's characterization. The urban masses were every bit as stupid, servile, and violent as he said they were. But rather than seeking to tap into the power of the mob, the answer that liberalism came up with was to do away with the mob altogether by restructuring society in such a way that it could never come together in the first place. The goal was to reengineer society so that the crowd would disperse before it could coalesce.

The result in the United States and in other countries that eventually accepted the U.S. model was a gigantic effort at social engineering, a process by which society was taken apart and reassembled so that the problem could be eliminated at the source. But because liberal society could never bring itself to admit that social engineering was what it was engaged in, it had to cover up its tracks even from itself. Even though the new order was artificial in the extreme, it had to be made to seem completely natural. Rather than advancing to something new, it had to appear that society was returning to its "normal," i.e., preexisting, state.

Among other things, this meant the creation of an entirely different class structure. By the end of the nineteenth century, American society consisted of a small number of plutocrats, a sizable but increasingly insecure middle class, and a proletariat that was increasingly hard-pressed and combative. In its quest for stability, twentieth-century U.S. society opted for a model based on an expanded middle that would absorb much of the upper class and working class on either side. Ostensibly, the new model was not new at all but a return to the old Jacksonian ideal in which everyone from the yeoman farmer to the small businessman was considered part of the productive classes. The class divisions created by industrial capitalism would be forgotten as America returned to a social scheme in which nearly the entire working population was brought back under a common national umbrella. Rather than the differences, the emphasis was to be on all the things that members of the new middle class had in common—the bills that everyone from the blue-collar worker to the local bank president had to pay, the mortgage payments they had to meet, the lawns they had to mow, the kids they had to put through school, and so on.

But if this reinvigorated middle class ideal represented a return to Jacksonian ideals in one respect, in another it represented a clear departure. In the 1800s, the emphasis had been on the individual as producer, whether of food for his own table or goods for the marketplace. But the chief problem facing America at the turn of the century was that production was no longer in the hands of yeoman farmers, artisans, or owners of small workshops. Instead, it was hopelessly collectivized, which is to say increasingly performed by large numbers of people laboring together in large factories and offices. Collectivized production led to class conflict— if there was one lesson that the industrial age drove home again and again, this was it. Yet collectivized production was unavoidable. At the same time, though, it was apparent that another aspect of the economic process was not only much less collectivized but had the potential to be rendered even less so by removing it from the city and centering it around the detached, freestanding single-family home. This was consumption. As employees, Americans were cogs in the machine and were destined to remain so for as long as anyone could see. But, as consumers, their individuality could blossom anew. If the new order could not do away with the factory or large-scale corporation, it could dissolve the ties of community and class that otherwise bound Americans together. If it couldn't change the workplace, it could transform society outside the workplace into a kind of lattice of individual atoms, separate from one another yet fixed in place. The urban masses would be no more. In their place would be the new phenomenon of the mass market, "an aggregation of individuals and families," in the words of one social historian, "living apart, addressed through the mass media."[1]

Consumerism was thus the key to reorganizing society and putting an end to class conflict. If one thing was certain, it was that the key to pacifying the masses was to create a new kind of mass market that would neutralize them by turning them into eager recipients of a growing quantity of consumer goods. As early as 1913, a left-leaning economist named Walter Weyl, a founding editor of the *New Republic* magazine, noticed that ordinary people had begun spending in a way that would have once been unthinkable:

> Street car riding for pleasure, city pleasure parks, summer vacations, the purchases of books, magazines, and newspapers, the enormous extension of the five-cent cigar, the democratization of watches, bicycles, cameras, carpets, etc., signify a change within the last half a century of the farthest reaching proportions.[2]

Instead of a day-in, day-out struggle for the bare necessities, a certain portion of the urban working class had reached a point where it could begin to afford a few petty luxuries. Naively, Weyl argued that city pleasure parks and summer vacations would soon lead to socialism as workers demanded that government make such pleasures available to a broader and broader portion of the working public. In fact, they would lead to the opposite because in order to make the great leap from the democratization of watches to the democratization of cars and suburban homes, the working class would have to be scattered and dispersed. The democratic renaissance that Weyl had in mind required a working class that was more organized and politically conscious than it had been previously, whereas consumerism, if it was to be successful, required one that was less.

The story of this great transformation is a complicated one. According to Merrill Peterson's masterful 1962 study, *The Jefferson Image in the American Mind,* the United States has seen three great ideological shifts since its founding. The first occurred in 1800 when the Federalists were smashed and the country was locked into a seemingly permanent Jeffersonian political framework. The second occurred in the 1860s when the Jeffersonian framework was destroyed in turn and the country was sent swinging back in a quasi-Hamiltonian direction. The third began in the late nineteenth century after the South had been readmitted to the Union and the middle and upper classes in the North began having second thoughts about where headlong urbanization and industrialization were leading. No one wanted to throw out all the good things that industry had wrought—the sanitary sewers, the mechanized transport, the telephones, and other consumer goods. Yet bourgeois opinion was coming around to the point of view that unless industry was somehow "Jeffersonized," the ancient republic would not survive. A way had to be found to harmonize a fast-growing industrial system with a slow-moving preindustrial Constitution, although no one as yet could say what that might be.

As Peterson pointed out, the South played a crucial role in this growing Jeffersonian resurgence. Prior to 1861, Southern "fire-eaters" had scorned Jefferson as a trimmer and compromiser who, rather than embracing slavery as a positive good, had apologized for it as a temporary evil that would fade away if only the South was allowed to handle matters on its own. After 1865, however, Southerners gained a new appreciation for Jefferson's political value in the context of a reunited republic. As a fervent advocate of states' rights, Jefferson was a source of not only invaluable ideological ammunition for use in the battle against Reconstruction and Republican-imposed military rule, but he could also be used to defend the "Southern way of life" once the troops were withdrawn and the position of the former Confederate states was normalized.

As a racist, he could be used to fend off Republican demands that ex-slaves be granted a measure of civil rights. As an anticapitalist (albeit of a reactionary stripe), he could be used to turn tables on post–Civil War Republicans who were more and more identified with the new crop of corporate robber barons. If Republicanism equaled economic royalism, then the refurbished Jeffersonian ideology of the 1870s and 1880s stood for a return to the rough-hewn white-male egalitarianism of the ancient republic.

The results were a testament to the deep-seated conservatism of American politics. Once again, the contest was between upper-class Federalists (or Republicans, as they were now known) and Jeffersonian Democrats who championed the farmer, small businessman, and the Southern Bourbon class, successor to the old slavocracy. But because the South was too weak, too politically discredited in the wake of the Civil War, to engineer such a shift on its own, it needed help from other sectors that were also coming into conflict with the economic power centers in the Ohio Valley and the Northeast. This was the role of populism, a movement that burst out of the prairies in the late 1880s, spread like wildfire to hard-pressed farmers in Texas and the Southeast, and then, under the leadership of William Jennings Bryan in 1896, seemed poised for a time to take over the entire country. Populism is an extremely confusing phenomenon since, like Jeffersonianism in general, it seems to face two ways simultaneously. Its politics were nostalgic, even reactionary—antiurban, tinged with racism and xenophobia, devoted to the belief that the holy writ of the Founders (minus, of course, the arch-villain Hamilton) contained the answer to every problem the modern world might serve up. On the other hand, the movement, at least until the debacle of 1896, seemingly leaned in a socialist direction as well. Populists favored the nationalization of the railroads, supported the rights of labor (if only for white men), and spoke out in favor of the eight-hour day.

As a consequence, populism has evolved over the decades into a kind of ideological Rorschach test, something for historians to read into whatever they wish to see. For a Cold War liberal like Richard Hofstadter, the populist explosion of the 1880s and 1890s was yet another example of "the paranoid style in American politics," one in which farmers blamed a host of distant forces—bankers, railroad magnates, international financiers, etc.—for their growing list of misfortunes. For more recent left-leaning scholars such as Michael Kazin and Lawrence Goodwyn, populism was a thoroughly justified rebellion against the dictatorship of big capital, an upsurge whose negative features have been greatly exaggerated by establishment historians eager to discredit any and all manifestations of popular revolt.[3]

Yet while some of Kazin's and Goodwyn's points are justified, the uncomfortable fact after all these years is that Hofstadter remains a good deal closer to the mark. America was not Europe, and its farmers were not peasants. Rather, the farmers were small businessmen who "carry their businesslike qualities into agriculture . . . [where] their trading passions are displayed in that as in their other pursuits," as Tocqueville put it in the 1830s.[4] They were "petty bourgeois" in the classic Marxist sense, which in the context of the late-nineteenth-century U.S. economy meant that they occupied a middle position between the robber barons and the emerging urban proletariat. Depending on the mood or circumstance, they might be hostile to one or the other or both. At the same time, however, the logic of their world view could not help but propel them farther and farther to the right. If, as they believed, the ancient republic was still a beacon of light and morality, then it followed that all the bad things that had happened since the Civil War were somehow the work of what Jefferson had once described as "the subtle corps of sappers and miners constantly working under ground to undermine the foundations of our confederated fabric."[5] The goal, therefore, was to return the republic to its ancient purity, to wrest it away from elements that were foreign in one sense or another and put it back in the hands of the people—the *real* people, that is—who had established the republic in the first place. And, of course, there was no better symbol of incipient foreign domination than the American city, overflowing with immigrants and brimming with strange new ideas and art forms.

But it was not only their political assumptions that were propelling the populist movement toward the right—it was the utter hopelessness of their cause. American agriculture was so overextended that some sort of shakeout was inevitable. Between 1860 and 1900, the number of American farms had nearly tripled, while the amount of land under cultivation had more than doubled. Beginning in 1870, output per acre had risen 86 percent. Yet not only were Americans producing more wheat but, as we have seen, so were Canadians, Argentines, Ukrainians, and others. Markets were fairly drowning in grain, which meant that prices had only one way to go: down. Between 1870 and 1895, cotton prices fell 27 percent, while wheat and corn plunged an even more sickening 50 percent.[6]

There was no arguing with those numbers, no way of disguising the fact that American agriculture was suffering from a vast crisis of overproduction. This is not to say that a progressive U.S. government could not have come up with various innovative ways to deal with the problem. It could have devised incentive programs to persuade marginal farmers to take up other occupations or benefit programs to cushion the blow. It could have encouraged rural cooperatives in order to bolster and stabilize some of the more hard-hit local economies. Instead, Washington offered nothing. Vetoing a relief bill for drought-stricken farmers, Grover Cleveland declared in 1887 that "the lesson should constantly be enforced that though the people support the Government, the Government should not support the people."[7] Rural Americans were on their own. Crushed by forces they didn't understand, the only solution they could come up with was to somehow turn back the clock to the glory days of the Jeffersonian republic when farmers were at the apex of the republican moral pyramid.

This explains the populist obsession with the silver standard ("the dollar of our daddies"), the fervent patriotism, and the ever more passionate invocation of ancient folk heroes. "The time has arrived," declared Leonidas Lafayette Polk, a leader of the newly organized Populist Party in 1892, "for the great West, the great South, and the great Northwest, to link their hands and hearts together and march to the ballot box and take possession of the government, restore it to the principles of our fathers, and run it in the interests of the people."[8] The Jeffersonian alliance between the South and the West against the urban Northeast was thus reborn. James B. Weaver, the party's 1892 presidential candidate, declared that there was enough good sense in the "rugged utterances" of Jefferson and Jackson "to completely transform and re-invigorate our present suppliant and helpless state of public opinion."[9] James H. "Cyclone" Davis, the lanky populist spellbinder from Texas, urged his followers to "bow in adoration of the sainted sire of American liberty . . . [and] waft a message to Mr. Jefferson and tell him that there is another hereditary high-handed aristocracy in our land."[10]

Inevitably, populist nostalgia of this sort acquired a nativist, anti-urban edge. The Populist Party's 1892 platform called for an end to "undesirable immigration" on the part of "the pauper and criminal classes of the world."[11] Yet what immigrant arriving at Ellis Island was not a pauper to some degree or another and perhaps a criminal as well? Although some historians have argued that obsessive populist attacks on the Rothschilds were more anti-British than anti-Semitic (London being the banking family's chief headquarters at the time),[12] the distinction was lost on Jews in New York, Chicago, and other big cities. All they knew was that populists, in classic anti-Semitic fashion, blamed all the world's troubles on a small number of almost magically powerful Jews. In 1894, a Texas populist warned that it was "from the cities, with their brothels, their low-down grogeries, their sweatshops, from districts where dirt, and disease, and rats, and hunger, and despair blot out all that is god-like in man and

makes him a ravening beast, that the red hand of anarchy is raised"[13]—
rhetoric indistinguishable from that of a Jacob Riis, General Miles, or
Gustave Le Bon. Two years before drafting the Populist Party's 1892 platform, a Minnesota politician and writer named Ignatius Donnelly dashed
off an apocalyptic novel entitled *Caesar's Column* in which starving farmers descend upon the cities of the world and reduce them to cinders. It
was an updated version of the medieval French jacquerie in which peasants, maddened by oppression, would burn down the manor house, rape
the lord's wife and daughters, and, for good measure, roast the proprietor
himself over an open fire. Interestingly, Donnelly ended his novel with a
vision of a new republic arising out of the ashes of the old, one in which
partisan politics were banned, dissenters expelled, banks forbidden, and
cities eliminated through the simple expedient of requiring everyone to
live in owner-occupied homes on minimum half-acre lots.[14]

Although not strictly speaking a populist—he spurned the party's
nomination in 1896 and ran for president as a Democrat instead—William
Jennings Bryan was nonetheless the idol of the populist masses and an
example of how "silverism," agrarianism, and religious fundamentalism
were coming together in one increasingly lethal package. In his usual
florid, Old Testament style, he denounced cities as

> embodied paganism . . . composed of people of this
> world . . . seeking the ends of this world . . . satiating
> the animal man with the riches, with the lavish luxury of
> things . . . Babylon the great, the mother of harlots and of
> the abominations of the earth . . . drunken with the blood
> of the saints, and with the blood of the martyrs of Jesus . . .
> [who] reigneth over the kings of the earth.[15]

Bryan's famous speech at the 1896 Democratic national convention
sounded many of the same themes:

You tell us that the great cities are in favor of the gold standard; we reply that the great cities rest upon our broad and
fertile prairies. Burn down your cities and leave our farms,
and your cities will spring up again as if by magic; but destroy
our farms and the grass will grow in the streets of every city in
the country. . . . It is the issue of 1776 all over again.[16]

This was almost comically wrongheaded. The city was not dependent on the countryside; to the contrary, the countryside was increasingly
dependent on the city—not only for markets but for the industrial know-
how needed to upgrade agriculture and put it on a more modern footing.
If the U.S. was to continue as an agricultural powerhouse, it would not be
by returning to hallowed old ways but by moving forward to a new kind
of farming, one that was increasingly capital intensive and mechanized.
Yet not only was the city parasitic and in league with foreign powers,
according to Bryan, it was also anti-Christian, a point he drove home with
the words: "You shall not press down upon the brow of labor this crown
of thorns, you shall not crucify mankind upon a cross of gold." If
American farming was dying, it was because urban apostasy was killing it
off—or so Bryan contended.

But in another respect, Bryan's speech was remarkably prescient. All
Americans had something valuable to contribute, he told the convention,
because fundamentally all Americans were businessmen:

The man who is employed for wages is as much a businessman as his employer; the attorney in a country town is as much
a businessman as the corporation counsel in a great metropolis; the merchant at the crossroads store is as much a businessman as the merchant of New York; the farmer who goes
forth in the morning and toils all day—who begins in the
spring and toils all summer—and who by the application of

brain and muscle to the natural resources of the country creates wealth, is as much a businessman as the man who goes
upon the board of trade and bets upon the price of grain.[17]

Every farmer was as good as J. P. Morgan because in the final analysis every farmer was the same as J. P. Morgan. In a 1994 study, a Rutgers
University historian named James Livingston pointed out that in the loftiest regions of the American bourgeoisie, "democratic" capitalism of this
sort was viewed with the deepest suspicion. Encouraging ordinary folk to
think of themselves as businessmen, it was believed, was irresponsible and
counterproductive. It would encourage them to take on more debt than
they could handle and engage in "reckless speculation." As a business
spokesman named Henry Farquhar argued:

> [I]t may well be doubted whether an avowed and deliberate
> encouragement of debtors as a class is good policy, notwith-
> standing their enterprise and progressiveness. The objection
> that too much encouragement may make them too enterprising
> and too progressive is not less well-founded than obvious.[18]

This was harsh and snobbish but not without a certain economic
logic. As in agriculture, the chief problem facing the larger U.S. economy
in a deflationary epoch was that of overproduction—overproduction of
goods, of investment capital, even entrepreneurial spirit. The classic solution was to constrict the flow of capital by jacking up interest rates, which
among other things would serve to thin out the ranks of entrepreneurs.
Instead of encouraging Americans to enter the business class, the effect
would be to encourage them to stay put. Rather than dissolving class lines,
the result would be to harden them. As Livingston noted, the idea of the
man in the street as a small-scale businessman was "the object of both
criticism and ridicule in sound money literature."[19] Just as capitalism

required a strong currency, it required a "strong" class structure, one in which workers and capitalists both knew their place.

Yet this was not the direction in which America was moving. Although Bryan lost to William McKinley in 1896 and populism was all but destroyed as an electoral force, the victory proved short-lived. Over the next two decades, the hard-money forces found themselves losing ground to neopopulist advocates of a more elastic currency. In 1893, J. P. Morgan had not only bailed out the U.S. Treasury but had used the crisis as an opportunity to lecture Washington on the importance of getting its financial house in order. Yet, just fourteen years later, the same U.S. government had to mobilize its resources in order to bail out Wall Street during the financial crisis of 1907. Wall Street orthodoxy held that wages had to be continually slashed if profit margins were to be maintained. Yet the more wages were cut, the more financial stability seemed to decline. Not only did consumption have to be broadened, but Main Street had to be strengthened as well so that the economy could be widened at its base.

The upshot was the Federal Reserve System, created in 1913, and the looser monetary policies of the 1920s. Although the populists would be the last to admit it, the Fed, a deliberately decentralized federation of twelve district banks, was in a certain sense a delayed victory for the old populist cause, while the easy credit that followed was in many ways a delayed victory for Bryanesque capitalism. Both were attempts to broaden the economic base so as to stabilize the structure as a whole. Although it would be an exaggeration to say that every last American became a businessman during this period, it is fair to state that as the affluent began loading up on big-ticket items from cars to suburban homes, the notion of the middle-class family as a self-contained business enterprise gained accordingly. So did a concept of a specifically middle-class political landscape, one in which "strong" geopolitical class lines of industrial capitalism would be replaced by something more along the lines of a small town. If the middle class was to expand at the expense of both the bourgeoisie and the working class, then the middle-class community would have to expand at the expense of both Park Avenue and the slum.

· · · · · · · · · · · · ·

But populism was not the only force to hop on the Jeffersonian bandwagon during this period; another important component of the growing antiurban movement was prohibitionism. Like populism, with which it overlapped in many parts of the country, prohibitionism was a strongly agrarian movement whose leaders spoke openly of a strategy of encirclement in which they would first conquer the small towns and farms before turning their guns on the big cities.[20] In 1903, the Anti-Saloon League, the chief antialcohol group, declared that if America was to be cleaned up, it would be due to the efforts of "the vast and virile countryside where the bible is not yet effete, nor Christ a myth." It added in 1914, "The Gibraltar of the American liquor traffic is the American city," while a year later it announced that the time had come for "the pure stream of country sentiment and township morals to flush out the cesspools of the cities."[21] Another statement that the league issued around this time presented a lurid picture of a once-mighty American republic sinking in a swamp of booze and corruption:

> The vices of the cities have been the undoing of past empires and civilizations. It has been at the point where the urban population outnumbers the rural population that wrecked Republics have gone down. . . . The peril of this Republic likewise is now clearly seen to be in her cities; there is no greater menace to democratic institutions than the great segregation of an element which gathers its ideas of patriotism and citizenship from the low grogshop. . . . Already some of our cities are well-nigh submerged with this unpatriotic element, which is manipulated by the still baser element

engaged in the unAmerican drink traffic and by the kind of politician the saloon creates. . . . If our Republic is to be saved, the liquor traffic must be destroyed.[22]

Liquor, corruption, moral decay, loss of patriotism—the city was at the root of them all. Urban influence had to be reduced so that the balance of power between town and country could be restored to what it was in the early days of the republic.

• • • • • • • • • • • • •

Antiurbanism and class hatred explain the prohibitionist focus on the corner saloon. From fundamentalist preachers to "progressive" reformers such as Jane Addams, the antiliquor forces were as obsessed with the saloon as the populists were with the Rothschilds. In retrospect, it is not hard to understand why. The saloon was the point of convergence for all those forces that rural prohibitionists feared and loathed most intensely, not only alcohol but bossism, immigration, even sexual immorality. In the days before the Sherman Antitrust Act made such vertical integration impossible, breweries would put up the money for franchise holders to open saloons where their beer would be exclusively sold. Whether they were low dives or innocent watering holes depends on one's point of view. In cities such as New York, Chicago, St. Louis, San Francisco, Denver, Buffalo, and Baltimore, many saloons were linked to gambling and prostitution, although in other places such as Boston and Philadelphia they were not. Accusations that they fostered heavy drinking appear to be largely unfounded: In the course of some two hundred visits to working-class saloons in Chicago, a professor of sociology named E. C. Moore said he came across just three instances of visible drunkenness in all. Charges that unscrupulous bartenders encouraged innocent working men to squander their pay on alcohol appeared to be much exaggerated as well. One study found that only 5 percent of the typical working-class family budget was going to alcohol, which does not seem exorbitant for men working twelve hours a day, six days a week, in heavy labor.[23]

In other respects, however, working-class saloons were an affront to the wing of middle-class opinion that the temperance movement represented. First, the fact that they were owned or backed by the major breweries made them a direct arm of the "liquor power," enemy outposts that would have to be conquered one by one if the war against booze was to be victorious. Second, they were closely tied in with the political machines, which made them a symbol of urban political corruption. The saloon was not only a drinking establishment but a kind of front office for the local ward heeler, a place where he could hang out, dispense favors, call in his chits, and recruit foot soldiers. Third, and perhaps most important, not only were saloons places where alcohol was consumed but they were places where alcohol was consumed outside the home. They were an all-too-public venue at a time when reformers of various stripes were desperate to domesticate and privatize consumption, particularly consumption of a troublesome substance such as alcohol by a troublesome element in the form of the urban working class. With their swinging doors, sawdust-strewn floors, photos of sports heroes, and the obligatory picture of a naked odalisque reclining on a couch behind the bar, such "poor men's clubs" represented a form of urban freedom that the gathering American jacquerie found intolerable and was therefore determined to suppress.

"Our cities are growing much more rapidly than the whole population, as is the liquor power also," declared Josiah Strong. "If this power continues to keep the city under its heel, what of the nation, when the city dominates the country?"[24] Perhaps because they were so strong in the Midwest, prohibitionists seemed particularly obsessed with Chicago, "the town that Billy Sunday could not shut down." As one historian put it: "Full of Catholics, anarchists, socialists, railroad barons, trust-builders, commodity speculators, grasping bankers, saloonkeepers, and houses of ill repute, Chicago symbolized the consequences of a relaxation of the moral imperatives of the pietistic ethic."[25] It was as fascinating as it was repellent, which explains the sexually obsessive quality of so much turn-of-the-century temperance prose.

· · · · · · · · · · · ·

In addition to populism and prohibition, a third element in this growing turn-of-the-century Jeffersonian alliance was the amorphous but still highly important movement known as progressivism. It may seem strange to place progressivism in this camp since historians have traditionally described the movement as the Hamiltonian counterpart to Jeffersonian populism. Progressives were urban rather than rural, they enjoyed upper-class support, they were less than enthusiastic about trust-busting and other issues dear to populist hearts, and they tended to be aggressive and innovative in their use of state power—all hallmarks, supposedly, of latter-day Hamiltonianism. But the distinction is overstated. Politics in the United States, in which power is endlessly checked, balanced, and divided against itself, are rarely so straightforward. By the turn of the century, the quasi-Hamiltonian order that had taken hold during the Civil War period was showing clear signs of exhaustion. Associated as it was with robber-baron capitalism, urbanization, and class polarization, it was growing unpopular and frayed. Increasingly, progressives agreed with agrarians that the city had grown too large, that it needed to be cut down to size, and that the overriding goal should be to return to the "scattered democracy" (to use Henry Adams's phrase[26]) of small towns, single-family homes, and picket fences that America once was, supposedly, and could be again.

Moreover, in one respect the progressives were more Jeffersonian than the Jeffersonians. This had to do with the scattered, "localist" nature of their politics. The populists had moved to form a national political party as soon as the winds of revolt began blowing out of the Great Plains. However mistaken, their view of America as a people's republic that had been hijacked by various neo-Federalist "miners and sappers" at least offered a comprehensive, "totalizing" theory of where America had gone wrong and how it could be fixed. The progressives, however, reversed the process. They did not form a separate political party until 1912, and then almost as an afterthought. In the meantime, they devoted themselves to myriad "improvement societies"—by one count, some 2,400, as of 1905[27]—that strove to apply local solutions to local problems. It is easy to understand why localism of this sort was so attractive. It allowed the movement to flow around the political logjam in Washington, avoid getting bogged down in tedious ideological debates, and throw itself directly at problems in a way that would yield immediate tangible results. This is what made the movement seem so practical in the eyes of the businessmen and professionals who were its core constituency. But it is also what made it so conservative. Steering clear of ideology meant allowing the reigning ideology of the day to go unchallenged. Indeed, in a subtle way it meant strengthening it. By arguing that real progress arose from real people tackling real problems in their own backyards, progressives ended up reinforcing the minimalistic Jeffersonian view of government as something at best irrelevant to the problems of society and at worst a hindrance. Politics only gummed up the works. They interfered with effective community action. Therefore, they were something to avoid.

The upshot was the beginning of the wholesale depoliticization of American society that would continue rolling and building throughout the twentieth century. Social action was privatized via the creation of innumerable philanthropic agencies and do-gooder groups. If progressives did not banish politics altogether (although undoubtedly they would have liked to have tried), they sought to hamstring them by promoting nonpartisan forms of city government and subjecting elections and nominations to ever more stringent rules and regulations. To the degree the progressive movement differed with the Jeffersonians, it was only over the secondary question of the role of the state. Where Jefferson believed that a minimal national government would lead to minimal politics, the progressives, faced with bossism and corruption at every turn, felt they had no choice but to strengthen government in order to rein in politics that were overflowing their proper constitutional bounds. Where Jefferson hoped to use popular political power to cripple the nation-state, progressives hoped to use government at all levels—from the federal on down—to cripple political power. But the overall effect was the same: to turn democracy against itself so as to nullify it as a political force. Too much democracy and too much politics led to too much corruption. Both had to be reined in as a consequence.

Attitudes like these drove not-unsympathetic intellectuals like Walter Lippmann and Herbert Croly to despair. In his classic 1909 text, *The Promise of American Life,* Croly pointed out that the optimistic progressive belief that partisan differences were secondary and that men of goodwill could agree on fundamental issues concealed a subcurrent that was dangerously authoritarian:

> Reformers have always tended to believe that their agitation ought to be and essentially was non-partisan. They considered it inconceivable either that patriotic American citizens should hesitate about restoring the purity and vigor of American institutions, or such an object should not appeal to every disinterested man, irrespective of party. It was a fight between law and its violators, between the Faithful and the Heretic, between the Good and the Wicked.[28]

The result was tolerance toward those who agreed that the solution was to return republican institutions to their original "purity and vigor," and intolerance toward those who did not. The resultant moral atmosphere was so harsh and unforgiving that it made even corrupt Tammany Hall politicians seem tolerant and humane. Progressive morality was inevitably tinged with antiurbanism not only because the city fairly bubbled over with things progressives didn't like—bossism and corruption, left-wing radicalism, sexual freedom, and so forth—but because the city was plainly at odds with the middle-class progressive consensus. Not only was it big, fast moving, and all too modern, it was filled with people who plainly did not agree that "restoring the purity of American institutions" was the answer. Because they did not agree, they had to be cast out of the community of the faithful.

· · · · · · · · · · · ·

The consequences were especially dramatic in the West where the old-line political machines were weaker and progressives therefore had a freer hand. In Oregon, the reformist leader William S. U'Ren wielded such enormous clout, one political observer quipped, that "the state government is divided into four departments—the executive, judicial, legislative, and Mr. U'Ren—and it is still an open question who exerts the most power."[29] In California, progressives went their neighbors to the north one better not only by establishing themselves as a rival power center but by taking over the state government directly when their standard-bearer, Hiram Johnson, was elected governor in 1911. California promptly reinvented itself as a kind of open-air laboratory for the research and development of various progressive nostrums and cures.

From nearly every perspective, including that of urban development, the results were disastrous. In an excellent account written in the early 1950s, the historian George E. Mowry showed that, despite the movement's liberal reputation, the typical progressive was a conservative Republican, a businessman or professional, a Mason, and almost always a member of the local chamber of commerce.[30] Whatever their hostility to the monopolists, "goo-goos" and "pwogs" (to use the derisive names coined by their enemies) usually proved to be even more hostile to organized labor welling up from below. In San Francisco, one of the most tightly organized union towns on the entire Pacific Rim, progressives and laborites were at each other's throats from 1905 on. In Los Angeles, the progressive-controlled city council responded so ferociously to a union-organizing drive in 1910 that the resultant crackdown, as Mowry put it, made even "the old Southern Pacific–dominated government [seem] like a benevolent institution." When the Socialist Party seemed to be on the brink of taking over the city government in 1911, progressives put aside their scruples and joined forces with old enemies to combat what they saw as the greater threat from the left. "Churches and saloons, partisans and nonpartisans, Republicans, Democrats, and Independents, reformers and performers, . . . men who hate and distrust each other united against the menace of class rule," one progressive journalist observed.[31] Meanwhile, the state government under Hiram Johnson let loose with a blizzard of reforms, the ultimate effect of which was to confirm the popular stereotype of the "pwog" as a stiff-necked, small-town prig. To be sure, railroads and utilities were regulated. But slot machines were banned, a "local option" antiliquor law was approved, and everything from prizefighting and prostitution to slang and "indecent" literature were prohibited. In 1913, progressive lawmakers approved a measure limiting landholding by Japanese farmers. Although they passed a workmen's compensation law and another measure mandating the eight-hour day, a bill limiting the ability of judges to hand down antilabor injunctions went down in defeat. While some labor reforms were permissible, the right to strike was not.[32]

Initiative and referendum, the cornerstone of the progressive program, had especially far-reaching consequences. The theory behind "I&R" was all too simple. Because progressives viewed politicians as inherently self-interested and corrupt, they believed that a way had to be found for citizens to flow around them by initiating and enacting legislation on their own. It was a revolt against the very idea of representative democracy, one that, far from rendering government more efficient, tied it up more completely than ever in knots. Previously, legislators had been limited in their ability to duck the difficult issues of the day. But by allowing them to refer such questions in the form of referenda to the voters, it enhanced their ability to bob and weave. As politicians grew more slippery, government grew more ineffectual. As the crustily conservative but not imperceptive *New York Times* argued in a 1911 editorial:

> While pretending to give greater right to the voters, [I&R] deprives them of the opportunity effectively and intelligently to use their powers. They receive the right to vote much more often and on a larger number of matters than before, but the number and variety of the votes they are called on to cast does [sic] away with all chance of really using sense and discretion.[33]

Voters were overwhelmed, with the result that politics wound up more muddled than ever. With the primary system inviting Californians to vote the man rather than the party—another wrongheaded progressive reform—candidates evolved into free-floating political entrepreneurs unencumbered by old-fashioned notions of party loyalty. As the number of candidates rose, ideological distinctions were blurred. Not surprisingly, California saw the creation of the nation's first professional campaign-consulting firm when a couple of public-relations men named Clem Whittaker and Leone Baxter formed a partnership in 1933.[34] The small-town businessmen who were the progressive movement's core constituency were remaking politics in their own image.

· · · · · · · · · · · ·

The relationship between "reforms" like these and de-urbanization was subtle but important. Ultimately, such measures served not only to fragment political power but to fragment the political landscape. Unable to believe that democratic politics could ever be honest, efficient, and responsive, progressives believed that the only option was to tie them down, Gulliver-style, with various rules and regulations, to devolve power from the politician to the rank-and-file citizen, or to break government up into smaller and smaller units. Among other things, this led to a nearly endless proliferation of minute local governments, special agencies, and citizens' groups, the purpose of which was to institutionalize a local, small-scale vision of government. While San Francisco, for a variety of political and geographical reasons, was able to retain its big-city shape, Los Angeles evolved in a very different direction. It became the world's first noncity city, an Iowa-by-the-sea composed of low-density neighborhoods revolving around the bungalow and motorcar.

The turn-back-the-clock nature of progressive politics was also evident in the movement's attitude toward the political party. Progressive horror of partisan politics was fully in keeping with the Founders' horror of factionalism. Factions, according to eighteenth-century republican ideology, were by definition narrow and selfish. Great men avoided them like the plague, which is why Washington, for one, was determined to remain above petty factional disputes. Yet modern democratic theory had come to view the party differently—not as something inherently egotistical and corrupt but as the only frank and honest means by which rank-and-file citizens could band together to fight for common goals. Rather than a necessary evil, the emergence of the mass party in the mid-1800s was seen as a positive good, a means of analyzing and organizing politics in such a way as to make sense of an otherwise disparate array of issues, questions, and beliefs. The purpose of a party was not only to assemble a slate of candidates for everything from dogcatcher to president but, in more sophisticated terms, to create an overarching ideology that would enable the people to see the connection between the local and the national, the micro- and macrocosmic. If U.S. politics were fragmented, by the same token, it was due to America's failure to advance beyond a conception of the party as little more than a coterie of self-interested politicians. Rather than moving forward, the progressive answer to the problem of bossism was to return to some pristine state before "faction" had reared its ugly head. Rather than embracing the hurly-burly of democracy, it sought to substitute an eighteenth-century model in which disinterested statesmanship sought to rise above such petty concerns.

The relationship between the party and the city is also subtle but significant. Both are functions of the freedom to associate, the right to group oneself with like-minded individuals and fight for a common political program on the one hand versus the right to live in close proximity with one's fellow citizens in a city or community on the other. Because both forms of association were free and unstructured, both, from a prim, repressive, "pwog" point of view, were seen as dangerous and corrupt. An assault on one was necessarily an assault on the other, which is why progressive reforms had an antiurban edge even when they didn't take aim at the city directly.

. . . .

Progressives were thus the urban wing of the gathering antiurban offensive. Although the results were not quite as spectacular, progressivism scored some notable breakthroughs in the East also, particularly in housing, an area especially ripe for reform. Of the 3.5 million people living in greater New York around the turn of the century, more than two-thirds lived in some form of tenement, a catchall term for multistory housing that was cheap, crowded, ill-ventilated, and run-down. Most tenements were of the "dumbbell" variety, a type of design in which only four of the fourteen rooms on each floor received direct air and sunlight.[35] Yet not only did unscrupulous landlords (which is to say landlords who were scrupulous about maximizing profits) herd as many people as they could into each building, they erected rickety structures in the spaces behind them in order to house even more. Nearly every square inch of land was taken up as a result. Meanwhile, bathing facilities were rare, and at one for every 7.6 residents, according to one survey, flush toilets were in short supply. Public-health concerns were far from unjustified.[36]

Yet, it is also evident that progressives had more in mind than venti-lation and toilets. Lawrence Veiller, a giant of the tenement-reform move-ment who held a number of key housing-policy posts—head of New York City's first department of housing, resident-housing expert at the highly influential Charity Organization Society, director of the National Housing Association, and, finally, a member of a blue-ribbon panel in the early 1920s that drafted a model national-zoning code—made no bones as to his ultimate goal. It was nothing less than to put an end to the "congre-gate form of living." It didn't matter whether the congregate form in question was a rat-infested hovel or the Waldorf-Astoria—all types of multifamily housing stood condemned. Urban housing reform was the first step toward moving immigrants out of the cities altogether and plac-ing them in freestanding cottages in the countryside, where their children could romp amid the grass and trees. There is not the "slightest reason," Veiller declared, "why the greater part of our tremendous foreign popula-tion, which has come from rural peasant life in Europe, should not con-tinue in similar rural peasant life in this country—in fact, there is every reason why it should."[37] In 1910, he added that

the normal method of housing the working population in our American cities is in small houses, each house occupied by a separate family, often with a small bit of land, with privacy for all, and with a secure sense of individuality and opportunity for real domestic life. Under no other method can we expect American institutions to be maintained. It is useless to expect a conservative point of view in the workingman, if his home is but three or four rooms in some huge building in which dwell from twenty to thirty other families, and the home is his only from month to month. Where a man has a home of his own he has every incentive to be economical and thrifty, to take part in the duties of citizenship, to be a real sharer in government.

Democracy was not predicated upon a country made up of
tenement dwellers, nor can it so survive. . . . When there
are no homes there will be no nation.[38]

"Normal" democracy was conservative, while crowded city living gave
rise to radical ideologies that were threatening to "American institutions."
Veiller's deep belief in the overriding importance of owner-occupied single-
family housing led him to oppose city-owned apartment projects for a
number of reasons: because he believed that the city would make for an
inefficient landlord, because he worried that such programs would drive
private builders out of business, but mostly because he believed that they
would lead to a "sacrifice of self-dependence" by encouraging slum dwellers
to rent in the city rather than moving to the countryside where they could
own.[39] His fear was not that public housing would work poorly but that it
would work all too well by providing working-class New Yorkers with an
alternative to de-urbanization.

Another progressive group, the Committee on Congestion of
Population, organized in 1907, zeroed in more directly on the problem of
high population densities. The committee's chairman, Henry Morgenthau,
a real-estate investor who had gone into reform politics (and whose son,
Henry Jr., would serve as Franklin D. Roosevelt's treasury secretary),
blamed crowded neighborhoods for "disease, moral depravity, discontent,
and socialism."[40] As its longtime director Benjamin Marsh put it, congestion profited "the undertaker, the saloon keeper, the land speculator, the
tenement sweater [i.e., sweatshop owner], the politician, [and] some trust
companies." Although some reformers hoped that improved mass transit
would solve the problem by allowing the urban population to spread itself
more evenly, Marsh was more realistic in recognizing that trolleys and subways compounded the problem by luring ever more workers into the city
in search of jobs.[41] Rather than reducing urbanization, they wound up

intensifying it. As a result, the Committee on Congestion of Population settled on a different strategy. Instead of trying to lure immigrants out of the slums by improving mass transit, the committee hit upon the simple expedient of holding down population growth by restricting building heights and lot coverage. The idea was a variation of what is sometimes called the "push down–pop up" effect: Repressing population growth at the center, it was hoped, would cause it to pop up at the periphery, thereby distributing the burden over a broader area. In the name of sunlight and ventilation, the aim was to leave slum dwellers with no choice but to decamp for the "healthier" environment of the countryside.

The impact of an exceedingly simple idea like this cannot be exaggerated. The Committee on Congestion put together an exhibit showing that the most densely populated sections of New York were also the poorest and had the highest rates of infectious disease. Politicians, socialites, and various opinion-makers were dutifully shocked and demanded that something be done. In 1909, the committee helped organize the National Conference on City Planning in Washington, D.C. Attended by some of the leading progressive luminaries of the day, the conference marked the formal start of American urban planning, not only as a profession but as a movement devoted to the low-density gospel.[42] As urban planners fanned out across the country, fully half of America's nonrural population found itself living under one kind of zoning code or another by 1927, all dedicated to the proposition that reduced population density would lead to an enhanced sense of community and a higher quality of life.[43] As John Nolen, a participant in the 1909 conference and perhaps the leading planner of his day, put it in 1932:

The future city will be spread out, it will be regional, it will be the natural product of the automobile, the good road, electricity, the telephone, and the radio, combined with the growing desire to live a more natural, biological life under pleasanter and more natural conditions.[44]

If the city refused to "de-densify" on its own, the idea was to use the new power of zoning, so as to leave it no choice. Artificial means had to be used to create a more "natural" existence.

. . . .

In one form or another, zoning is as old as the city itself. When medieval Venice ordered its glassmakers to move their dangerous furnaces to the nearby island of Murano, that was zoning. When it ordered its Jewish population to move to an out-of-the-way neighborhood known as the Ghetto, that, unfortunately, was zoning, too. In the United States, zoning had had its first stirrings as a formal legal device in San Francisco in the 1870s when property owners were able to make use of it to stem an "invasion" of Chinese laundries.[45] But the practice did not really take off until 1916 when New York City drafted and approved one of the first comprehensive zoning codes in the nation. Not only did the New York code seek to restrict building heights and lot coverage, it also represented an important step in the direction of the closely related principle of "separation of uses." If cities were crowded and volatile, it was because economic uses were jumbled together in a way that was dangerous and unsettling. The key to solving the problem of the city was to separate urban functions into neat little piles and assign each one its proper place. Only when manufacturing was confined to one zone, retail to a second, and residences to a third would harmony be restored.

But the real goal was to limit the growth and influence of the urban working class. In New York, the municipal zoning code grew out of a heated political battle that arose shortly after the turn of the century, when Grand Central Terminal, Pennsylvania Station, and the first subways all came on line within a few years of one another. In combination, the three new additions to the city's transportation system transformed both travel patterns and ways of doing business. Where previously garment shops had crowded into the Lower East Side to be close to their workers, they now began migrating to the area now known as the Garment District in order to gain access to the exciting new openings to the outside world. Thanks to the subways, their workforce was able to follow.

The resulting *volkerwanderungen* triggered panic and outrage among the posh retailers on a stretch of Fifth Avenue north of Fourteenth Street known as Ladies' Mile. "One year, things were going as usual," one observer recounted. "The carriage trade parked its conveyances in University Place or along the side streets. Next year the carriage folk, shopping in the fashionable hour between twelve and one, found themselves struggling for passage with ten thousand operatives [i.e., garment workers]."[46] The Fifth Avenue Association, the main merchants' group, was outraged. Complained one leader: "Nothing so blasting to the best class of business and property interests has ever been seen or known in any great retail district in any large city as this vast flood of workers which now sweeps down the pavement at noontime every day and literally overwhelms and engulfs shops, shopkeepers, and the shopping public."[47] Another merchant declared:

> The employees from these [manufacturing] loft buildings cannot be controlled. They spend their time—lunch hour and before business—on the avenue, congregating in crowds that are doing more than any other thing to destroy the exclusiveness of Fifth Avenue. If the exclusiveness and desirability of Fifth Avenue are destroyed, the value of real estate on Fifth Avenue will degenerate immediately.[48]

The exclusiveness of Fifth Avenue required the exclusion of those lowly beings who manufactured the items that upscale retailers were offering for sale. So determined were the merchants to force out the workers that, in the aftermath of the Triangle Shirtwaist Fire in 1911, they even fought against a measure requiring garment shops to install overhead sprinklers.[49] Anything that made working conditions safer or more comfortable encouraged the operatives to stay put, whereas the one thing the merchants wanted was for them to go away.

The battle over the midtown garment industry has been described as the opening salvo in a prolonged effort to safeguard urban real estate by purging industry and the working class from the most desirable locations. By 1915, the Fifth Avenue merchants had succeeded in closing down some two hundred garment shops employing some thirty thousand workers. "Shall we save New York?" asked a newspaper ad taken out by some of the city's leading merchants, bankers, and realtors.

Shall we save it from unnatural and unnecessary crowding, from high rents, from excessive and illy distributed taxation? We can save it from all of these, so far at least as they are caused by one special evil . . . the erection of factories in the residential and famous retail sections.[50]

Separation of uses was a way to prevent workers from going where they weren't wanted and to force them out of areas where they were already ensconced. By the 1920s, Brookline, Massachusetts, had decided that the best way to preserve real-estate values was to forbid multifamily housing in single-family districts, while the nearby town of Milton decided that the best way was to forbid retail outlets in residential districts.[51] Los Angeles adopted a comprehensive zoning code designed to preserve its low-density character, while Atlanta hired Robert Whitten, a prominent planner who believed that bankers should live in one part of town, shopkeepers in another, and manual laborers in a third, to draw up an ordinance dividing the city into separate racial zones as well. Whitten drew up detailed maps showing where whites and blacks could live and where they could not, although, in the spirit of fairness, the zoning code he developed allowed both groups to employ members of the other race as live-in servants. (It is not known if any black Atlantans availed themselves of this privilege.)[52]

Meanwhile, there is no question as to whom the zoning movement benefited. "By the 1920s," one historian noted, "the . . . districts that accepted the most stringent zoning codes were those occupied by the most expensive residential uses."[53] The zoning codes were stringent because they were designed to screen or push out both people and activities deemed harmful to the municipal bottom line and, by implication, to shunt them onto someone else. While a small number of communities benefited from the practice, more found their position undermined.

· · · · · · · · · · · ·

The progressive assault on the city was successful in other areas as well. One was child labor. Nowadays, of course, it is all but impossible to say anything positive about child labor. The very phrase conjures up images of pale, undernourished creatures toiling away in coal mines and cotton mills. But the child labor at which progressives took aim around the turn of the century was very different from the child labor that reformers had battled a generation or two earlier. Instead of children condemned to work in noisy, dimly lit factories, the targets this time were the swarms of "newsies," shoe-shine boys, messengers, and underage peddlers who could be found on nearly every corner in certain neighborhoods selling everything from trinkets to chewing gum. These were not industrial slaves who rarely saw the light of day, but bold adventurers who symbolized all that was free and anarchic about the turn-of-the-century metropolis. To quote the historian David Nasaw:

> The child labor reformers and their allies feared for the street traders not because they were exposed to physical danger or

deprived of sensory stimulation or physically confined during the daylight hours. They set out to save them from a different order of evils: from too much, not too little freedom, stimulation, and excitement.[54]

This is not to sentimentalize turn-of-the-century street life. Newsies and other street urchins often skipped school, sometimes slept on sidewalks, and were almost always dirty. But compared to the suburban ennui that would be the lot of middle-class children in subsequent decades, their existence was in many ways a childhood idyll. In the absence of heavy motorized traffic, streets served crowded immigrant neighborhoods as open-air markets, meeting places, and playgrounds. Children were free to roam high and low, earning a few dollars here and there selling newspapers and hiring on in various odd jobs. Although parents worried, the lure of the streets was irresistible. Recalled Irving Howe:

> The streets were ours. Everyplace else—home, school, shop—belonged to the grownups. But the streets belonged to us. We would roam through the city tasting the delights of freedom, discovering possibilities far beyond the reach of our parents. The streets taught us the deceits of commerce, introduced us to the excitement of sex, schooled us in the strategies of survival, and gave us our first clear idea of what life in America was really going to be like.[55]

Reformers responded to this aspect of urban freedom as they did to all others: by crusading to shut it down. They launched campaigns against the casual jobs that lured children out into the world and against the amusements that drew their pennies. Lillian Wald, founder of the Henry Street Settlement in 1893, regularly called the police to chase away children selling trinkets at the foot of the Williamsburg Bridge.[56] When not campaigning against saloons and brothels, Jane Addams was fulminating against vaudeville houses for promoting a "debased form of dramatic art, and a vulgar type of music," thereby promoting "hallucination and mental disorder" among the young. Nickelodeons, she warned, were contributing to a wholesale moral breakdown:

> [W]hile the occasional child is driven distraught, a hundred permanently injure their eyes watching the moving films, and hundreds more seriously model their conduct upon the standards set before them on this mimic stage. Three boys, aged nine, eleven, and thirteen years, who had recently seen depicted the adventures of frontier life including the holding up of a stage coach and the lassoing of the driver, spent weeks planning to lasso, murder, and rob a neighborhood milkman. . . .[57]

Since the vaudeville houses and nickelodeons could not be shut down, the proper response to such horrors, it seemed, was to see to it that children were kept away. This was the idea behind the supervised playground movement, yet another progressive spin-off that began gathering speed during this period. In Pittsburgh, one advocate argued that supervised playgrounds would promote "civic unity," improve children's "moral nature," and instill "social training and discipline." Another said they would encourage "new social notions, and a better standard of what is acceptable to those 'higher up.'" In 1917, Henry Stoddard Curtis, secretary of the newly formed Playground Association of America, said that adult-supervised playgrounds were the only alternative to children hanging out on the streets where they would "watch the drunken people, listen to the leader of the gang, hear the shady story, [and] smoke cigarettes." "No one who has observed children carefully in any city," he added, ". . . between the close of school and supper, has found that any considerable percentage of them were doing anything that was worth while."[58] Roaming about, looking for adventure, savoring the freedom of the city—these were all a waste of time. Meanwhile, street children had no better opinion of the playground advocates than the advocates had of them. "I can't go to the playgrounds now," said an eleven-year-old in Worcester, Massachusetts. "They get on me nerves with so many men and women around telling you what to do."[59]

An example of what was really at stake occurred in 1899 when two of New York's most notorious publishers, Joseph Pulitzer and William Randolph Hearst, suddenly raised the wholesale price of newspapers that newsboys hawked on nearly every corner. Thousands of newsies responded by going on strike. The consequences were tumultuous. Mobs of children and adolescents battled police and scabs, destroyed papers, and over-turned delivery vans. Messengers and shoe-shine boys walked out in sympathy, as did newsboys in Jersey City, Newark, Yonkers, Troy, Rochester, New Haven, and Providence. The result was something approaching a general strike of children, one that ultimately forced both newspaper magnates to back down and rescind the increases. Predictably, progressives responded not by blaming the publishers and certainly not by commending the strikers for their spirited response and high degree of organization. Rather, they responded by attempting to do away with the newsies once and for all by requiring them to be licensed. When newsboys attempted a repeat performance in the auspicious year of 1917 with help from the American Federation of Labor and the Industrial Workers of the World, reformers, wringing their hands over "the effect of street life upon growing boys," declared that "it would be for the ultimate welfare of the newsboys themselves to eliminate their business entirely."[60] Eventually, the publishers solved the problem by moving toward a system of stationary, adult-operated newsstands. The urban newsie gave way to the boy tossing papers from a two-wheeler onto front lawns. Somehow, child labor was less problematic when it occurred amid suburban greenery.

. . . .

Progressives also warred on the city by warring on prostitution and sin. The former was wide open around the turn of the century, both winked at and milked by police and politicians as a never-ending source of payoffs and bribes. Ministers thundered from the pulpit, reformers inveighed from the lectern, but otherwise, no one seemed particularly eager to interfere with a practice in which some of society's most respected members were implicated. Virtually every large city had its red-light district—Memphis its Gayosa Avenue, New Orleans its Storyville, Chicago its Levee, and San Francisco its Barbary Coast. In Chicago, two madams from Omaha, Ada and Minna Everleigh, opened a luxurious brothel called the Everleigh Club that soon became the talk of the town.[61] In Pittsburgh, whorehouses were left undisturbed as long as they purchased their furniture from the "official furniture man," their beer from the "official bottler," their liquor from the "official liquor commissioner," and their clothes from the "official wrapper maker."[62] In New York, whole stretches of the Lower East Side resembled open-air meat markets. "On sunshiny days the whores sat on chairs along the sidewalks," recounted Mike Gold in his memoir *Jews Without Money*. "They sprawled indolently, their legs taking up half the pavements. People stumbled over a gauntlet of whores' meaty legs."[63]

All that soon changed. In city after city, well-organized citizens' committees went into action during the Progressive Era, forcing the establishments out of business or driving them underground. In New York, the crypto-brothels known as Raines Law hotels, which had numbered in the thousands as late as 1905, all but disappeared. Higher-class brothels were also forced to close, while the number of brothels overall was greatly reduced.[64] Whores were forced to take to the streets, where they became prey to pimps and thieves. What made the antiprostitution movement so successful was not merely that it was better funded and more determined but that it had been organized on an entirely new ideological basis. Old-fashioned thunder and damnation were out, while the new and seemingly more modern language of public health was in. One antiprostitution group, headed by a prominent dermatologist named Prince A. Morrow, called itself the American Society of Sanitary and Moral Prophylaxis, while another, described by one historian as little more than a front for the Rockefellers, called itself the Bureau of Social Hygiene. In 1917, a publication called *Social Hygiene* predicted that New Orleans would soon conquer prostitution the way it had conquered yellow fever, which is to say by adopting the most up-to-date scientific techniques.[65] As one sociologist noted:

Social-policy debates were pervaded by broad metaphors linking personal and class interests with health and morality. . . . Social problems created "degradations" and "diseases" that spread "corruptions" and "infections." Industrialism and urbanization had greatly increased social density, so that lower-class immorality might infect all classes, as their germs certainly did.[66]

Predictably, yet another progressive antiprostitution group, New York's so-called Committee of Fifteen, founded in 1902, zeroed in on crowded tenement districts as a "prolific source of sexual immorality."[67] The committee did not say how tenements were a source of sexual immorality or why. But, then, it didn't have to. Prostitution was an affront to morality, while a substantial body of opinion held that crowded tenement districts were a threat to republican institutions. Since republican institutions and morality were one and the same, crowding and prostitution had to be causally linked.

It was left to an antiprostitution campaigner named George Kibbe Turner to take the inevitable next step. Writing in *McClure's* magazine in

1909, he observed that "the acute and often unscrupulous Jewish type of mind" was the driving force behind the liquor business. "The Jewish dealer in women," he wrote, had done more to erode "the moral life of the great cities of America in the past ten years" than anyone else.[68] According to one credulous historian, Turner's article had a "sensational" effect in "la[ying] bare the connection between liquor, gambling, crime, political corruption and prostitution. . . ."[69] But, of course, it didn't lay anything bare at all; rather, it covered it over with layers of prejudice and mystification.

The war against sex, the nonpaying as well as the paying kind, was in some ways even more feverish. In this instance, the problem was not just the overcrowded tenement but the city itself. The city was where one went to escape small-town social controls; hence, it was the place where dark desires were able to flourish. "In a great city one has no neighbours," observed the Committee of Fifteen. "No man knows the doings of even his close friends; few men care what the secret life of their friends may be. Thus, with his moral sensibilities blunted, the young man is left free to follow his own inclinations."[70] Obviously, this had to stop.

At the same time, though, the city's mazelike character, the fact that it was filled with byways and hiding places where the authorities could see nothing that people didn't want them to see, made it impossible to stop. Yet reformers were determined to do their utmost. In Chicago, members of the local vice commission inveighed against a long list of modern phenomena they regarded as vulgar and salacious: immoral movies, divorce, dance halls, dangerous crazes like the Turkey Trot, vaudeville, suggestive advertising, homosexuality, even ice-cream parlors, excursion boats, and amusement parks. To deal with the problem of couples necking on secluded park benches, the commission advocated searchlights for "the proper policing of such spots as are not covered by arc lights." In Syracuse, New York, the vice commission said of a local lovers' lane: "It is so dark there that you will scarcely see your hand before your face. As you go slowly along you can see nothing, but you can *hear* whispering all about." One town banned unclothed department-store mannequins, while another made it a misdemeanor to "stare at, or make what is commonly called 'goo-goo eyes' at, or in any other manner look at or make remarks to or concerning, or cough or whistle at, or do any other act to attract the attention of any woman or female person."[71] Sex, other than the domesticated variety, was another freedom that had to be curtailed.

· · · · · · · · · · · · ·

The turn-of-the-century revolt against the city was not solely an American phenomenon but, in a slightly different form, was hardly less powerful in Europe as well. As Arno J. Mayer pointed out:

> [U]ltraconservatives in particular decried urban life as the main seedbed of the modernity they loathed and stood against. In turn, they advanced the wholesome towns and villages of peasants, burghers, clerics, and notables as a counterideal to the profligate city. . . . Not too surprisingly the glorification and defense of soil and peasant became permanently inscribed on the banner of truculent nationalism that eventually rallied all conservatives.[72]

Yet nowhere else, it seems safe to say, did antiurbanism reach such a pitch of sexual hysteria as in the U.S. The question is: why? What was it about American society that caused it to react to the stresses of modernity in such a singularly feverish way? What caused nearly all sections of middle-class society—urban no less than rural—to gang up on the city en masse?

Although any connection between antiurbanism and the Constitution would no doubt strike most analysts today as far-fetched, observers did not feel that way at the time. Walter Lippmann, for example, dwelt on the connection at considerable length in *A Preface to Politics,* a book he published in 1914, as a young man a few years out of Harvard. America's devotion to eighteenth-century republicanism, he wrote, had rendered it ill equipped to deal with the problems of the modern age. "We cling to constitutions out of 'loyalty,'" he wrote. "We trudge in the treadmill and call it love of our ancient institutions. We emulate the mule, that greatest of all routineers."[73] When confronted with something new and disturbing, the American tendency was not to analyze and think. Rather, its immediate response was to strike out blindly on the assumption that anything new must be wrong. If "all wisdom is enfolded" in the Constitution, as John Milton once said about the Bible,[74] then any phenomenon that was contrary to the Founders had to be eradicated if Americans were to remain true to the faith of their forefathers.

Yet sex in the city, Lippmann went on, could not be eradicated. It had found "a thousand avenues. The brothel, the flat, the assignation house, steamers, ice-cream parlors, Turkish baths, massage parlors, street-walking—the thing has woven itself into the texture of city life."[75] Rather than coolly working their way through the problem, the American impulse was to resist at all costs—to close its eyes and, as the modern slogan would have it, just say no. Lippmann noted that a recent Chicago report had observed quite sensibly that "[s]o long as there is lust in the hearts of men," prostitution would persist in one fashion or another. Yet the same report also called for "[c]onstant and persistent repression," with "absolute annihilation the ultimate ideal."[76] Prostitution could not be eliminated, yet society must not stop trying. It was a recipe for ever escalating repression, not only against sex but against the city in which it had been allowed to proliferate.

5

FORDISM

The modern city is the most unlovely and artificial sight
this planet affords. The ultimate solution is to abandon it.
We shall solve the city problem by leaving the city.

HENRY FORD

HE CITY was untamable yet unstoppable. All the experts said so. In 1894, the sociologist Charles Cooley declared flatly that "any efficient organization of industry is quite inconceivable without the concentration of men and other industrial forces in cities and other foci of industrial activity."[1] Five years later, Adna Ferrin Weber, a pioneering urban demographer, declared that as long as agricultural productivity continued to grow, the agricultural portion of the workforce could only diminish, which meant that the countryside would continue to lose population at the expense of the cities. Any alternative was "too remote to be predicted."[2] Literati such as Ignatius Donnelly, Jack London, H. G. Wells, and Anatole France agreed: Urban concentration would continue until the built-up forces exploded like a volcano.[3]

Just how wrong they were was about to be proved by a pioneering auto manufacturer in the Midwestern city of Detroit. Any attempt to come to grips with American urban policy means coming to grips with the monumental personality of Henry Ford. Ford was a bigot and a reactionary, a half-educated businessman whose tyrannical tendencies grew increasingly pronounced as his empire expanded. But he was also a genius. The Model T was one of capitalism's great economic breakthroughs, indeed probably the last time in industrial history that an ordinary mechanic with no formal training would be able to have such an extraordinary impact. Ford's achievement was not only economic and technological, however. It was also social, political, even aesthetic. He didn't invent the automobile—that was the achievement of the German inventors Gottlieb Daimler, Wilhelm Maybach, and Karl Benz in 1885–87. But he radically simplified it, emphasizing sturdiness and durability over sleekness, style, and fancy engineering. Where other pioneer automakers were gearing their products to the upscale urban market, Ford, for both business and political reasons, aimed his car at rural and small-town folk in need of a utilitarian vehicle capable of navigating rutted and muddy country roads. He eschewed gimmicks such as color schemes or annual style updates not only because he thought marketing tricks like these were dishonest and effete but because his business sense told him that middle-class consumers would take to a car that was as homely as it was functional. "It Gets You There and It Gets You Back"—this was the decidedly unsexy slogan that Ford used to peddle the Model T. Yet that was precisely why he liked it. He wanted a car that would be plain and practical in keeping with the no-nonsense Midwestern values with which he had grown up.

Ford's intellect was crude and raw but, at the same time, encyclopedic. Thanks to his populist upbringing in rural Michigan, he viewed society in classic Jeffersonian-Jacksonian terms of honest country folk versus villainous urban elements who were forever trying to usurp the ancient republic. In Jefferson's day, these "miners and sappers" had consisted of bankers, merchants, and other Federalist types, whereas by the late nineteenth and early twentieth century the list had expanded to include everyone from Wall Street financiers to Bolsheviks, imperialists, the Illuminati, and that perennial favorite, the Jews. But although the characters had changed somewhat, the underlying logic had not. The people stood for the old-fashioned agrarian republic. They were honest, simple, and homespun. The enemy represented the forces of urbanization, capitalism, or, even worse, international socialism. He was clever, duplicitous, and ever watchful. Therefore, it was the duty of latter-day Paul Reveres to alert the people to the danger at hand. The moneylenders had to be driven out of the temple, the Constitution restored to its rightful place of honor, and, last but not least, the city, the great enemy stronghold, expunged from the landscape.

"America is made, not to be remade or unmade, but to go on being made according to the original pattern of a land and a government for all peoples capable of receiving liberty," Ford wrote in 1924. "Amid all the writing now done on efficiency and freedom in politics, none is more modern than Jefferson."[4] If Jefferson represented the pinnacle of wisdom, then everything that had happened since his death in 1826 represented a falling away, a lapse from grace. Newfangled political ideas were not progress. To the contrary, real progress meant purification and a return to founding principles.

The importance that Ford attached to ideas like these cannot be overstated. Politics were not a hobby for him but central to his makeup, the thing that drove him forward. As he declared in 1914:

I do not consider the machines that bear my name simply as machines. If that was all there was to it I would simply do something else. I take them as concrete evidence of the working out of a theory of business which I hope is more than a theory of business—a theory towards making this world a better place to live.[5]

There was nothing the least bit cynical about this statement. To be sure, Ford wanted money. But he wanted it as part of his grand scheme for retooling America so as to return it to its Jeffersonian roots. His breakthrough idea, his lifelong mission, was to recreate the old Jeffersonian order by reconstructing America around the automobile. By advancing into the motor age, he intended to return society to its former purity. By going forward technologically, he aimed to go backward politically and socially. This was quite impossible—in fact, it was the contradiction on which "Fordism" would eventually founder. But initially, at least, the Fordist revolution to end all revolutions proved spectacularly successful.

· · · · · · · · · · · · ·

One of the most penetrating accounts of the great Fordist transformation of the early twentieth century can be found in Booth Tarkington's Pulitzer Prize–winning novel *The Magnificent Ambersons* (1918). Tarkington, who in addition wrote *Penrod* (1914), *Seventeen* (1916), and *Alice Adams* (1921), also had something of an encyclopedic mind, which is what gives his portrait of a representative Midwestern town in the throes of the auto revolution a certain epic quality. In essence, his book describes a politico-industrial coup d'état in which the new auto technocracy topples the old horse-and-carriage elite. Autos, Tarkington emphasizes throughout, were not just a novel form of transportation, but the basis of an entirely different social order. "They are here," one of his characters says, "and almost all outward things are going to be different because of what they bring. They are going to alter war, and they are going to alter peace. I think men's minds are going to be changed in subtle ways because of automobiles; just how, though, I could hardly guess."[6] Tarkington was too much the good Republican to quarrel with the progress that the auto seemed to represent. The old ruling class, he clearly believed, was closed and snobbish and deserved to be taken down a peg or two. Still, he couldn't help mourning the passing of the old regime.

　　Much of *The Magnificent Ambersons* is an elegy for a relaxed, preauto way of life. It is one in which women stop for a chat in the middle of the street while wagons and buggies flow around them and houses come equipped not only with front porches so people can enjoy the evening air, but side and back porches as well. The pace is so leisurely that passengers on a mule-drawn "streetcar" think nothing of waiting while a housewife, who hailed them from an upstairs room, "shut the window, put on her hat and cloak, went downstairs, found an umbrella, told the 'girl' what to have for dinner, and [came] forth from the house."[7] One of the most charming scenes in the novel is a description of a moonlit summer night in which the only traffic is an occasional horse and buggy followed by

> the firefly lights of silent bicycles gliding by in pairs and trios—or sometimes a dozen at a time might come, and not so silent, striking their little bells; the riders' voices calling and laughing; while now and then a pair of invisible experts would pass, playing mandolin and guitar as if handle-bars were of no account in the world—their music would come swiftly, and then too swiftly die away.[8]

But this peaceful scene, Tarkington continues, proves short-lived:

> Then, like a cowboy shooting up a peaceful camp, a frantic devil would hurtle out of the distance, bellowing, exhaust racketing like a machine gun gone amuck—and at these horrid sounds the surreys and buggies would hug the curbstone, and the bicycles scatter to cover, cursing; while children rushed from the sidewalks to drag pet dogs from the street. The thing would roar by, leaving a long wake of turbulence; then the indignant street would quiet down for a few minutes—till another came.[9]

And another and another. If a single flivver was like a cowboy shooting up a peaceful camp, then hundreds or thousands were like a war on one's very doorstep. Where previously children and pets had been forced to take cover due to the occasional passing auto, now they were driven entirely off the field. Instead of buggies and bicycles, the streets now offered a stream of

> constantly passing automobile headlights, shifting in vast geo-
> metric demonstrations against the darkness. Now and then a
> bicycle wound its nervous way among these portents, or, at
> long intervals, a surrey or buggy plodded forlornly by.[10]

Yet, they were soon driven off the road as well. Tarkington was, quite consciously, describing a new social structure, one in which the motorist was king and everyone else was reduced to the status of servant or serf. Although he was probably unaware of it, he was also describing a new economic order, one in the process of redefining such things as consumption and waste. Items like noise and pollution are what economists, beginning with an Englishman named Arthur Cecil Pigou in 1920, have labeled external costs or, simply, "externalities," the economic consequences of individual actions that are displaced onto others. Externalities may be insignificant, as in the case of the gentle clip-clop of a passing horse and carriage. They may be pleasurable and hence "positive," as in the case of a cyclist whose mandolin strumming is pleasing to all within earshot. But they can be both massive and negative, as in the case of a growing number of sputtering, backfiring automobiles. They impose costs on children who are deprived of the use of the streets and on residents deprived of the pleasure of sitting on their front porch on summer evenings. They undermine the value of stately old homes located along handsome boulevards now choked with traffic and fumes. These are real costs, yet their distribution could not have been more inequitable. Particularly in the early years of the automobile, they were borne most heavily by nonmotorists, who were not in a position to reap any of the auto's benefits. People who did not drive were forced to absorb costs generated by those who did.

An imbalance of this sort may sound trivial. Yet, even if he was a bit fuzzy on the economics, Tarkington's genius was to show how the cumulative effect of such costs could upset the balance of power in a surprisingly short time. The Amberson clan, for instance, owed its wealth and standing to something called the Amberson Addition, a parklike development that the family patriarch had built on the edge of the city in the 1870s, complete with fancy touches such as white cast-iron statues and oversize octagonal fountains. But now that a growing volume of cars was careening around its too-tight corners, the statues were covered by a layer of pollution and grit and property values were plunging. Observed Tarkington:

> These were bad times for Amberson Addition. This quarter, already old, lay within a mile of the centre of the town, but business moved in other directions; and the Addition's share of Prosperity was only the smoke and dirt, with the bank credit left out. The owners of the original big houses sold them, or rented them to boarding-house keepers, and the tenants of the multitude of small houses moved "farther out" (where the smoke was thinner). . . . And with the coming of the new speed, "farther out" was now as close to business as the Addition had been in the days of its prosperity. Distances had ceased to matter.[11]

Although the American system would seem to be endlessly protective of the rights of property, no compensation was offered for such losses and none was received. When a member of the Amberson clan, frightened and alarmed by the growing destruction, suggests that cars should simply be banned—"You see how they spoil the bicycling and the [carriage] driving; people just seem to hate them!"—the reaction is one of shocked disbelief. "Fanny! You're not in earnest?" another family member replies.[12] The new regime was noisier and more polluted, yet people were unable to respond. In the old days, they were indignant when George Minafer, the spoiled rich boy who is the novel's antihero, raced his pony through the streets, scattering the townsfolk like geese. But now that the automobile was doing the same on a far wider scale, they were paralyzed.

. . . .

For years after the introduction of the automobile, history was written by the victors. The auto was the wave of the future, and anyone who said otherwise was nothing more than a Luddite trying to hold back progress. If people found technological change unsettling, it was because technological change was always unsettling, yet in the end always for the better. But this version of history is as simplistic and one-sided as any other. In reality, motorization was a highly complex phenomenon. On one hand, there is no doubt that it represented a titanic explosion in human productive capability. In 1860, U.S. output from steam engines, waterwheels, windmills, and draught animals totaled 13 million horsepower. In 1930, U.S. output totaled 1.6 billion horsepower, 87 percent of which came from motor vehicles.[13] When population growth is taken into account, this means that, thanks largely to the Fordist revolution, the average American had roughly thirty-five times more power at his fingertips than his forebears two or three generations earlier. The bulldozer effect that Tarkington described in *The Magnificent Ambersons*, the ease with which the automobile shoved all other modes of transport off the road, was a tribute to its overpowering brute strength.

On the other hand, if the auto created benefits, it also generated costs. Despite efforts to discount such costs as minor or to dismiss them as "the price of progress" (an all but meaningless phrase), there is no question that they were immense. Pedestrian fatalities rose dramatically after the turn of the century when motor vehicles began invading city streets in significant numbers. By 1907, a year prior to the introduction of the Model T, traffic fatalities in New York City were running at more than seven hundred annually, double the level of five years earlier.[14] If the victims had been motorists, there might have been certain rough justice in this since the deaths would have represented a self-imposed cost. But they were not. Rather, three-fourths of the victims were pedestrians, mostly tenement children who had not gotten the message that it was no longer safe to play in city streets. When a car ran down a two-year-old named Louis Camille, in an Italian neighborhood in Lower Manhattan, rioting broke out. Over the next five years, the *New York Times* reported thirty-four other such violent protests plus a full-scale shoot-out between residents and police in nearby Hoboken when yet another child was struck by a passing vehicle. Schools instructed children to stay off the streets, and at one point, police even began arresting those who stepped off the curb. But still the carnage continued. By World War I, this slaughter of the innocents had claimed the lives of more than a thousand children in New York City alone.[15]

Deaths like these represented an external cost that motorists displaced onto pedestrians who, on average, were significantly lower on the economic scale—in other words, a wealth transfer from the poor to the well-to-do. Yet another auto externality took the form of rising municipal outlays for new and wider roads, plus the replacement of picturesque cobblestones (which cause motor vehicles to skid) with more auto-friendly asphalt and concrete.[16] As traffic volumes multiplied, New York widened Twenty-third Street—a major east-west thoroughfare—in 1910 and cut back on sidewalk space so as to create two additional lanes of traffic on Fifth Avenue in 1912. Whether or not the city wanted to take such steps, it felt it had no choice. Without them, congestion would have multiplied even faster, which meant that merchants would have been cut off from their customers, motorized and foot-borne alike, all the more surely.

Again, no one compensated the city for the cost of such "improvements," neither motorists nor higher levels of government. Although sidewalks "transported" more people per square foot, they had to be narrowed to make way for streets that, due to rising congestion, moved fewer and fewer. Rural-dominated state legislatures responded by taxing urbanites in order to construct paved highways out into the hinterlands. Although the *New York Times* protested the effect of doubly penalizing urban economies, and the Cleveland chamber of commerce complained that such practices were driving city budgets into the red, such protests were ignored. Even something as simple as snow added to the burden. Prior to the car, cities had not bothered to clean up after a snowstorm, knowing that carriage owners would simply switch to sleighs. But because motor vehicles were less efficient in snow than horse-drawn vehicles, cities now had to hire laborers to shovel the streets, some twenty-four thousand temporary workers following each major snowfall in New York alone.[17]

Congestion imposed costs on trolley riders, who now found the going a good deal slower, and on pedestrians, who had to pick their way through a sea of stalled vehicles whenever they crossed the street. As early as 1907, one transportation writer noted that no matter how quickly cities acted to expand roadway capacity, traffic rose just as quickly to fill it.[18] In 1913, a travel writer named Edward Hungerford found growing traffic paralysis in one city after another in the course of a cross-country tour. Pittsburgh and San Francisco, both located on narrow peninsulas, were jammed twice a day, while heavy traffic was driving down property values along Cleveland's posh Euclid Avenue and Philadelphia's Wissashickon Drive. In New York, a 1915 study found that pedestrians were making better time along Fifth Avenue than drivers, while rush-hour speeds in Washington, D.C., had fallen to under six miles per hour, roughly the pace of a slow jog. In Chicago, trolley companies complained that street-car speeds were down 45 percent due to rising auto traffic. Police departments were finding that they had to assign 25 percent or more of their officers to traffic duty to prevent gridlock.[19]

Americans were learning an important fact about the automobile: it was less efficient than billed. While creating miracles of mobility in some areas, it was creating nightmares of immobility in others. Its use of urban space was nothing short of profligate. Because cars have a larger turning radius than trolleys, bikes, or horse-drawn transport, intersections had to be widened. Because they are greedy for places to park, trees had to be cut down along broad avenues, while marginal old buildings, rather than being upgraded and repaired, had to be knocked down to make way for parking lots. Early traffic writers calculated that a typical auto took up ten to twenty times as much road space per passenger as a trolley. Yet it was all too common to see a hundred straphangers held up by a single motorist waiting to make a left turn.[20]

Urban efficiency took a nosedive. In Los Angeles, the number of people entering the central business district fell 24 percent between 1923 and 1931 despite booming population in the metropolitan region as a whole.[21] New York saw a similar drop in human traffic across the major East River bridges. After peaking at 426,000 people a day in 1907, human traffic across the Brooklyn Bridge subsequently declined nearly 60 percent. The number of people making their way across the Williamsburg Bridge fell 52 percent after peaking in 1924, human traffic across the Manhattan Bridge declined 50 percent after peaking in 1939, while the number of people crossing via the Queensboro Bridge fell 24 percent from its peak in 1940.[22] For a variety of reasons—the high-rise office boom of the 1920s, the growth of the commuter railroads, and the fact that auto-ownership rates in New York lagged well behind those of the nation as a whole—travel into and out of Manhattan's central business district continued to rise right through World War II. But then, after peaking at some 3.7 million people a day in 1948, it, too, fell back—by 9 percent as of 1960, by another 15 percent as of 1976.[23] As the number of motor vehicles entering midtown rose, the number of people fell.

Two statements by a couple of pioneering champions of the automobile are useful in shedding light on Americans' thinking, or nonthinking, during this period. The first is by an auto enthusiast named Frank Munsey in 1903:

I have never known a case where the viewpoint differed so radically as they do from the inside and outside of an automobile. The man who knows it from the outside despises it and damns it on general principles . . . but once inside of a really first rate automobile a marvelous change comes over him.[24]

This was typical of the cheerful boosterism of the day. No one, Munsey believed, was immune to the auto's wiles—and considering the enthusiastic public reaction, he may very well have been right. Yet what was significant was not so much what Munsey said as what he didn't. He did not say, for instance, that the auto had been maligned or that complaints about its being noisy, smelly, and dangerous were untrue. All he said was that such things didn't matter. Once an individual allowed himself to be seduced, he no longer cared about its broader social impact. Surrendering to the auto meant surrendering to the urge to elevate one's enjoyment over the well-being of others. Rather than grappling with the problem posed by auto-generated externalities, it meant learning to ignore them. This was not the first time consumers had been invited to behave in an antisocial manner. But it was the first time they had been invited to do so en masse with such a powerful instrument at their disposal.

The second quote is from an auto booster named William F. Dix in 1904:

Imagine a healthier race of workingmen, toiling in cheerful and sanitary factories, with mechanical skill and trade-craft developed to the highest, . . . who, in the late afternoon, glide away in their own comfortable vehicles to their little farms or houses in the country or by the sea twenty or thirty miles distant! They will be healthier, happier, more intelligent and self-respecting citizens because of the chance to live among the meadows and flowers of the country instead of the crowded city streets.[25]

This was the old progressive dream of a working class that is less threatening by virtue of being de-urbanized. It is a reverie that looks forward to the day when factory work is so advanced it hardly seems like labor at all, while simultaneously looking backward to a rural idyll straight out of Thomas Hardy. The underlying political message was obvious: "healthier, happier, more intelligent and self-respecting citizens" meant workers who, because they owned property, would be less prone to grumbling, more inclined to see their interests as consonant with those of capital. It was a happy state of mind that would be achieved when workers were removed from "crowded city streets," with all their dangerous political doctrines, and relocated "among the meadows and flowers," where such influences were absent.

As these statements show, the automobile accomplished two things seemingly at a stroke. It promoted a form of extreme individualism in which each person was encouraged to define his own interests in opposition to those of society around him; and it promised to bring within reach a social goal of a de-urbanized working class that, during the hell-bent industrialization of the previous decades, had seemed more and more remote. Putting two and two together, middle-class Americans concluded that the key to solving the city problem lay in universalizing this increasingly antisocial form of individualism so that a wider and wider portion of the population could partake. In 1906, Woodrow Wilson had complained that cars were playing into the hands of radicals by fueling the resentment of the poor: "Nothing has spread socialistic feeling in this country more than the automobile; to the countryman they [i.e., automobiles] are a picture of arrogance of wealth, with all its independence and carelessness."[26] Rather than doing away with the arrogance of wealth, the solution that American capitalism seized upon was to "democratize" it so that "independence and carelessness" would be available to a broader and broader portion of the population.

. . . .

By most accounts, Henry Ford was not such a bad egg during his early years. To be sure, he was hard driving and fanatical in pursuit of his goal of a low-priced people's automobile. But he was the very model of a shirtsleeves boss who labors alongside his workers, laughing, kidding, and urging them along. "He was like a kid with a new toy," recalled one employee. "God, he could get anything out of us," added another. "He'd never say, 'I *want* this done.' He'd say, 'I wonder if we can do this? I wonder?' Well, the men would break their necks to see if they could do it." As Ford no doubt sensed (although he would never have put it in such terms), this was in keeping with the Jacksonian ideal of the boss who is not a boss but rather a first among equals. Once he became wealthy, Ford was famously absentminded about money. One story told of his wife finding a crumpled $75,000 check that he had shoved in his pants pocket weeks earlier and forgotten to deposit.[27] This was in keeping with the faux-modest Jacksonian ideal as well. Money was important, but only for its utilitarian value. Patriotism, public service, the respect of one's fellow citizens—in the Jeffersonian-Jacksonian hierarchy of values, all these ranked higher.

This combination of Jeffersonian ideology and modern industry led to a curious dialectic. The more Ford's empire expanded, the more determined he became not to use his money merely to make more money but to serve the people by restoring the ancient republic. Yet the more he resisted the traditional role of capitalist, the more tyrannical he grew. In the old days, associates had noticed a certain cruel streak—a tendency to tease, a penchant for rough practical jokes. But by the time Ford opened his Model T factory in the Detroit suburb of Highland Park in 1910, his personality was turning increasingly explosive, while by the time he opened his gargantuan River Rouge complex a bit farther out of town in 1919–20 it was even worse—secretive, dictatorial, increasingly malevolent. Unlike his rival Alfred P. Sloan Jr., who around this time was transforming General Motors into a model of modern corporate efficiency, Ford was contemptuous of sales meetings, paperwork, and organizational charts. As a consequence, conditions inside his company grew ever more chaotic. Old associates who remembered their boss from the days before he could walk on water were purged. More and more power fell into the hands of shady thugs led by a five-foot-six ex-boxer named Harry Bennett, who bragged about his underworld connections and seemed to have a sixth sense when it came to flattering and entertaining the boss. Ford appointed Bennett to head up his blandly named Service Department. Supposedly created to combat pilferage, it was turned by Bennett into a company-wide secret police force whose chief occupation was ferreting out and terrorizing union organizers.[28] Bennett's enforcers interrogated workers and ransacked lunch pails and overcoats looking for union literature. They lurked around taverns and marketplaces that Ford employees were known to frequent, sniffing about for signs of disloyalty.

Two of Ford's biographers, the writing team of Peter Collier and David Horowitz, compare what was happening inside the Ford empire during this period to what was happening in certain parts of Europe. The atmosphere was growing dark, fearful, and violent. Conditions on the assembly line were verging on the totalitarian. According to Collier and Horowitz:

> There was no sitting, squatting, singing, talking, or whistling on the job. Smiling was frowned upon. Workers learned to communicate without moving their lips, in what became known as "the Ford whisper." Their frozen features were called "Fordization of the Face." The workers fought back by taping messages onto the parts moving along the assembly

line, a technique that allowed them not only to communicate but also to uncover the informers in their ranks when the information on the messages was revealed to men of the Service Department. . . . Anyone even suspected of being a UAW sympathizer was not only summarily fired but usually beaten up as well.[29]

Ford's foremen patrolled the assembly line like concentration-camp guards, shouting, cursing, and punching. "The average worker," the great man declared, "I am sorry to say, wants a job in which he does not have to put forth much physical exertion—above all, he wants a job in which he does not have to think."[30] Yet the rigorous controls that Ford was imposing suggested the opposite. If workers were lazy and docile, why was it necessary to go to such lengths to terrorize them into submission?

Meanwhile, Ford's political views were also evolving. In this respect, he doesn't seem to have been such a bad egg at the beginning, either. He managed to make a colossal fool of himself in 1915 when he launched his famous "Peace Ship" to Europe in an ill-conceived effort to single-handedly put a stop to World War I. Yet members of the press found themselves touched by the spectacle of a naive businessman yanked this way and that by a motley crew of Russian bohemians, pacifists, and idealistic clergymen. One reporter described him as "a mechanical genius with the heart of a child," while another called him "a sort of inarticulate Christ."[31] In 1919, Ford bought a local Michigan newspaper, the *Dearborn Independent,* and with the help of William J. Cameron, his handpicked editor, turned it into a personal vehicle for his various opinions and views. The paper began innocuously enough with articles about hay making, quilting, and other rural pursuits. But then, as America plunged into yet another of its periodic red scares, the tone turned angry and violent. An article in November 1919 congratulated Seattle's "two-fisted Irish chief of police" for crushing a general strike. Another asked: "Wouldn't it solve a lot of our problems to have fewer half-million or million-people cities, and more of the 25,000, 50,000, or 100,000 sort?"[32] In an article about the new Communist regime in Russia, the paper informed its readers: "The so-called 'dictatorship of the proletariat' is really and practically the dictatorship of the Jews."[33]

As a Midwestern populist, Ford was both anti-imperialist and anti–Wall Street. He enjoyed portraying himself as the rare enlightened boss who is a friend of the workingman, and he was far from completely hostile to the Russian Communists—as long as they stayed in Russia, that is. But the slightest hint of Bolshevism in the United States drove him to wild fantasies in which Communists somehow blended with international financiers and so-called "forces of darkness" until they became one and the same. Jews, meanwhile, the arch-puppeteers, were behind them all, pulling the strings. As the *Dearborn Independent* declared in 1921, Jews

are at the heart of the problems that disturb the world today. The immigration problem is Jewish. The money question is Jewish. The tie-up of world politics is Jewish. The terms of the [Versailles] Peace Treaty are Jewish. The diplomacy of the world is Jewish. The moral question in movies and theaters is Jewish. The mystery of the illicit liquor business is Jewish.[34]

If bootleggers were able to smuggle booze past Coast Guard patrol boats, it was because Jews had somehow arranged for their crews to look the other way. If Hollywood was turning out biblical epics filled with writhing, half-naked slave girls, it was because Jewish movie moguls were out to subvert Christian morals. Yet amid all this feverish paranoia about "Jew York,"[35] the paper was also capable of publishing a down-to-earth article by a thoroughly respectable urban planner named Hugh C. Mitchell on how to retool community design so as to meet the needs of the motor age.

Antiurbanism is what tied the various strands together. Jews were dangerous because they were the quintessentially urban people. Cities were dangerous because they were filled with Jews. Urban planners were useful because they saw the city as an obstacle to be conquered and believed its crowds needed to be thinned out, its crooked lines made straight so that the motorist would be able to race right through it as if it weren't there. As Hugh C. Mitchell wrote in his 1924 article on community design:

> The city planner must make it easier and easier for automobiles to move along certain routes, harder and harder for them to stop. In widening a street he gives it greater capacity; by eliminating a left-hand turn he removes an obstacle. He makes streets in the congested districts one-way streets, alternating the direction of travel on successive streets. [36]

By making it "easier for automobiles to move" and "harder for them to stop," Mitchell and his fellow planners were reconfiguring the city so that auto traffic, and hence auto-borne commerce, would bypass it entirely. If one-way streets, narrower sidewalks, and other such "reforms" made the city less pleasant as a place to live, work, and stroll about, that was not unintentional. Since congestion is "[u]ndoubtedly one of the greatest single problems which today confronts the city planner," as Mitchell put it, the solution was to de-congest the city by persuading more and more people to leave. Where Jefferson had hoped that yellow fever would thin out the urban ranks, the automobile was serving the same function far more effectively.

Mitchell also turned his attention to the ongoing carnage in the city streets:

> The time is not far past when the streets were regarded by many as the legitimate playground for children. It has not

been many years since a prominent member of the House of Representatives, objecting to an appropriation for playgrounds, defended the use of the streets as a playground by his children—by all children. But the extreme hazard of such use of the streets to those so using it has convinced the most skeptical . . . of the necessity for providing proper play places, and this the cities are doing, often at great cost. . . . But even at a very high cost the playgrounds are worth it.[37]

This was progress as the new ideology of Fordism was coming to define it. Because motorization had made streets hazardous, cities were forced "at a very high cost" to provide play spaces that formerly were free. Such costs were a benefit—a positive externality, according to the Fordist theoretical framework—because they weighed heavily on urban budgets, thereby rendering the city less and less efficient.

Ford used his weekly column in the *Independent* to rage against the city and everything it stood for in much the same way that he raged against the Jews:

Every social ailment from which we suffer today originates and centers in the great cities. . . . There is something about a city of a million people which is untamed and threatening. . . . A great city is really a helpless mass. Everything it uses is carried to it. Stop the transport and the city stops. It lives off the shelves of stores, but the shelves produce nothing.[38]

The city was helpless, yet threatening. It was the natural habitat of intellectuals whose influence on the nation at large, according to Ford, was increasingly unhealthy: "We are a nation of casual readers. We read to escape thinking. Reading has become a dope habit with us. Learning has become a thing of accent and of facts."[39] The city was the natural habitat of the crowd, which Ford, not surprisingly, viewed in essentially Le Bonist terms as something stupid and degraded: "Men are never so much like a herd as when they are organized. When they are free to go afoot and alone and across lots, they are intelligent individuals."[40] The city was where political and economic power was concentrated, which is why power had to be decentralized and rural self-sufficiency promoted:

> The ideal community is self-sustaining. . . . If near flowing water, every community should be self-sustaining in matters of power, heating and lighting. Every community in the midst of an agricultural district should be self-sustaining in the matter of food. The grain grown near by should be milled near by. . . . Every community should be constructed out of material near at hand and thus preserve unity with its basic soil.[41]

Finally, as we know from Washington Irving and others, the city was where history was most concentrated, which is why historical consciousness had to be overthrown. Ford's famous remark that "history is bunk"—the exact quote is, "history is more or less bunk"—was no chance utterance. Rather, it was a theme he returned to repeatedly. The past, he believed, was a burden that the people had to cast off so they could be free to make their way in the present. As he put it in his 1926 autobiography: "You may fill your head with all the 'facts' of all the ages, and your head may be just an over-loaded fact-box when you get through. . . . It must be perfectly clear to everyone that the past learning cannot be allowed to hinder our future learning."[42] Although elsewhere Ford proclaimed himself in favor of facts, facts, facts—

> we shall not bother about good feeling in industry or life; we shall not bother about masses and classes, or closed and open shops, or such matters as have nothing at all to do with the

real business of living. We can get down to facts. We stand in need of facts. . . .

—some facts were more equal than others.[43] Facts that aided in "the real business of living," i.e., the Fordist reconstruction of society, were good. Facts that were inconvenient, that got in the way, that somehow suggested that the Fordist orthodoxy was less than 100 percent sound, were not.

De-urbanization was thus the way to free Americans from the double burden of history and intellect. In the city, one was weighed down by book learning, but as soon as one left the tall buildings and stepped into the bright sunshine, all that nonsense fell away. Cities "were a school for the race," Ford wrote in 1921. "They taught us something. They filled their place and did their work of education. But an end comes to every place of education, and it seems clear that an end is coming to this also."[44] Having learned as much as they needed to know, it was time for Americans to move on.

What made a collection of bigoted, half-baked opinions like these important was Ford's unique ability to put them into effect. Twentieth-century America followed with remarkable fidelity the blueprint he laid out. His solution to the urban problem—"We shall solve the city problem by leaving the city"—became national policy. His forecast that urban economies would run into the ground due to mounting costs imposed by the automobile proved deadly accurate. Not only did the working class eventually de-urbanize once the Depression and World War II were out of the way, but, as he also forecast, industry did as well.[45] Despite the enormous strength for a time of the United Auto Workers and other industrial unions, Ford's prediction that de-urbanization would prove ultimately crippling to organized labor also turned out accurate. Hyper-mobility allowed factories to escape first to the suburbs and then to the Sunbelt, where organized labor was slow to follow. If "great cities are the birthplace of labour movements," as Engels put it in 1844,[46] then their demise was the start of labor's great unraveling—as Ford well understood.

. . . .

There is a good deal that Ford got wrong, of course. Anti-Semitism never caught on with the American public the way he would have liked. No matter how much he tried to promote square dancing and other rural pursuits, young people preferred the Charleston and the jitterbug. Still, when it came to the all-important question of class, his successes clearly outweighed his failures. The purpose of mass motorization, in the final analysis, was to destroy the urban class structure and replace it with something more amorphous, a middle-class utopia that would lead to the abolition of class society altogether. After a false start in the 1920s, he and his successors were eventually successful. Even though American workers continued to go on strike in massive numbers until the early 1980s, they tended to think of themselves less as workers in the classic sense and more as hard-pressed consumers. As conservatives were happy to point out, their chief complaint regarding the Fordist system was not that it had gone too far but that it had not gone far enough in turning out cars, consumer goods, and suburban homes.

The repressive atmosphere inside Ford's factories also served to pump up consumerism. Nothing drove rank-and-file workers more quickly into the arms of the UAW than violent and abusive foremen. Yet while the union's hard-fought organizing victory in 1941 forced the company to restrain its foremen while handing over more in the form of wages and benefits, it bore unexpected fruits. Mind-deadening regimentation plus steady wage hikes combined to drive home a message that Ford and his successors did not find unpalatable. Work was painful and degrading. The only thing that made it bearable was the promise of consumption at the end of the day. Prior to the Fordist assembly line, labor had been a source of identity and self-worth. Hours were long, but the pace was slower, and owners were so far removed from the task of daily management that the time-and-motion pioneer Frederick W. Taylor once complained that the typical factory "was really run by the workers and not by the bosses."[47] Now, with bosses micromanaging workers' every move, there was no doubt as to who was in charge. For workers, the only relief was to be obtained off-hours through the process of owning and consuming.

. . . .

Moreover, Fordist discipline, no longer confined to the assembly line, was extending itself into society at large. Ford himself had always been ferociously self-disciplined. Whip thin, he did not smoke or drink, seldom ate meat, and seemed to get his second wind at a time when most men were getting ready to retire. Now the demands of the motor age, he insisted, demanded a corresponding commitment on the part of every last citizen. Because Americans couldn't drink and drive, he became a vocal supporter of Prohibition. Because he wanted his workers to make use of the famous five-dollars-a-day wage to lift themselves up, he had his "Sociology Department" send inspectors into their homes to make sure that they were clean, that there was food on the table, that the children were in school, that the wife was not taking in boarders (a practice believed to lead to dangerous sexual entanglements), and in the case of recent immigrants, that they were learning English. Prior to the assembly line, the prevailing attitude among bosses, to quote one efficiency expert, was not to "care a hoot what became of the workman after he left the factory at night, so long as he was able to show up the next morning in fit condition for a hard day's toil." If he drank or gambled, it was nobody's business but his own; the boss's only concern was how he performed on the job. But as a social system rather than merely a means of production, Fordism could not afford anything so laissez-faire. Society had to be as intensively engineered as the factory in order to ratchet up both consumption and production to the highest level.

"We employers who feel that management is to become a true science," declared a factory manager in 1916, "must begin to think less of the science of material things and more of the science of human relationships."[48] The new suburbs that blossomed after 1945 were the upshot. With their broad lawns and evenly spaced bungalows, they offered as few places to hide as the Pullman model town had fifty or sixty years earlier. There were no saloons, no alleyways, no meeting halls, no "whores' meaty legs" taking up half the sidewalk. It was a relentlessly sunny and green environment that imposed an equally relentless code of behavior. Home owners had to mow the lawn, accumulate the requisite number of consumer goods, and work day in and day out to meet the mortgage, a far more demanding taskmaster than the old landlords had been. "No man who owns his own house and lot can be a Communist," declared William J. Levitt, builder of Levittown, in 1948. "He has too much to do."[49] While unorthodox political beliefs were not exactly prohibited under the postwar suburban regime, there is no question that they were strongly discouraged. The new communities were structured in such a way as to promote a certain body of core beliefs: conformity, privatism, and the notion of individual accumulation as an index of moral worth. No one was shipped off to the gulag for failing to comply, but, still, the great majority complied regardless.

THE URBAN WAVE
CRESTS AND CRASHES

6

One of the more important city planning aspects
of housing is the removal of the factory and the home
to the city outskirts, thus instituting a process of
industrial and residential decentralization.

JOHN NOLEN, THE FATHER OF AMERICAN URBAN PLANNING, 1919

The suburb is a public acknowledgement of the fact
that congestion and bad housing and blank vistas and lack
of recreational opportunity and endless subway rides are not
humanly endurable. The suburbanite is merely an
intelligent heretic who has discovered that the mass of
New York or Chicago or Zenith is a mean environment.

LEWIS MUMFORD, *HARPER'S*, 1926

Our Ruskinian boys and girls keep talking about
the evils of present day standardization, and the robot
crowds on the subways, and the horrors of cleanliness and order.
They make me sick, they make me tired.

GENEVIEVE TAGGARD, *THE NEW MASSES*, 1927

A NYONE WHO has ever lain on a beach and watched the tide beat against the shore knows that a wave is never more impressive than in its final moments. From a low-lying swell, it rears up and arches forward. Foam forms around the edges, and swimmers seem in danger of disappearing into the maw. And then it crashes. In seconds, it vanishes into the sand.

Twentieth-century development followed a similar pattern in the United States. From an urban perspective, the writing was on the wall as early as 1908, when the first Model T rolled off the line. Not only did motorization impose an increasingly inefficient form of transportation on the city but by liberating millions of middle-class motorists from having to sleep in the same town in which they worked, it deprived the city of much of its revenue base as well. Newark, to cite one particularly horrendous example, was an important manufacturing, retail, and financial center during the first decades of the twentieth century. Yet even as its prosperity was rising, the local business elite was deserting it in droves. By 1925, some 40 percent of the city's attorneys already lived in one of the nearby bedroom communities. By 1947, the same figure stood at 63 percent, while by 1965, as the city was nearing collapse, it hit 78 percent.[1] Yet there was little that Newark could do to stop the hemorrhage. At just twenty-three square miles, it was painfully aware that motorists could escape its jurisdiction in minutes, while, thanks to a rural-dominated state legislature, the days were long gone when it could annex nearby suburbs at will. Middle-class professionals were absconding with its wealth. Yet all it could do was watch as its economic base dwindled to nothing.

This was not urban decay but a form of urban manslaughter in which a wide array of social policies came together in such a way as to reduce one city after another literally to rubble. A combination of federal tax breaks and direct government outlays fueled suburban development at the expense of the cities, while an equally broad network of federal policies, most of them hidden in one way or another from direct public oversight, subsidized motor vehicles at the expense of public transit.

The American system of limited government and fragmented political power allowed suburban communities to turn themselves into middle-class redoubts whose raison d'être was to screen out blacks, Jews, and anyone else deemed harmful to the municipal bottom line, while at the same time rendering cities powerless to fight back.

Not only did the system permit suburban communities to turn themselves into middle-class redoubts, moreover, it fairly *mandated* that they do so by penalizing those that did not. With its run-down housing projects and overgrown vacant lots, Newark would seem to have absolutely nothing in common with New Canaan, Connecticut, located some fifty miles to the east, one of America's most elite communities. Yet a century ago, as the urban historian Kenneth T. Jackson has pointed out, they were not nearly as dissimilar as one might suppose. Although smaller, New Canaan was also an important manufacturing center with a sizable working class. Differences only emerged after the turn of the century when wealthy New Yorkers discovered New Canaan and began transforming it into a fashionable country retreat. From then on, the two communities' paths diverged. While its policies were hardly ideal, Newark struggled to hold on to its industrial base by, among other things, maintaining an open-door policy to successive waves of newcomers, including blacks from the Deep South. In 1909, it became one of the first major cities to integrate its schools, and during the 1930s, it became a national leader in the construction of low-income housing. New Canaan, by contrast, set about expelling industry by adopting a zoning code establishing a two-acre-minimum lot size in the 1930s and then, a few years later, upping the ante to a four-acre minimum. Anyone who could not afford such enormous estates was effectively barred from entering. Not only did local shopkeepers refuse to serve blacks but home owners and realtors refused to sell to Jews. After hanging up the phone, a local realtor told a waiting couple as late as 1974 that the caller was his mother "want[ing] to make sure I am not showing any houses to Jews." Where Newark hosted more public units per capita than any other municipality in the country, New Canaan closed its doors to multifamily housing of nearly any sort whatsoever.

"Newark's problems became more severe *because* the city attempted to help poor and minority citizens and *because* it was a leader in civil rights, at least in comparison with the suburbs," to quote Jackson, while New Canaan prospered by virtue of opposing those very same reforms. Where Newark was an urban disaster area of international renown by the 1960s, New Canaan was emerging as perhaps the wealthiest single enclave on the entire East Coast. Today, it is one of the top ten municipalities in the nation in terms of *Who's Who in America* listings per capita. It is filled with expensive shops, fleets of Mercedes and BMWs, luxuriously equipped public schools, and attractive and well-kept parks. Where Newark real estate is so devalued it cannot be given away, the average new home in New Canaan by 1999 was selling for more than $1 million.[2] It was an example of how the new Fordist regime systematically punished generous impulses and rewarded mean-spirited ones.

What made such policies so hypocritical, of course, is that they were instituted in the name of civic responsibility and rugged individualism. In 1923, at the very dawn of the auto-suburban age, the U.S. Commerce Department, then under the leadership of a dynamic young politician named Herbert Hoover, issued a pamphlet declaring that suburban home ownership and good citizenship were mutually reinforcing:

> A family that owns its own home takes pride in it, maintains it better, gets more pleasure out of it, and has a more whole-some, healthful, and happy atmosphere in which to bring up children. The homeowner . . . works harder outside his home. . . . A husband and wife who own their own home are more apt to save. They have an interest in advancement of a social system that permits the individual to store up the fruits

of his labor. As direct taxpayers, they take a more active part in local government. Above all, the love of home is one of the finest instincts and the greatest inspiration of our people.[3]

Nothing by way of data was offered to back such assertions up. No evidence was offered to the effect that home owners had a more rewarding home life, worked harder, or were more apt to save. Indeed, by fueling spending and consumption, the "wealth effect" created by rising real-estate values actually encouraged home owners to save less, which is one reason why the 1920s per-capita savings rate declined nearly 50 percent below pre-1917 levels.[4] The Commerce Department also offered nothing to back up its assertion that home owners, as direct taxpayers, tended to take a more active part in local government. But even if true, they were doing so at a time when participation in national politics was plunging. Voter turnout in presidential elections fell to around 50 percent in the decade following World War I, some thirty points less than the levels of the late nineteenth century, while turnout in the 1926 congressional elections reached a low of 33 percent, a level that would not be equaled until 1998.[5] Even if Hoover's Commerce Department was correct in asserting that local political participation was growing as a consequence of rising home ownership, the trend was more than offset by declining participation at the national level.

Of course, this may have been the desired effect. Just as Henry Ford didn't want Americans to "bother about masses and classes, or closed and open shops," politicians like Herbert Hoover didn't want them troubling themselves over issues of national or international policy. Instead, these politicians preferred that citizens narrow their focus to such things as school boards, zoning codes, and other minutiae, since anything larger might disturb the status quo. From an establishment point of view, only one thing mattered. When home ownership was stagnant—in 1920, the nonfarm-ownership rate had hit an all-time low of 45.6 percent, while in the Bronx and Manhattan by the turn of the century it had fallen to just 6 percent[6]—social unrest had risen. If home ownership could be made to go back up, then presumably unrest would fall. Walter Weyl had argued some years earlier that declining home ownership was an indication of economic advancement. Just as Americans were taking advantage of economies of scale by shopping in large department stores, he argued, they were doing the same by renting in large apartment buildings.[7] If so, postwar politicians were happy to turn their backs on modernization in exchange for a return to political stability.

Not surprisingly, Hoover was yet another Le Bonist when it came to the nature of the urban masses. As he wrote in 1922:

> Acts and deeds leading to progress are born of the individual mind, not out of the mind of the crowd. The crowd only feels, it has no mind of its own which can plan. The crowd is credulous, it destroys, it hates and it dreams, but it never builds. It is one of the most profound of exact psychological truths that man in the mass does not think, but only feels.[8]

The idea, therefore, was to create a social structure that would systemically dissolve the crowd into its individual parts. Although Hoover would later be tagged as a conservative due to his do-nothing policy following the Crash of '29, he was actually a progressive Republican who had supported Teddy Roosevelt's Bull Moose party in 1912 and, as secretary of commerce, had managed to win over "the leftists of the *New Republic,* the machine-worshippers of the Taylor Society, and the new breed of management engineers," as one historian put it, which was no mean feat.[9] His suburbanizing policies represented the most advanced bourgeois thinking of the day.

But the initial impact of the mass-motorization policies of the 1910s and 1920s was paradoxical. Rather than undermining urbanization, they seemed for a time to be driving it to new heights. The 1920s were the era of Fritz Lang's *Metropolis* (1927) and Hugh Ferriss's drawings of an imaginary New York composed of huge Babylonian-style skyscrapers, auto speedways, and pedestrian catwalks strung every which way in between. It was a vision of a futuristic hyper-city that was simultaneously high-speed, massive, and immovable. Rather than a sign of impending disaster, the dense swarms of motor vehicles nosing their way into every major downtown at this time seemed to be a sign of urban vitality. They were a tribute to the city's immense drawing power rather than a sign of declining efficiency.

In truth, the urban economy was falling between the cracks of two socio-industrial systems. Rail and trolley ridership had peaked in 1908, and although transit use was still going up in a few areas, most notably New York, the national trend was downward.[10] Cars and trucks were stealing more and more of rail's business, while government regulatory agencies, still fighting the populist battles of yesteryear, were refusing the railroads permission to raise rates. Not only were trolleys mired in traffic but they were under continuous assault by various goo-goo elements for whom the entire mode was synonymous with sweetheart deals and municipal corruption. As Owen D. Young, chairman of General Electric, a major supplier of trolley equipment, put it in 1928, "it is indeed a rather dull morning when the public, in one form or another, does not threaten to lick the industry before the day is done."[11] Moreover, rail transport was labor-intensive and therefore vulnerable to strikes, whereas Detroit at this point was, from a manufacturer's point of view, still an open-shop paradise.

But the auto sector also had its problems. Congestion was not just clogging city streets but clogging up sales. By the mid-1920s, those middle-class consumers who were inclined to purchase a motor vehicle had already done so for the most part, while in traffic-laden cities still well served by mass transit, those not so inclined saw little reason to change their minds. The marketing innovations that were allowing General Motors to catch up with and surpass Ford during this period—yearly style changes, a growing array of makes and models, planned obsolescence, and so forth—were, in the final analysis, a desperate attempt to shoehorn more cars into an already overloaded market. A wave of ads touting the auto as a status symbol, a dream machine, and a sex object was a tacit acknowledgment that, amid rising traffic, the car's practical benefits were tapering off. One solution would have been to build more highways so cars would have more room to romp and play. Yet the federal role in highway construction was still undeveloped, while state and local governments were too fragmented and resource poor to do it on their own.

Housing was another trouble spot. There was no point building a highway from one congested city to another since, for a motorist, the effect would be that of a pipe plugged at both ends. If interurban transport was all cars were good for, then city dwellers might as well take the train. What auto manufacturers needed, rather, was a system of in*tra*-urban auto transport—i.e., diffuse, low-density communities in which residents would be able to use their cars not just for long-distance travel but short-distance errands. They needed suburbs, in other words, which meant a mass market in suburban housing. America must "make houses like Fords," declared Edward Filene, the department-store magnate, in 1925.[12] Yet the middle-class buying public in the 1920s was still too small to support such a market, while the real-estate business was too narrow and unaccommodating. Between 1885 and 1925, the price of an entry-level home had risen at better than two and a half times the rate of inflation. Builders had tried to compensate by shifting to cheaper, multifamily construction, yet the overall effect was to drive up single-family home prices all the more.[13] With "close to three-quarters of the suburban houses built in 1929 . . . within reach of only a tenth of the nation's families," as one historian put it, suburbia was still an elite preserve.[14] Making matters worse was a fragmented, cumbersome mortgage system that seemed all but designed to shoo away borrowers before they entered the door. Banks required as much as 50 percent down, with the balance due in just five to ten years and sometimes as little as three.[15] Only buyers with ample cash reserves could even think of entering the market, which meant that the bulk of the population would remain shut out for years to come. The auto-suburban system needed to broaden itself if it was to survive, yet growth seemed to be pushing up against structural limits.

The result was yet another crisis of overproduction. As markets grew more and more saturated and industrial output began to falter, capital raced about in an increasingly frenzied search for new places in which to invest. In tandem with the stock market, urban real-estate values rose unsustainably as contractors built bigger and bigger buildings in the belief that the supply of tenants would always expand to fill them. When, by 1929, it became apparent that this wasn't the case and that developers had seriously overestimated demand, real-estate values began a long, sickening slide. Completed in 1931, the Empire State Building, the capstone of the 1920s office-construction boom, would not be fully rented until the late 1940s. Even as it rose higher and higher, the urban real-estate boom was weakening at the base.

. . . .

Among other things, this led to a perceptual lag in which planners, urbanologists, and ordinary members of the public continued to think of the city as something massive and inexorable long after this was in fact the case. There is no better example of this phenomenon than Lewis Mumford, a public intellectual whose very name was synonymous with urban planning for nearly forty years. Mumford had his moments of eloquence and insight. But when it came to the real condition of American cities, he displayed a remarkable combination of willful blindness and dogmatism. From the 1920s through the 1950s, he flailed away at the metropolis as something stifling and oppressive. The city, he complained again and again, cut its inhabitants off from nature, bombarded them with ads, robbed them of their sex drive, and reduced life to a hollow shell. This was the old progressive complaint about the city as unnatural and degrading, with a soupçon of *The Wasteland* and *Lady Chatterley's Lover* thrown in to make it seem more up to date. Yet for all his anger and anticommercialism, Mumford was, in a sense, oddly complacent. No matter how much he whaled away at the city, he assumed that it would always be there, huge and immovable, ready for more. When, by the late 1950s, it was apparent even to Mumford that this was no longer the case and that urban America was in serious trouble, he did an about-face. From a city basher, he promptly reinvented himself as a passionate champion of "the complex, many-sided civilization that the city makes possible."[16] Yet what he failed to acknowledge, and what he clearly hoped readers wouldn't notice, was his own role in the debacle.

Mumford was another American tory-radical, this time by way of John Ruskin and William Morris, a couple of English aesthetes who personified some of the more glaring contradictions in a certain strain of nineteenth-century left-wing thought. Both were critics of industrial production, not only of the things that factories turned out but of the productive process itself—the way it turned workers into appendages of machines and labor into drudgery. Both called themselves socialists, with Morris especially militant at certain stages of his career. But both were fundamentally backward-looking in their critique. The aesthetic values they espoused were neo-Gothic, while, in terms of production, they longed for a return to the days of the eighteenth-century rural craftsmen, the same craftsmen Engels had lambasted for their lack of politics and intellect in his 1844 "pre-Marxist" classic, *The Condition of the Working-Class in England*.[17] Ruskin and Morris extolled this preindustrial mode of production for all the reasons Engels did not—because it was small-scale and self-contained; because it took place in rural villages, where nature was close at hand; and because technology had not yet reached the point where the laborer was dwarfed by the machines he tended. By returning to some supposedly idyllic premodern state, they believed that workers could re-create an existence that was innocent, unified, and complete—a cozy little world in which all the necessities of life would be close at hand.

Mumford's modest contribution was to take such ideas and carry them forward into the age of Hollywood and Madison Avenue. Instead of the factory, the enemy was now urban commercial culture. Instead of long hours, low wages, and unemployment, modern society's failure was evident in such things as canned foods, magazines, and commodified sex. Especially in his early years, Mumford's stance was that of the self-conscious aesthete—not the simpering, overrefined urban variety, but the lusty, rural, Mellors-the-gamekeeper sort who likes to go romping barefoot through the meadows and entwine daisies in his lover's hair. His indictment of the city was that it was deracinated and devitalized. It substituted tasteless, factory-made food in place of honest regional cooking, Tin Pan Alley in place of genuine folk music, and Hollywood-style titillation in place of genuine eroticism. As Mumford wrote in 1938, "Bawdiness, no longer the goatlike outburst of animal spirits after the abstentions and rigors of the winter, becomes in itself a jaded, night-in-night-out part of metropolitan routine: it measures its titillation and charges accordingly."[18]

But where ideas like these seemed passionate and thrilling in the hands of a master like D. H. Lawrence, in Mumford they seemed derivative and unconvincing. He was the type of personality who seemed prim and uptight the more down and dirty he tried to be. In *The Culture of Cities,* a long, antiurban screed that he published in 1938, he complained that:

What is called the "growth" of the metropolis is in fact the constant recruitment of a proletariat . . . people who do without pure air, who do without sound sleep, who do without a cheerful garden or playing spaces, who do without the very sight of the sky and the sunlight, who do without free motion, spontaneous play, or a robust sex life.[19]

How on earth did Mumford know that working-class sex was *not* robust? How many workers had he surveyed or even spoken to? *The Culture of Cities* gave no hint. The metropolis, he went on, undermined cultural diversity by teaching "inhabitants of the rural areas . . . to despise their local history, to avoid their local languages and their regional accents, in favor of the colorless language of metropolitan journalism." As a result,

> to scorn one's roots in one's own region and admiringly to pluck the paper flowers manufactured and sold by the metro-
> polis becomes the whole duty of man. Though the physical radius of the metropolis may be only twenty or thirty miles, its effective radius is much greater: its blight is carried in the air, like the spores of a mold.[20]

Virtually everything about the city repelled Mumford—the hustle and bustle of midtown ("solidified chaos"), the press ("trivial anesthesia"), even the goods on sale in the shops ("rootless . . . removed from the sources of life"). Interestingly, though, it was the subways that he found most degrading. One reason was the old progressive complaint that by "thicken[ing] the crowding at the center," as he put it, the subways worked against the "decentralization of the metropolis . . . [into] subcenters of industry, business, and residence." But Mumford's complaint was also visceral: subways literally made him sick. They were "metropolitan man-sewers" that crammed people into hot and smelly holes, forced them to rub up against one another, and left them gasping for air: "one becomes physically oppressed with the concrete fact of congestion in the . . . tightly jammed subway train, rank with the odor of human bodies on a summer's evening." The "depression of the uncomfortable journey," he added, "the exposure to infectious diseases in the over crowded car, the disturbance to the gastrointestinal functions caused by the strain and anxiety of having to reach the office or factory on time"— for someone who celebrated goatlike sex, Mumford could be curiously finicky when it came to some of the earthier aspects of city life.[21]

These crowded and smelly straphangers were essentially the same urban throngs that Walt Whitman had celebrated in the 1850s. But where Whitman found them inspiring and even erotically charged, Mumford found them a turnoff—sickly, pasty-faced creatures who were alien to sexuality and a threat to sound democracy. The irony, of course, is that once these same desexed urbanites began finding their way to the countryside after World War II, Mumford found them even more repellent than ever. Where urban culture had struck him as shallow and commercial, the postwar suburbs with their shopping centers and subdivisions struck him as even more so. Backpedaling furiously, the same man who had once lauded Henry Ford now attacked cars as "insolent chariots." Overinvestment in highways, he wrote in 1958, had created "a crudely over-simplified and inefficient method of mass-transportation: a regression from the complex, many-sided transportation system we once boasted." Highways were "a tomb of concrete roads and ramps covering the dead corpse of a city." Rather than laying down more concrete, the answer lay in "rebuilding the mass transportation in our cities." After spending much of his career attacking subways because they inhibited decentralization, Mumford now pronounced himself in favor of subways because they . . . inhibited decentralization.[22]

To be fair, Mumford was striving for a middle ground between the hypertrophied metropolis of the early twentieth century and the lifeless, highway-bound, postwar landscape of the 1950s and after. His Aristotelian ideal was the *garden city,* a term coined in the 1890s by an amateur English planner named Ebenezer Howard, which to Mumford's way of thinking meant a low-density community of no more than fifty thousand people, with plenty of greenery within its boundaries and unbroken "greenbelts" beyond. No residential building in such a community should be taller than three stories, Mumford wrote in 1926, and no office building taller than five.[23] Although the casual observer might assume that the garden city of pre–World War II imagination and the auto-based suburb of postwar reality were one and the same, Mumford insisted otherwise. The difference, he wrote, was that the garden city was compact and walkable, a genuine community clustered around a compact business district, whereas the postwar suburb was nothing more than a shapeless blob. "[B]oth metropolitan congestion and urban scattering are obsolete," he wrote in 1958. "This means that good planning must work to produce a radically new pattern of urban growth," i.e., a revival of the nineteenth-century small town.[24]

. . . .

As in the case of Herbert Hoover, this was dogma masquerading as analysis. The fact that Mumford was playing essentially the same tune in the 1950s that he had in the 1920s was indicative of how static his thinking had become. But while Mumford was hardly the first writer to repeat himself, it was his singular misfortune to run headlong into a diminutive force of nature in the person of Jane Jacobs. Jacobs was a magazine writer with an interest in urban planning and design and an unsettling tendency to think for herself rather than merely parrot the experts. As she recounted decades later in a newspaper interview, the turning point came in 1958 when *Architectural Forum,* a magazine she was working for at the time, sent her to Philadelphia to do a piece on a visionary housing project that a prominent urban planner named Edmund Bacon was supervising. Bacon showed her neat little schematic drawings of what the project was going to look like. Recalled Jacobs:

The drawings looked wonderful with all these little people in them. And I went down to see it. It was just like the picture—except all those little people weren't in it. The only person in it, in the whole thing, for blocks, was a little boy—one lone little boy who was sort of disconsolately kicking at a tire. . . . I kept saying, "Where's the people?" And he [Edmund Bacon] kept saying, "Look at this vista. Stand here and look." And I said, "Don't you think it's funny that the people aren't here? Where are they?" . . . So then we went over to the old neighborhood—just one block away. And the streets were just teeming with people. And they were sitting around on steps and they were shopping and they were talking with one another and they were all ages. And one reason there was so many of them, I soon figured out, was that all those people from over there in the new place had gone a block away. . . . He'd taken me [to the old neighborhood] to show me how bad things were and what was the next thing that was going to be wiped out.[25]

What Jacobs had come across was an all too typical case of "modern" urban planning based on straight lines and unobstructed vistas, a type of design that flowed from a decades-old "progressive" ideology that was fundamentally cold, authoritarian, and misanthropic. Such designs were perfectly in keeping with an Eisenhower-era ethos that viewed with horror families lounging on front stoops or teenagers hanging out on street corners. But what was the point of a housing project that was clearly cold and inhospitable to the people it was supposed to serve? Jacobs returned to her office, mulling over what she had seen and heard. The result three years later was *The Death and Life of Great American Cities,* a 450-page demolition job on the profession of urban planning as it was then known. Jacobs's tone was brisk, self-confident, and curtly dismissive of more than half a century of accumulated wisdom as to how cities were supposed to work:

Reformers have long observed city people loitering on busy corners, hanging around in candy stores and bars and drinking soda pop on stoops, and have passed a judgment, the gist of which is: "This is deplorable! If these people had decent homes and a more private or bosky outdoor place, they wouldn't be on the street." This judgment represents a profound misunderstanding of cities. It makes no more sense than to drop in at a testimonial banquet in a hotel and conclude that if these people had wives who could cook, they would give their parties at home.[26]

Rather than the typical social worker's view of the street as something dangerous and degrading, Jacobs pointed out that a city street functions as an arena for a wide range of activities, everything from shopping and running errands to playing stickball or hopscotch, hanging out, gossiping, or flirting. Where planners and social workers viewed with disdain the mishmash of uses in a typical urban neighborhood—the hardware store next to the wholesale meat market next to the brownstone next to the luncheonette—Jacobs pointed out that the result of such "clutter" was an urban symbiosis in which the whole wound up greater than the sum of its parts. Hudson Street in Greenwich Village was a mixed-up ball of confusion according to the conventional view, yet it *worked:*

The workers from the laboratories, meat-packing plants, warehouses, plus those from a bewildering variety of small manufacturers, printers, and other little industries and offices, give all the eating places and much of the other commerce support at midday. We residents on the street and on its more purely residential tributaries could and would support a modicum of commerce by ourselves, but relatively little. We possess more convenience, liveliness, variety and choice than we "deserve" in our own right. The people who work in the neighborhood also possess, on account of us residents, more variety than they "deserve" in their own right.[27]

Large, mixed-use urban neighborhoods benefited from economies of scale that allowed them to support more business and services than smaller, more specialized neighborhoods could separately. Zoning, the chief weapon in the urban planner's armory, was not a means of bringing order out of chaos but an assault on an urban organism that was rich, subtle, and complex:

> The leaves dropping from the trees in autumn, the interior of an airplane engine, the entrails of a dissected rabbit, the city desk of a newspaper, all appear to be chaos if they are seen without comprehension. Once they are understood as system of order, they actually *look* different.[28]

Similarly, a sidewalk filled with children playing hopscotch, an old woman peeking out of an upstairs apartment, a shopper gazing idly at a store window—all seemed to be aimless as well. But once understood as part of a larger social system, they, too, took on new meaning. They were an essential part of urban ecology, a complex interplay that helped hold the city together. Kids playing on the sidewalk were a signal to passersby that a neighborhood was lively and safe. An old woman peeking out her window was providing an important neighborhood service by watching out for suspicious characters. The window-shopper was a reminder that the city was not just for the busy and purposeful but for loungers, idlers, and daydreamers—Walter Benjamin's famous flâneurs.

All of which was a dig at urban planners and social workers who wished to reduce human activity to a set number of "uses," all neatly stowed away in their separate compartments. But the dig turned into a frontal assault when Jacobs took aim at the planners' most sacred cow of all, the garden city. The garden city was not just misconceived, she wrote, but an insidious attempt to force a lively and variegated urban culture to conform to a narrow aesthetic ideal, that of the English country town. The results were more than futile, but "deeply reactionary" and "authoritarian."[29] It was a "powerful and city-destroying" idea that rested on the premise that the way to "sav[e] the people was to do the city in." Ebenezer Howard, Jacobs went on,

> conceived that the way to deal with the city's functions was to sort and sift out of the whole certain simple uses, and to arrange each of these in relative self-containment. He focused on the provision of wholesome housing as the central problem, to which everything else was subsidiary; furthermore he defined wholesome housing in terms only of suburban physical qualities and small-town social qualities. . . . He was uninterested in aspects of the city which could not be abstracted to serve his Utopia. In particular, he simply wrote off the intricate, many-faceted, cultural life of the metropolis. He was uninterested in such problems as the way great cities police themselves, or exchange ideas, or operate politically, or invent new economic arrangements, and he was oblivious to devising ways to strengthen these functions because, after all, he was not designing for this kind of life in any case.[30]

This was an attack on what might be called the Platonic school of urban planning, the notion that planners should begin with some ideal of how a city should function and what it should look like and then proceed accordingly. Whether the results were successful or not was irrelevant; the important thing was that the ideal was honored and upheld. Jacobs was not as studiedly bohemian in her private life as Mumford was in his, but she was far less of a prude. She appreciated all aspects of urban culture, the high and the low. As a mother with young children, she might have been expected to regard the Village's White Horse Tavern, the bar where Dylan Thomas drank himself to death in 1953, as a neighborhood blight, an offense to children and other delicate creatures. Instead, her description of it as a hangout for stevedores, college students, and writers bordered on the lyrical: "On a cold winter's night, as you pass the White Horse, and the doors open, a solid wave of conversation and animation surges out and hits you; very warming."[31] Philadelphia's Franklin Square, she wrote, was "a good Skid Row park," which is to say one that efficiently served the needs of the winos who frequented it.[32] Where progressives were horrified by tall buildings—they obscure the sky, block the sun, cut people off from nature, etc.—Jacobs loved the feeling of being dwarfed by giant skyscrapers on every side:

> What is more dramatic, even romantic, than the tumbled towers of Lower Manhattan, rising suddenly to the clouds like a magic castle girded by water? Its very touch of jumbled jaggedness, its towering-sided canyons, are its magnificence.[33]

Where progressives campaigned for setbacks and other restrictions on the portion of a lot that a building could cover, Jacobs contended that such restrictions encouraged builders to put up tall, needlelike structures that were in fact more monotonous than the old brownstones and tenements. Where the progressives had fought against high population density, Jacobs argued that they had made a total hash of the question by failing to understand how malleable a concept like urban space could be:

> The Garden City planners and their disciples looked at slums which had both many dwelling units on the land (high densities) and too many people within individual dwellings

(overcrowding), and failed to make any distinction between the fact of overcrowded rooms and the entirely different fact of densely built up land. They hated both equally.[34]

More people could enjoy more room on a given acre of urban land than the reformers realized, provided city dwellers were permitted to approach the problem of urban space freely and creatively.

Jacobs understood the city in ways that Mumford did not, despite his years of writing on the subject. Where he valued "beauty, order, spaciousness, clarity of purpose" (as he put it in a pained reply to Jacobs that ran in the *New Yorker* in 1962[35]), she understood that what the city dweller values most is often the jumbled, crowded quality that comes from heaping together goods and services in no particular order—until one gets the hang of it, that is, and understands how subtly and cleverly it is all arranged. Instead of order and spaciousness, what an urbanite appreciates is a retail district crowded with a wide variety of shops, a cheap restaurant next to a movie theater, or a dozen types of ethnic cuisine within strolling distance of one's apartment. While "clarity of purpose" might have its place, the city dweller also values obscurity and multiple layers of meaning: the out-of-the-way neighborhood, the "secret" restaurant that no one else has discovered, the rundown shop filled with cheap pleasures. Where Jacobs contended that even decrepit old buildings have their place in an urban economy, it is a measure of Mumford's thinking on the subject that by the 1950s he was actually arguing that Venice should tear down old buildings of no special artistic or historic value and replace them with more up-to-date structures.[36]

. . . .

Of course, in the nearly four decades since *The Death and Life of Great American Cities* appeared, Jacobs has spawned an orthodoxy of her own every bit as overwhelming as the one she toppled. There are Jane Jacobs

Web sites, Jane Jacobs videos, and Jane Jacobs academic conferences, not to mention hordes of Jane Jacobs acolytes who regard her every word as gospel. Considering how she slaughtered the Goliath of the urban-planning establishment with just one book, it is all quite understandable. But, like any cult, it is more than a bit one-sided. Jacobs's understanding of the details of city life was nonpareil. But when it came to the city in a larger historical context, she was all but oblivious. While Mumford's political judgments were often wretched, at least he recognized the importance of politics. Based on *The Death and Life of Great American Cities,* however, it is apparent Jacobs did not—she was as blind in her way as he was in his. She confessed to being mystified as to why congressmen and other politicians allowed themselves to be misled by wrongheaded urban planners: "This is the most amazing event in the whole sorry tale: that finally people who sincerely wanted to strengthen great cities should adopt recipes frankly devised for undermining their economies and killing them."[37] But more amazing was Jacobs's failure to comprehend the deep *political* animosity that led legislators to embrace such antiurban doctrines. By blaming planners rather than politics, she ended up paying planners a backhanded compliment by exaggerating their clout.

The upshot was Jacobs's rather naive belief that if bad plans were killing American cities, good plans would revive them. "American downtowns are not declining because they are anachronisms, nor because their uses have been drained away by automobiles," she wrote. "They are being witlessly murdered, in good part by deliberate policies of sorting out leisure uses from work uses." Abolish separation of uses, in other words, and the murder would cease.[38] But this was as simplistic as anything the garden-city people had to offer. If separation of uses was fostering motorization, then motorization was fostering separation of uses. The two were so closely intertwined that it was difficult to tell where one began and the other left off. It was impossible to attack one without attacking the other.

But it was precisely naivete of this sort that made Jacobs so popular. Her ideas were simple and easy to grasp. As with the progressive nostrums of two or three generations earlier, the absence of any political or historical dimension made her proposals seem "practical" and hence easier to sell. One could put them into effect without getting bogged down in discussions about class structure, philosophy, or political theory—what some community activists would later call the "paralysis of analysis." Within a few years after her book appeared, New York fairly teemed with local activists convinced that one had only to utter the magic words *neighborhood* and *community* to make any and all urban problems go away. Crime, corruption, deteriorating conditions in the public schools—there was no problem that ordinary people working together in their own communities could not solve. Activism of this sort reached its reductio ad absurdum in 1968 when black nationalists seized control of a local school board in the Ocean Hill–Brownsville district in Brooklyn and, in the name of community control, set about busting the city teachers' union, which they saw as an agent of outside and specifically Jewish influence. "Community control" revealed itself as a euphemism for parochialism, xenophobia, and political fragmentation—which is undoubtedly why the Ford Foundation backed it so enthusiastically.

It is unfair, of course, to blame Jacobs for such excesses. Nonetheless, "Jacobean" analysis of this sort was not the answer to what ailed urban America. To the degree it encouraged a fragmented urban view, her analysis may actually have made things worse. Jacobs's microscopic approach was both her strength and her undoing.

. . . .

But this is getting ahead of our story. Jane Jacobs belongs to the tentative, contradictory, and decidedly incomplete urban revival of the 1960s and 1970s, whereas Mumford's chief contribution (if that is the right word) was to the climactic antiurban offensive of the 1920s, 1930s, and 1940s.

Rather than a respite, the New Deal marked a vast intensification of the suburbanization process that had begun some twenty-five years earlier. Despite his aggressive use of governmental power, Roosevelt's goals, at least as far as housing was concerned, were fundamentally no different than those of his predecessor. He wanted to stabilize home ownership after a tidal wave of bankruptcies and defaults in 1929–33 and, once that was accomplished, use the full power of government to make home ownership available to an ever broader segment of the public. As he stated in his "declaration of national policy" in 1935, "the broad interests of the Nation requir[e] that special safeguards should be thrown around home ownership as a guarantee of social and economic stability"—a sentiment that Hoover could not have agreed with more.[39] Previously, overinvestment in real estate had been a source of ongoing economic turbulence. As a New Deal study group put it in 1937, "Gambling in land values has contributed to alternate booms and depressions . . . [and] has been one of the major tragedies of American urban life."[40] The Roosevelt administration's answer was not to eliminate the problem by scaling back the market, but, to the contrary, to stabilize the market by expanding it. More home owners pouring more money into real estate would somehow make for safer economic conditions. The answer to persistent real-estate bubbles was to create a bubble so big it could never be allowed to burst.

Since suburbanization was impossible without highways, the New Deal poured resources into that sector also. Of the two million people on the Works Project Administration payroll as of 1939, more than nine hundred thousand were employed on various road and highway projects. A 1941 study by yet another New Deal agency, the Natural Resources Planning Board, stressed the importance of building "express highways and off-street parking in urban areas" to accommodate projected traffic growth, while in 1944, with victory over the Axis in sight, the administration began laying plans for what would eventually become the interstate highway system.[41] A senior Federal Housing Administration official summed up administration thinking in 1939 in a speech before the American Institute of Planners: "Decentralization is not a policy, it is a reality—and it is as impossible for us to change this trend as it is for us to change the desire of birds to migrate to a more suitable location." Recalled Rexford G. Tugwell, a garden-city enthusiast who headed up FDR's Resettlement Administration: "My idea was to go just outside centers of population, pick up cheap land, build a whole community, and entice people into them. Then go back into the cities and tear down whole slums and make parks of them."[42] Rather than putting a halt to de-urbanization, the Roosevelt administration's goal—indeed the goal of virtually the entire liberal intelligentsia—was to use every available resource to speed it up.

The Roosevelt administration believed in the virtues of suburbanization and motorization for all the usual reasons: because cities bred disease, criminality, and political instability; because class conflict could not be fully eliminated unless workers were de-urbanized; because America was incomprehensible as anything other than a "scattered democracy" of small-scale Jeffersonian communities. There was also the technological factor to consider. Rail was yesterday's technology, signifying regimentation, collectivism, and the tyranny of the timetable. The auto was today's, signifying individualism and escape. The result was a further shift in transportation investment. Already hard hit in the 1920s by competition from a fast-expanding auto-and-truck sector, railroads saw their revenues plunge another 50 percent in the early 1930s in the wake of the Crash. Rather than pouring in money as it was doing with homes and highways, the Roosevelt administration's response was to force the eastern railroads to accept further fare cuts in 1936, thereby undermining railroad revenues all the more.[43] From a populist point of view, this made perfect sense. The railroad companies had been gouging the public for years, and now it was the public's turn to strike back. New Dealers felt no sorrier for rail companies than they did for banks "forced" to kick widows into the street for failing to pay their mortgages. Yet the administration was moving to strengthen the banking sector through the creation of agencies like the Federal Deposit Insurance Corporation. When it came to transportation, however, the only thing it could do was punish the railroads all the more while clearing more space for the automobile.

Franklin Delano Roosevelt, the man at the center of this unfolding social policy, was a much more problematic figure than liberal iconography would have it. In an interesting study published in the 1950s, the economic historian Daniel R. Fusfeld argued that FDR's antiurbanism was the result of his upbringing in rural Dutchess County in upstate New York. Roosevelt's childhood on his family's estate was, by all accounts, happy, carefree, and secluded. His somewhat overprotective mother shielded him from the outside world and arranged for him to be tutored at home before sending him off to Groton and Harvard. As a result, he grew up at a certain remove from members of his class. Despite his considerable family wealth, his outlook was less that of a conventional capitalist in the thick of the business world than a country squire viewing events from afar. One result was an unusually thick layer of Jeffersonian beliefs that apparently settled on FDR at an early age: the notion that labor was not really to blame for spiraling class conflict, that the real villain was the city, that if only the world were more like Dutchess County, social problems would disappear. The only thing that made such time-honored beliefs at all unusual was the way Roosevelt gave them a certain plebeian spin. If monopolists were intent on holding urban workers in situ so as to exploit them more effectively—and who could argue that they weren't?—then the revolt against the city was part and parcel of the revolt against economic oligarchy. Not only peace, stability, and good citizenship were to be found out beyond the city walls but freedom from both the landlord and the boss. If the city represented oppression, the countryside represented liberation.

Thus, Roosevelt warned in 1921 that the continued "growth of the cities while the country population stands still will eventually bring disaster to the United States." In 1933, he promised in his inaugural address to take immediate steps to reduce "the overwhelming imbalance of population in our industrial centers." A year or so later, he wrote to Henry Ford to express his agreement on the importance of de-urbanization and decentralization.[44] Although FDR has traditionally been described as a pragmatist who cared less about ideology than results, there is no doubt that he was a serious student of Jeffersonian theory. Reviewing Claude Bowers's 1924 study *Jefferson and Hamilton* (itself a milestone in the neo-Jeffersonian revival), he wrote in the pages of the New York *World:*

> I have a breathless feeling as I lay down this book—a picture of escape after escape which this nation passed through in those first ten years; a picture of what might have been if the Republic had been fully organized as Alexander Hamilton had sought. But I have a breathless feeling, too, as I wonder if, a century and a quarter later, the same contending forces are not mobilizing. Hamiltons we have today. Is a Jefferson on the horizon?[45]

"We are approaching a period similar to that of 1790–1800," he added in 1925, "when Alexander Hamilton ran the Federal government for the primary good of the chambers of commerce, the speculators and the inside ring of the national government."[46] If so, it followed that what America needed in another age of Republican ascendancy was a second "Revolution of 1800" to put it back on track.

It is often said (by Merrill Peterson, among others) that even as Roosevelt was honoring Jefferson, he was betraying his legacy by creating a leviathan-like federal government that would have had the "sage of Monticello" spinning in his grave.[47] But this ignores both Jefferson's and FDR's finely nuanced stance vis-à-vis federal authority. When Jefferson perceived the nation-state as allied with the forces of capitalism, urbanization, and centralism, he was opposed. But when he saw an opportunity to use the nation-state to further states' rights and agrarianism—to turn the nation-state against itself, so to speak—his attitude was more pragmatic. Similarly, Roosevelt was prepared to use federal power in novel ways to promote an analogous program of de-urbanization, motorization, and suburban home ownership. As he put it in 1932, the "methods of government" may have changed, but "the principles of their actions are still wholly his [i.e., Jefferson's] own."[48] If the results were in many ways the opposite of what was intended—if rather than creating a nation of sturdily independent home owners, the New Deal wound up creating a class of suburbanites ever more dependent on federal tax subsidies, infrastructure investments, and environmental allowances—Jefferson's results were in many ways the opposite of what was intended as well. Both men's thinking was beset by many of the same contradictions.

The New Deal represented a rare unity of symbolism and substance. Images of Jefferson were hardly less ubiquitous in Washington than images of Stalin in Moscow. Roosevelt put Jefferson on the nickel and the three-cent stamp and made a point of delivering an Independence Day address from Monticello in 1936. Observed Merrill Peterson: "Every executive department or office seemed to have its own Jefferson specialist and project."[49] As a newspaper columnist named Simon Strunsky noted in 1936: "This is a very prosperous time for Thomas Jefferson. Everybody has a kind word for him. Nearly everybody writes a book about him. Every political party and faction in the end calls him father."[50] The climax came in 1943 when FDR presided over the opening of the Jefferson Memorial, a structure whose clean lines, sparkling white columns, and verdant setting overlooking the Tidal Basin seemed to represent the Arcadian spirit at its most classical. Jefferson had been more than rehabilitated; he had come to symbolize American political aspirations as it prepared for global hegemony.

. . . .

Once he had stabilized home ownership, Roosevelt's goal was to get it going at a faster rate than ever before. By 1933, housing starts had fallen to ninety-three thousand a year, barely a seventh of the pre-Crash rate. Half of all mortgages were technically in default, while in Philadelphia, sheriff's sales reached thirteen hundred during the first half of 1933 alone.[51] The administration's response was to ram through two emergency measures, an Emergency Farm Mortgage Act to prevent rural foreclosures and the Home Owners Loan Corporation to shore up home ownership in nonfarm areas. By mid-1935, the HOLC had pumped $3 billion into the housing market and was providing backing for one out of every ten owner-occupied nonfarm residences. Where previously the length of a typical mortgage had been from five to ten years, the HOLC urged bankers to stretch out repayment over twenty years or more. Instead of 50 percent down, it pressured them to accept 20 percent or less. The idea was not only to make it easier to borrow but easier to borrow larger sums.[52] While cracking down on margin buying on Wall Street—a practice that allowed investors to borrow nine dollars for every dollar they put toward the purchase of a stock—the New Deal was encouraging essentially the same practice in housing. Indeed, it was restructuring the market in such a way as to make borrowing unavoidable.

The Federal Housing Administration, formed in 1934, took things a step farther. Rather than lending money outright, the FHA confined itself to insuring private bank loans. This behind-the-scenes role gave it immense leverage in reshaping the credit market. Following up on the HOLC, it pushed for even longer repayment periods—thirty years instead of just twenty or twenty-five—and for full amortization of the loans, a reform that saved buyers approximately 15 percent on the cost of a new home. By announcing that it would not insure mortgages for homes that did not meet certain minimum standards, the FHA extended its sway over construction. Soon, virtually every new home was being built to FHA standards whether it was to be purchased with an FHA-insured mortgage or not. The result was to impose an unprecedented degree of uniformity and standardization on what had been a fragmented, helter-skelter industry. Uniformity led to mass production and lower costs. Despite a delay of a decade or two, Fordism was finally invading home construction.

In a taste of things to come, a developer just north of Wilmington, Delaware, offered for sale in 1939 four hundred six-room bungalows for just $550 down and a mere $29.61 a month in mortgage charges.[53] Although no one grasped the significance at the time, the implications were little short of revolutionary. For perhaps the first time in the modern era, it was becoming cheaper in nonrural areas to own than to rent. Middle-class families were about to discover that they could not afford *not* to abandon their cramped city apartments and head for the open countryside. Indeed, the thriftier the household, the sooner they arrived at that conclusion. The most economically ambitious were the first to go.

World War II revolutionized home ownership in another way also. Thanks to a combination of rising federal expenditures and bracket creep caused by fatter paychecks, income taxes now took a far bigger bite out of the average wage-earner's paycheck. Where a typical middle-class family of four had handed over just 1.5 percent of its income to the federal government in 1940, by 1945 that same family was handing over 15.1 percent, a tenfold increase.[54] One result was to multiply the value of tax loopholes, most especially the mortgage deduction. A previously insignificant savings now blossomed into a major tax asset, not just for the affluent but for a growing portion of the middle class. The tax code thus emerged as perhaps the most powerful single engine driving the U.S. housing market. Not only could middle-class Americans not afford to rent but, thanks to the complicated array of carrots and sticks that the tax code represented, they could not afford *not* to pump more and more of their wealth into real estate. The result was like providing farmers with an open-ended subsidy to grow more wheat: Federal policies effectively left them no choice but to grow more and more, no matter how big their crops. Suburban homes, consequently, spread like crabgrass. Four-room houses in Levittown sprouted extra bed-rooms and backyard patios as if by magic. Bungalows gave way to split levels and colonials. The five-thousand-square-foot trophy home of the 1980s metastasized into the ten-thousand-square-foot "McMansion" of the 1990s. At a time when upper-class Americans were celebrating the wonders of free-market capitalism, they were putting their wealth into a real-estate market that benefited at every turn from a dense network of government subsidies.

The connection between such trends and America's great bleeding sore of race is fairly direct. Intrinsically, of course, there is nothing racist about wanting to live in a cottage of one's own amid a bit of greenery, and it would be vastly unfair to home owners to suggest otherwise. Nonetheless, the relationship between racism and suburbanization over the course of the twentieth century has been a close one. Once the flow of immigrants ceased and blacks began arriving in growing numbers from the Deep South to take their place, the ability to live in "racially pure" sur-roundings quickly became an all-important suburban "amenity," one of the key forces propelling suburbanization onward. FDR's role in this process was once again central. With the New Deal all but nationalizing the mortgage industry, both the Home Owners Loan Corporation and the Federal Housing Administration adopted frankly racist and anti-Semitic criteria for determining which areas were worthy of federal mort-gage guarantees and which were not. Top honors went to upscale, homogeneous neighborhoods filled with "American business and profes-sional men," free of any "infiltration of Jews." "High-class Jewish" areas were considered second-tier, while more run-down working-class areas were rated third. Black neighborhoods, no matter how neat or well main-tained, received the fourth, or lowest, ranking, rendering them ineligible for benefits. Where New Canaan's homes were ranked in the first and sec-ond category, those in Newark, with its abundance of what the HOLC called "inhospitable racial or minority groups," were ranked mostly in the third and fourth. In St. Louis, the HOLC expressed repeated concern about what the "rapidly increasing Negro population" was doing to real-estate values, while in Brooklyn, the presence of a single black family was enough to place an entire block off limits.[55]

Rules like these remained in effect until the civil rights movement of the 1960s. Their effect was twofold. Economically, they penalized not only blacks, but whites who were less than careful to live in racially pure surroundings. But they also skewed perceptions by creating a value system in which blacks were automatically considered to be economically destructive. Wherever black people went, wealth fled—or so the mass of middle-class American home owners came to believe. Buildings would become run-down, broken windows would go unfixed, and neighborhoods would grow seedier and seedier. Washington could have used its immense power to shore up property values in minority areas. Instead, under liberal administrations no less than conservative ones, federal lending agencies used their power to drive them down. White Americans were free to live in segregated areas only. Black Americans had to pay a penalty for living anywhere at all.

7

THE ANTISOCIAL

SOCIETY

If we are to have the full use of the
automobile, entire cities must be remade.

PAUL HOFFMAN, PRESIDENT,

STUDEBAKER CORPORATION, 1939

A NY DISCUSSION of the Fordist transformation of the twentieth century would be incomplete without at least some mention of Ford's most notorious student, Adolf Hitler. The two men were something of a mutual admiration society. Hitler singled out Ford for praise in the pages of *Mein Kampf,* put up a photo of him in his party headquarters in Munich, and presented him with the Grand Cross of the German Eagle, the highest civilian award that he could bestow on a foreigner, on the occasion of Ford's seventy-fifth birthday in 1938. Ford returned the compliment by endorsing Charles Lindbergh's pro-Nazi "America First" campaign to keep the United States out of the war, by opposing arms sales to Britain and France, and by arguing as late as 1940, if only privately, that the entire phony war had been cooked up "by the Jew bankers" to make money.[1] Hitler admired Ford not only for his anti-Semitism but for the constellation of social, economic, and industrial policies that went with it. The German leader was every bit as urbanophobic as the American auto magnate and every bit as convinced that moral and racial regeneration could only come about through a wholesale transfer of city dwellers to the countryside. "The more I witnessed [urbanization]," Hitler wrote in *Mein Kampf,* "the greater grew my revulsion for the big city which first avidly sucked men in and then so cruelly crushed them. When they arrived, they belonged to their people; after remaining for a few years, they were lost to it."[2] De-urbanizing the proletariat would undermine working-class solidarity, promote an ethos of individual achievement, and in the process, to quote Hitler's labor minister, foster the creation of "racially pure people's communities" out in the countryside.[3] Pastoralization would also help shore up the ranks of Germany's depleted peasantry, "a foundation for the whole nation," as Hitler wrote in *Mein Kampf,* "[that] can never be valued highly enough."[4]

As in America, motorization was the thread needed to tie it all together. As Hitler told Louis Renault in 1935 in words that must have been music to the French auto magnate's ears:

The endeavor of the National Socialist leadership is directed toward decentralizing the industrial working population from the production centers to the countryside. Factory work must be supplemented by field work. For the conveyance from living quarters to work quarters a cheaper means of transportation than heretofore available must be created.[5]

Other factors were also at work. Hitler was eager to move from what he regarded as an overreliance on steel, electrical production, and mining, the basis for the German economy since the nineteenth century, to autos, oil, and rubber, the magic triad in which the U.S., the economy that everyone wished to emulate, was surging ahead. Not only did these appear to be the new growth industries of the twentieth century, but—in what was much the same thing—they were industries in which organized labor had a far less powerful grip. No longer would a small number of strategically placed rail workers be able to bring an entire economy to its knees. Instead, motorized transport would supposedly flow around any such labor blockages the way water flows around a rock. The military factor was another consideration. World War I had been the ultimate railroad war—a grinding, drawn-out conflict in which trains delivered men and matériel to front lines that hardly budged from one year to the next. But as Hitler and his general staff were well aware, the next war would be different, an infinitely more mobile affair in which tanks, half-tracks, and the lowly truck would sweep across hundreds of miles of territory in a week. Instead of running on coal, the next war would run on diesel fuel and gasoline.

The upshot is that, following a shakedown period in 1933–34, the Nazis embarked on a full-tilt policy of mass motorization. For years, the parties of the left—the Communists, who regarded the automobile as a bourgeois conveyance, and the Social Democrats, who were somewhat less hostile, but still kept their distance—had vetoed motorization, but Hitler's rise to power broke the logjam. The Nazis lowered auto taxes and fees, simplified ownership rules and traffic laws, encouraged auto vacations, gave car designer Ferdinand Porsche the go-ahead to develop a cheap and simple "people's car," and inaugurated a crash program to cover the countryside with a dense network of state-of-the-art *autobahnen*.[6] Not only was the fuehrer determined to catch up with America, he aimed to forge ahead. Although only a small number of Volkswagens were actually produced before war broke out, motorization and highway construction were nonetheless the key ingredients in the Nazi economic revival of the mid-1930s.[7]

All of which established Hitler as an unusually devoted follower of the master of Highland Park. But, of course, one way in which Hitler differed from Ford concerned the military question. Where Hitler was a militarist nonpareil, Ford was all but oblivious. Judging from his writings, he had absolutely no interest in war, guns, uniforms, or any of those other things so dear to Nazi hearts. Yet this did not necessarily make Ford intrinsically more liberal. Rather, if he was uninterested in all things military, it was because he could afford to be. America's unparalleled geographical position—it is a country, as has been said, bordered by insignificant military powers to the north and south and fishes to the east and west—allowed him the luxury of pacifism, while his Midwest upbringing added to his sense of detachment from the outside world. The isolationist argument that America had nothing to worry about from foreign armies unless it deliberately went looking for trouble was one he felt in his bones to be true. The German bourgeoisie, by contrast, had no such luxury. In the wake of Versailles, it felt hemmed in on every side, threatened from the east by Soviet Russia and from the west by Britain and France. Somehow, it had to break through this ring of steel, which is why in right-wing circles Hitler's truculent nationalism seemed more and more justified. Where Ford saw the car primarily as a means of escape—from the city, from Jewish influence, from monopoly capitalism—Hitler saw motorization as a means of mobilization and conquest.

Otherwise, the two men saw eye to eye on a broad range of issues—on the city as a stronghold of "Judeo-Bolshevism," on the countryside as a source of moral and racial regeneration, on the political virtues of a new economy based on mass production and mass consumption. "The cure of poverty is not in personal saving, but in better production," observed Ford in the early 1920s. "Parsimony is the rule of half-alive minds."[8] Hitler similarly sought to ignite a boom in the mid-1930s based on easy credit and generous subsidies for middle-class consumerism. If Ford had been a manufacturer in France, Denmark, or Norway, he would have been prime Quisling material after the Nazi takeover. If he had been British, the Churchill government, knowing of his political sympathies, would have likely put him under lock and key. In America, the Roosevelt administration was content to see Ford's long-suffering son, Edsel, ease the old man out of office so that the Ford Motor Company could be retooled for military production.

In the end, however, it was not Fordism that crashed and burned in 1945 but Nazism. German industrial capacity proved too limited, Hitler's military policies too erratic and extreme. After producing only a few thousand cars, the VW factory where Hitler personally laid the cornerstone in 1938 had to discontinue civilian production the following year and devote itself to military vehicles; in 1944, it suffered heavy damage from Allied bombers. Fordism, on the other hand, emerged triumphant. The payoff after four years of military retooling came when the Axis was defeated and the Fordist system at long last gained the momentum it needed to take flight. Previously, infrastructure had been lacking to accommodate the millions of cars that Detroit was turning out each year, while suburban homes were beyond the reach of all but the most affluent. But now, due to a combination of falling home prices, rising incomes, and stepped-up government spending, the base had been broadened.

. . . .

In retrospect, what seems so remarkable about the great transformation of the 1940s and 1950s was its organic quality, the way it seemed to grow of its own accord with a minimum of formal direction. Where Henry Ford had located his Highland Park plant on the outskirts of Detroit in 1910 and his gigantic River Rouge complex only a few miles farther out in 1919–20, the Willow Run bomber plant that the Ford Motor Company completed in 1941 was located in rural Washtenaw County, some thirty miles distant from downtown Detroit. No one questioned why the new facility had to be located so far out in the countryside—the answer seemed self-evident. Land was cheap, access was easier than in crowded urban centers, while, notwithstanding wartime gasoline rationing, rising mobility made it easier for workers to join in the great outward trek. By 1944, more than 40 percent of Washtenaw's population consisted of war workers and their families who had moved to the area within the previous four years. The War Production Board, the all-powerful committee of corporate executives and military planners that FDR assembled to take charge of the industrial mobilization, made full use of its power to encourage other companies to follow suit. Of $872 million in military investment that the board approved for the New York metropolitan area between 1940 and 1945, only $380 million went to the city itself, while the remaining 56 percent went to the various suburbs. Of the more than $1 billion that it approved for the Detroit metropolitan region, less than a third went to Detroit proper, while the remainder—$713 million in all—went to the outlying areas.[9] Was this a deliberate effort on the part of conservative businessmen to strike at the Democratic Party's urban base? One suspects so, yet ultimately the question is irrelevant. The only thing that mattered from the point of view of the business elements that dominated the War Production Board was that cities were congested, they were expensive to build and operate in, and they were a breeding ground for labor strife. The geopolitics of industrial investment had changed little from the time some twenty-five years earlier when a planner named Graham Taylor had explained:

> Some company officials act in the belief that by removing workingmen from a large city, it is possible to get them away from the influences which foment discontent and labor disturbances. The satellite city is looked to as *a sort of isolation hospital for the cure of chronic trouble.*[10]

In hindsight, 1933–45 was a gestational period, one in which America devoted itself to marshaling its resources for the great leap forward after the war. In 1929, just 13.4 percent of American households earned the equivalent of what, in 1950, would be a comfortable middle-class income of $5,000 a year. By 1941, 18.5 percent of households had crossed that threshold, while nine years later the proportion would reach

28.2 percent. While the number of U.S. households had risen by less than 50 percent, the number of middle-class households had more than doubled.[11] This was the beginnings of what the conservative sociologist Kevin Phillips has labeled the "incipient middle-class majority,"[12] one that not only possessed growing buying power but was imbued with the belief that its own interests and those of democracy in general were one and the same. As a Hoover Vacuum ad put it in 1944, "freedom of choice," the ability to walk into a store and choose from a cornucopia of consumer goods, was nothing less than the fifth freedom, right up there with freedom from want and fear and freedom of expression and belief.[13] "Our enormously productive economy," the retailing analyst Victor Lebow observed a few years later, "demands that we make consumption our way of life, that we convert the buying and use of goods into rituals, that we seek our spiritual satisfaction, or egoistic satisfaction, in consumption. . . . We need things consumed, burned up, worn out, replaced, and discarded at an ever increasing rate."[14] The commodification of freedom reached something of a pinnacle in the famous "kitchen debate" between Nixon and Khrushchev in 1959, in which the vice president tallied all the wonderful things that U.S. capitalism had showered on the American people— 56 million cars, 50 million television sets, 143 million radios, 31 million individually owned homes, and so forth.[15] Liberty was nothing if not the liberty to consume.

By requiring no money down and minimal monthly payments for those who qualified for Veterans Administration loans, Levittown, which opened in 1949, established the suburban home as an all-important moral and economic reward for those who had fought against Germany and Japan. Where the infant American republic had rewarded Revolutionary War veterans with land grants, the Truman and Eisenhower administrations effectively did the same for veterans of World War II. The interstate highway system (full name: the National System of Interstate and Defense Highways) sent an equally important message by combining the goals of individual mobility and national defense in one neat package. Although the idea seems laughable to us today, the *Bulletin of Atomic Scientists* devoted an entire issue in 1951 to "Defense through Decentralization," the notion that the best way to mitigate the effects of nuclear attack was to persuade Americans to forsake large cities for scattered low-density housing. Under mounting political pressure, Eisenhower appointed a blue-ribbon panel headed by General Lucius D. Clay, the former military governor of West Germany, to examine the question of an interstate highway system. To no one's surprise, the panel dutifully reported back that, "in case of atomic attack on our key cities, the road network must permit quick evacuation of target areas." A new highway system was needed not only to speed traffic but to improve civil defense. Not only did Fordist individualism make for a richer America, it made for a stronger America as well.[16]

In his irreverent 1986 study *Populuxe,* Thomas Hine described the middle-class utopia that existed from roughly 1954 to 1964—from the Army-McCarthy hearings to the Tonkin Gulf Resolution—as one of seemingly inexhaustible bounty:

> There was so much wealth it did not need to be shared. Every householder was able to have his own little Versailles along a cul-de-sac. People were physically separated, out on their own in a new muddy and unfinished landscape, but they were also linked as never before through advertising, television, and magazines.[17]

In the popular mind, facts like these were connected with one another by a seamless web of causality. Americans were wealthy *because* they had walled themselves off in their own minichâteaus. America's bounty was limitless *because* people were linked via advertising and the media. If Americans now existed primarily as consumers rather than as citizens (literal meaning: city dwellers), what of it? Consumerism made them affluent and powerful. If society was narrower, it was so that the market could expand—and since the market meant freedom, who could possibly disagree?

Society had to be reconfigured so as to make room for the bulky consumer "durables" that the postwar economy was producing in such startling quantities. In a 1981 essay, an academic named David Gross made the intriguing argument that the great postwar expansion across space in terms of highways, cars, and ever larger homes was accompanied by a withdrawal across another dimension, that of time. Where nineteenth-century architecture paid tribute to history by appropriating various styles of the past, twentieth-century architecture turned its back on history in order to concentrate on the present. Out went the gargoyles, half-timbered houses, and other historicist doodads. In came the futuristic design and nontraditional materials of the so-called international style.[18] Not only was history bunk out among the split-levels and ranch houses but even *duration* was losing its meaning. Where patience had once been a virtue, consumers now demanded the right to have what they wanted when they wanted it— i.e., right now. Rather than measuring their lives in years, people measured their success in terms of their ability to acquire bigger and bigger homes filled with more and more goods. Wrote Gross:

> Even the concept of "becoming" is losing its durational aspect. Under the pressure of advertising and the culture industry, becoming is now defined as spreading out and claiming for oneself a greater amount of space, or owning a larger number of things that occupy space. The tremendous amount of objects that proliferate and stretch themselves out in a spatial dimension is the American experience of consumption.[19]

Owning was a substitute for living and experience. "I need something new / Something trivial will do / I need to satisfy this empty feeling"—so sang a rock group called the Slits in a 1979 song entitled "Spend, Spend, Spend."[20] As a resident of a fast-growing suburb outside Carson City, Nevada, told a *New York Times* reporter in 1997: "My whole philosophy is live my own life, make money and stay out of politics as much as possible."[21] Where the ancient Greeks believed that politics were an essential part of the human experience, the suburbs taught that they weighed one down. Freedom was defined as not only the ability to escape urban society but to outrun history, politics, and all the other intellectual baggage that went with it.

. . . .

Despite their reputation for conformity and passivity, the Eisenhower years were actually something of a golden age of social criticism. If it was the age of William F. Buckley's *God and Man at Yale* (1951) and Russell Kirk's *The Conservative Mind* (1953), it was also the age of David Riesman's *The Lonely Crowd* (1950), John Keats's *The Crack in the Picture Window* (1956), Vance Packard's *The Status Seekers* (1959), and Dwight Macdonald's widely cited essay "Masscult and Midcult" (1960). Despite complaints from latter-day historians that "those who focused on the debasement of American esthetic life tended to exaggerate their case,"[22] in fact the very opposite may have been the case: Rather than exaggerating, intellectuals may have tempered their arguments so as not to appear out of step with their middle-class reading public. At least that is what John Kenneth Galbraith said in a subsequent edition of his 1958 classic, *The Affluent Society,* in which he confessed that he had been afraid to say at the time what he really thought about the environmental consequences of the new suburban lifestyle for fear of how his readers would react:

> I had no great confidence in this issue when I first wrote; what we were doing to air, water, wilderness . . . seemed a

distant, even ethereal concern. I feared that on this I would be dismissed as a compulsive worrier, an impractical aesthete.[23]

Galbraith was right—in the Age of Eisenhower, he *would* have been dismissed as an impractical aesthete. Nonetheless, the fact that readers did not want to hear about such things as air quality, billboards, and sprawl did not make them any less pressing. To the contrary, the environmental question was not distant and ethereal, but immediate and concrete. The more it was ignored, the more heavily it weighed. Society was already paying an enormous price, and in a few years it would pay a great deal more.

Galbraith's book was the first to grapple with the great paradox of postwar development, the side-by-side growth of private opulence and public poverty. As subdivisions, highways, and cars multiplied, private wealth was exploding. Yet the more it exploded, the more the public sector seemed to wither. Commuter railroads were sliding into bankruptcy, city streets were growing empty and rundown, while, as the hit 1957 Broadway musical *West Side Story* indicated, the very word *urban* was becoming synonymous with crime, racial strife, and decay. As Galbraith put it:

> The family which takes its mauve and cerise, air-conditioned, power-steered, and power-braked automobile out for a tour passes through cities that are badly paved, made hideous by litter, blighted buildings, billboards, and posts for wires that should long since have been put underground. They pass on into a country side that has been rendered largely invisible by commercial art.[24]

As bad as all this was, conditions were about to grow even worse. Whereas the road system still carried middle-class motorists through the cities, within a few years the interstate highway system would allow them to bypass urban centers entirely. As hideous as American cities might have been in the late 1950s, within ten years many of the biggest would go up in flames as race riots erupted from one end of the country to the other. As the number of motor vehicles in the United States tripled over the next four decades and traffic volume nearly quadrupled,[25] the roadside clutter that Galbraith found so offensive would soon give way to a far more gargantuan form of sprawl. Galbraith may have been a touch hyperbolic in complaining about a countryside "rendered largely invisible by commercial art." But reality would soon catch up with his rhetoric. Rather than rendering the countryside "largely invisible," hypersprawl would obliterate it.

In one respect, however, Galbraith's analysis fell short. Either because he did not know the answer himself or because he feared that the reading public was not yet ready to hear it, he seemed reluctant to probe too deeply into the why's and wherefore's—why private wealth seemed to be marching in tandem with deepening public squalor; what, precisely, suburban kitsch had to do with boarded-up windows and empty, wind-blown streets. Nearly half a century later, however, the search for an answer takes us back to A. C. Pigou, the aforementioned English economist who first touched on the relationship between private consumption and public costs in a work published in 1920. Motorization was still in its relative infancy, particularly in Britain where it lagged far behind the U.S. level. Nonetheless, Pigou was unquestionably on the right track in noting that "the public in general . . . suffer[s] incidental uncharged disservices from resources invested in the running of motor cars that wear out the surface of roads"—disservices, he added, that by rights should have been charged to the motorist or auto manufacturer responsible for such damage in the first place.[26] What Pigou could not know at the time was the degree to which such "disservices" would pile up in subsequent decades as motorization accelerated. The consequences were less apparent in low-density suburbs, which, with their ample spaces and greenery, were designed to reduce the impact of such costs by spreading them over a wide area. But in urban centers where traffic was thickest, the effects were more and more inescapable. As damage from noise, pollution, and other such phenomena mounted, one city after another collapsed under the strain.

What Galbraith was describing in 1958 was thus the same phenomenon that Pigou (and Booth Tarkington as well) had noticed decades earlier, but on a vastly greater scale. If urban streets were "badly paved," it was because rising traffic levels were tearing them apart. If they were "made hideous by litter," it was because cities no longer had the ability to deploy squads of broom pushers now that society was diverting more and more of its resources to suburban development. Although 1950s social critics were fond of attacking the American middle class for its philistinism in failing to support symphonies, museums, and other cultural institutions, Pigou's concept of external costs suggested that the problem was actually deeper. The middle class was guilty of an act not of omission but of commission, not of failing to come to the aid of cultural institutions but of depriving cities of the resources needed to support them in the first place. In displacing a growing volume of costs onto society, it was in effect misappropriating public wealth and using it for its own benefit. Urban blight was not the result of neglect but was an essential by-product of Fordist production and consumption.

In its hostility to society at large, the resurgent Jeffersonian ideology that was so evident in the 1950s assumed that individual actions were autonomous unless proven otherwise. Whether a motorist chose to drive or not to drive was nobody's business but his own; any suggestion to the contrary was positively un-American. But by emphasizing the public dimension of individual acts, the theory of externalities implied something very different. As motorization accelerated, the spillover effects accumulated with increasing rapidity. The more they piled up, the more inescapable the public consequences of individual acts became. Rather than regarding an individual act as private unless proven otherwise, the growing volume of external costs suggested that they had to be regarded as *public* acts—unless, that is, affirmative action was taken to mitigate the social consequences. To drive or not to drive, in other words, was no longer an individual decision but a social question because so many people were affected besides the motorist himself. It would remain a social question, moreover, until motorists took measures to absorb the social costs. The easy Lockean division between the private and public realm turned out, on closer inspection, to be not so easy after all. Indeed, as industrial production advanced and waste mounted, the dividing line was growing increasingly problematic. Where Jefferson had endlessly worried about the tyranny imposed by society on the individual, Pigou's analysis highlighted the tyranny that a mass of atomized individuals was imposing on society.

Not surprisingly, Pigou tilted to the left throughout his long career, going so far as to offer a bit of measured praise for the Soviet Union in a slim volume that he published in 1937.[27] But while this certainly put him out of step with "mainstream" economics, it did not make his ideas any less relevant. To the contrary, the more Fordism picked up steam, the more important these ideas became. Although capitalism is intrinsically egotistical, the twentieth-century American variety took this tendency to baroque extremes. Not only did the automobile allow the individual to displace growing costs onto society at large, but the miracle of the high-wage, high-consumption Fordist economy allowed a broader and broader portion of the population to join in the fun. The result was the curious paradox of the antisocial society, one that not only permitted individuals to strip the public sector bare of all accumulated social wealth but proclaimed the right of every last citizen to take part in the assault. Parks, cultural facilities such as museums and concert halls, basic urban amenities such as well-maintained neighborhoods and safe streets—all were redlined, allowed to go to seed, or demolished outright so that public resources could be shifted to suburban consumption. Indeed, whenever Fordist production has shown signs of faltering, the standard macroeconomic response has been to reduce interest rates and ratchet up public investment in highways and other forms of infrastructure so as to stimulate consumption and hence waste. Without waste there can be no consumption, and without consumption there can be no production. Eliminate one, and the chain is broken.

. . . .

As Paul Kennedy demonstrated in his 1989 study, *The Rise and Fall of the Great Powers*, the same qualities that contribute to imperial growth also contribute to imperial decay. During the 1950s, the American system seemed to be immortal. But the urban explosions of the 1960s should have been a signal that de-urbanization had gone too far and that it was saddling the United States with social costs far greater than anyone had anticipated. Unfortunately, the conclusion that nearly everyone involved drew from the riots was diametrically the opposite: Rather than going too far, de-urbanization had not gone far enough. In 1968, the Kerner Commission, appointed by President Johnson to investigate the causes of urban unrest, concluded that white flight to the suburbs had left blacks stranded in the inner cities, far removed from the engines of economic growth and the jobs they were generating. This was unquestionably the case. Yet the only solution that the panel could come up with was to allow inner-city blacks to join in the great suburban exodus. As the commission noted, racial integration would seem to

> call for large-scale improvement in the quality of ghetto life. But it would also involve creating strong incentives for Negro movement out of central-city ghettoes. . . . [I]f, over time, these residents began to find housing outside central cities, they would be exposed to more knowledge of job opportunities, would have shorter trips to reach jobs, and would have a far better chance of securing employment on a self-sustaining basis.[28]

This is what might be described as a strategy of "will the last one out please turn off the lights?" Decades of Fordism had drained the cities of wealth and employment. Yet the Kerner Commission's only response was to suggest that America drain them all the more completely by providing previously excluded racial groups with the means to flee as well. The flaws in this approach should have been obvious. Whatever the benefits to middle-class blacks, it should have been clear that a policy of redoubled de-urbanization would leave the lowest strata, unable to join the migration, in even worse shape than before. They would be more isolated, more thoroughly cut off. Yet America was so penetrated by Fordist logic by this point, so dogmatically committed to a goal of suburbanization *über alles,* that it was unable to conceive of an alternative.

This is not to argue in favor of suburban segregation, of course. If middle-class blacks wish to purchase a home in the suburbs, they should have the same right as middle-class whites. But rather than sending poor and working-class blacks on a wild goose chase after jobs in the suburbs, it would have been far more effective to take steps to reverse the exodus so that jobs would flow back to the inner cities where they never should have left. Not only would it have been more effective, but when the full range of social and environmental costs are taken into account, it would have been cheaper also. Because it ran counter to Fordist orthodoxy, however, it was unthinkable. Even as inner-city conditions continued to deteriorate, urban planning continued to be governed by the assumption that suburbanization was right and natural, that it was unchangeable, and that what was seen as an all-but-universal hankering for the "American Dream" of a single-family home and car (or two or three) would continue ad infinitum. Indeed, although population began flowing back to a few gentrified urban neighborhoods in the 1970s, suburbanization continued to accelerate. The wealth of public subsidies and environmental allowances that were needed to keep the system afloat accelerated also. In American politics, subsidies like these are known as "third rail" issues, meaning that any politician who touches them will see his career die on the spot. But if rein-ing in public giveaways is unrealistic, then it is unrealistic to interfere with an increasingly unrealistic social system. Subsidies must continue to expand so that the system can go on defying gravity indefinitely.

. . . .

The results could not be more perverse. Among other things, a funda-mentally uneconomical social system stands efficiency on its head. The old inner cities, which middle-class Americans currently regard as economic basket cases, were in fact far more efficient than anything that followed. Because they were compact and walkable, they allowed individuals to accomplish a multitude of tasks with minimal expenditures of resources and energy. It is estimated, for instance, that a nickel trolley fare in turn-of-the-century Chicago brought a typical worker within reach of an esti-mated forty-eight thousand jobs.[29] A century or so later, that same worker would have to invest thousands of dollars in a car, drive through endless miles of suburban sprawl, consume hundreds of gallons of gasoline, and generate dangerous levels of pollution and carbon dioxide in order to gain access to a fraction of that number. The only reason such a job search even begins to seem cost-effective is that the Fordist system serves to hide the true social and environmental costs. By the same token, if the inner city seems like an economic wasteland, it is only because the Fordist sys-tem serves to obscure the savings that accrue from living and working in a compact urban environment.

Subsidized suburbanization also stands fairness on its head. The ben-efits, tax subsidies, and government handouts needed to keep suburbia afloat dwarf those flowing to more traditional welfare recipients. Yet politi-cians since the 1970s have made a fine art of flattering one group while flag-ellating the other. In 1984, a conservative sociologist named Charles Murray made a name for himself with a book called *Losing Ground* in which he argued that welfare was hurting the poor by failing to penalize laziness, crime, and irresponsibility. As he put it, "the philosophical denial of personal responsibility for one's behavior prevents praise for worthy performance, and . . . has had a pernicious homogenizing effect on the status of poor people."[30] But if this was true for the inner-city poor, why was it any less true for suburbanites whose per capita benefits are many times greater? "[I]f the suburban resident was assessed the full value of the resources brought into play for his benefit," noted one labor historian, "you can be sure that many of them would quickly lose interest in the supposed joys of the Jeffersonian existence."[31] Yet the social structure depends on their not being assessed the full value. It rests, rather, on a cover-up of the true relationship between and among the individual, society, and the state.

As far back as 1959, a visiting Marxist argued along these lines in a conversation with a colleague in the United States. The American kicked things off by pointing to the nation's burgeoning highway system and expanding suburbs. Where once workers lived in crowded slums, they were now able to live in their own homes amid lawns and trees—surely, he said, this was something to applaud. But the Marxist begged to differ. The only thing impressive, he replied, was the waste. All that rushing about represented so much squandered time, money, and labor. Americans "do not seem to like the place where they live and always want to be on the move to go someplace else," he observed. Because mobility had detached itself from utility, it had become an end in itself. Besides, he continued, all those freestanding, single-family homes cost more to build, heat, and maintain than the multifamily housing he was used to back home. Rather than spreading out over the landscape, it was much more logical to build communities that were tighter and more compact.

The American was Dwight D. Eisenhower, the Marxist, Nikita Sergeyevich Khrushchev. The setting was Ike's farm in Gettysburg, Pennsylvania, while the socialist alternative that Khrushchev had in mind was the USSR.[32] It would be very easy to characterize Khrushchev's remarks as the self-serving comments of a politician whose nation was losing the international economic competition even if the world didn't yet know it. But Khrushchev's criticisms are not so easily dismissed. It was in the nature of the Fordist system to regard things like suburban homes and automobiles as ends in themselves, without tallying up the social costs. If Eisenhower had attended to such questions—if, for instance, he had troubled to ask himself what impact rising traffic levels were having on the quality of life—he might not have been so sure of himself in the first place.

Indeed, Khrushchev may have planted a seed of doubt. According to his biographer Stephen Ambrose, Eisenhower had been alarmed a few months earlier when he noticed highway contractors digging their way into downtown Washington. Turning to an aide, he demanded to know how much was being spent on mass transit in the district. When told it would be only $1 billion over twenty years, he made known "his concern that too much of the interstate highway money might be going into connections in the cities," suggesting that a tax might be useful in offsetting the cost of allowing a single individual to use a three-thousand-dollar vehicle to force his way into a crowded downtown where space was at a premium. A few months after Khrushchev's visit, Eisenhower made known his misgivings once again when he told his highway advisers that "running Interstate routes through the congested parts of the cities was entirely against his original conception and wishes, [and] that he never anticipated the program would turn out this way." Such projects were subtracting from society more than they were adding. Yet as dismayed as he was over the results, Eisenhower felt that "his hands were virtually tied," according to Ambrose. He might be president, but there was little he could do to reverse the process. Once underway, the highway builders were unstoppable.[33]

．．．．．．．．．．．．．

In the 1970s, the German political theorist Jurgen Habermas argued that the growing weight of Fordist externalities was driving society into a deepening crisis. As costs mounted, the individuals who made out best were those who succeeded in shielding themselves and their families while shifting the burden onto others. Increasingly, society divided itself up into winners and losers—those with the means to retreat into fortified communities and those left high and dry in hard-pressed towns where property taxes were rising, social problems were continuing to mount, and public services were going downhill. Society's inability or unwillingness to deal with widening social blight meant that every individual was left to his own devices. Yet the more each person was left to look after himself, the more society as a whole fell into decay. The result, said Habermas, is that "the social identity of class breaks down and class consciousness is fragmented"—meaning, in other words, that industrial workers, the backbone of democracy from Habermas's point of view, ceased thinking of themselves as a collective and responded instead as disconnected individuals blindly grappling with one another to remain afloat.[34]

This was not altogether undesirable from the point of view of a business class intent on reducing society to an inert mass of individual consumers. But it was agonizing from the standpoint of American liberals and European social democrats who were all too aware that as society corrodes, the consequences weigh most heavily on workers and the poor, the groups they felt most duty bound to protect. Because waste and the social decay that goes with it are unavoidable by-products of Fordist consumption, abolishing them by requiring individuals to pay the full bill for the costs they generate would mean pulling the plug on the Fordist productive machinery—an outcome that not even the most ardent reformer could contemplate without a shudder. Liberals and social democrats were thus paralyzed. No matter how they might rage against the system, they felt they had no choice but to keep it going.

This does much to explain the degeneration of American liberalism from John F. Kennedy's New Frontier and Lyndon Johnson's Great Society to the meaningless gestures of the Carter administration and the microreforms of the Clinton era. After burning his fingers badly on national health care in 1994, Bill Clinton spent the rest of his presidency backing away from any suggestion of serious reform whatsoever. Only the most minimal reforms would do. Thus, in mid-1997, he traveled to San Francisco to deliver a speech in which, with no small amount of fanfare, he unveiled three new urban initiatives: a one-year program giving police officers a 50 percent discount when they purchased homes owned by the Department of Housing and Urban Development in neighborhoods they patrol; another initiative that shaved a quarter of a percentage point off mortgages for first-time home buyers in inner cities; and a third that allowed a limited number of federal rent subsidy recipients to buy their own homes. The first was designed to benefit a thousand people, the second would allow twenty thousand eligible buyers to save about two hundred dollars each in closing costs, while the third was capped at two thousand families in all.[35]

It would be hard to imagine anything more microscopic. Yet such reforms were all the system could tolerate. When it came to social spending, Bill Clinton was in fact less adventurous and more timid than Dwight Eisenhower. As the economy expanded, the scope of social action narrowed.

. . . .

The old progressive stomping grounds of California provide further evidence of this deepening social impoverishment. As Peter Schrag, a former editorial writer for the *Sacramento Bee*, tells it in his 1998 study, *Paradise Lost*, California has gone from a place of almost limitless possibilities to one of meanness and confusion in the span of just three decades:

> California's schools, which thirty years ago had been among the most generously funded in the nation, are now in the bottom quarter among the states in virtually every major indicator—in their physical condition, in public funding, in

test scores—closer in most of them to Mississippi than to New York or Connecticut or New Jersey. The state has built some twenty new prisons in the past two decades. But it has not opened one new campus of the University of California for nearly three decades. Its once-celebrated freeway system is now rated as among the most dilapidated road networks in the country. Many of its public libraries operate at reduced hours, and some have closed altogether. The state and county parks charge hefty admission fees. The state's social benefits, once among the nation's most generous, have been cut, and cut again, and then cut again.[36]

Economic polarization, Schrag adds, has simultaneously accelerated. The number of "invisible poor"—illegal immigrants, subminimum-wage farmworkers living in toolsheds or garages, and so on—has multiplied, reaching as much as 20 percent of the population in some counties. At the same time, nearly a million middle- and upper-class Californians have retreated into various kinds of gated communities, some with walls and two-story guardhouses manned twenty-four hours a day.[37] Traffic congestion, a phenomenon whose importance as a social irritant cannot be overstated, has risen as well. When one considers the biblical plagues visited on California in the early 1990s—mud slides, earthquakes, rioting, and arson—it is not surprising that the public mood has grown nastier with nearly each passing year.

While zeroing in on the 1978 Proposition 13 tax revolt as the great divide in postwar California politics, Schrag, to his credit, has attempted to penetrate more deeply than most journalists into the dubious progressive reforms of the earlier part of the century that were still contributing so much to California's decay. Because they were aghast at the way old-line political bosses had tried to monopolize political power—and terrified that socialists would do so even more effectively—California progressives, as we have seen, sought to devolve political power to local citizens, to tie it down by encumbering it with a growing number of petty restrictions, or to break it up into smaller and smaller units. Although initiative and referendum—the effort to take legislative power out of the hands of the legislators and deliver it to the people themselves—predated World War I, it wasn't until the economic slowdown of the 1970s that the system truly became airborne. Since then, the state has seen one "citizen" initiative after another—dealing with term limits, anti-immigration measures, efforts to do away with bilingual education and affirmative action, a draconian "three-strikes" law mandating life in prison for anyone convicted of three felonies, and so on—all of which have left state government more hamstrung than ever and the political mood more vindictive. A progressive-era rule requiring the state budget to be approved by two-thirds majorities in both legislative houses has allowed well-organized minorities to bring state spending to a halt. Balkanized local power structures resulted in such a bewildering maze of local and regional governments that by the 1970s some Los Angeles home owners were paying property taxes to as many as twenty overlapping governmental agencies.[38] Politics were more than fragmented—they were downright pulverized. Citizens were not more empowered as a consequence, but less. They were lost in a maze of their own devising.

"[T]he more efforts were exerted to make the system manageable," observes Schrag, "the more unmanageable and incomprehensible it became, thus setting off an accelerated cycle of reform—in the legislature and increasingly in the initiative route—which made the process even more unmanageable."[39] An unmanageable system was tolerable as long as it was offset by economic growth. But as the economy slowed, the inefficiency of the larger social system grew more and more unbearable. Given the structure of California politics, voters responded the only way they knew how, which was to balkanize power all the more thoroughly. Beggar-thy-neighbor politics proliferated, stiff fees were imposed for the use of everything from golf courses to parks, and the state turned into a breeding ground for angry right-wing forces. By the early 1990s, Arizona, Colorado, the Pacific Northwest, and other points were filling up with well-heeled Californians seeking to escape the breakdown. So rapid has the deterioration been that California in the 1990s has given rise to a whole new genre of West Coast apocalyptic literature—not only Schrag's *Paradise Lost* but Mike Davis's *Ecology of Fear,* William Finnegan's harrowing *Cold New World,* Joel Schumacher's 1993 film *Falling Down,* and Warren Beatty's black-comic 1998 movie, *Bulworth.* When John Carpenter was considering updating his 1981 hit movie *Escape from New York,* he realized that the new, yuppified Manhattan was no longer believable as a postapocalyptic urban terror zone. Instead, he decided to call his sequel *Escape from L.A.* In the 1960s, California had been a model to be emulated. By the 1990s, it was an object lesson in what to avoid.

· · · · · · · · · · · · ·

But California's experience is merely a variation on a national theme. Its fragmented political culture is recognizable as a subspecies of Jeffersonian republicanism in which distrust of political power has been taken to its logical extreme. As Madison wrote to Jefferson a few days after the close of the Constitutional Convention, "*Divide et impera* [divide and conquer], the reprobate axiom of tyranny, is under certain conditions, the only policy, by which a republic can be administered on just principles."[40] But since the republic that Madison was talking about was a *people's* republic, this meant that the people had to continually divide up their own power in order to conquer themselves. The upshot has been a process of self-fragmentation that has accelerated as the stresses on the body politic have grown. As Walter Lippmann noted in the 1920s, Jeffersonian democracy is programmed to create a world in which "[c]onditions . . . approximate those of the isolated rural township." The only things that matter, the only things that citizens are equipped to handle, are those that fall "within the range of every man's direct and certain knowledge."[41] Therefore, government must be continually reduced to something that the individual and his neighbors can see and feel. Since anything larger is beyond the citizen's ability to understand and control, democracy means continually cutting larger structures down to size. Government must be reduced until it approaches the dimensions of a petty hamlet, and when that doesn't work (as, of course, it never does), it must be reduced even more.

Thanks to its amazing natural abundance, California was able to prosper for a time despite such an absurd theory of government. But it could not do so indefinitely. Once the initial layer of wealth was skimmed off, the state found itself dragged down by the growing inefficiency of an increasingly fragmented suburban system. The more it buried itself in waste, the more helplessly it flailed about. The more it flailed about, the narrower its vision grew. Suburbs seemed capable of moving in one direction only: toward greater and greater fragmentation.

8

THE THIRD
URBAN CRISIS

A parking map or aerial photo of any American
city center reveals devastation as obvious as that
resulting from the London Blitz. Saturation bombing is
the only adequate comparison. Hundreds of buildings
around the immediate center have been wiped out.

URBANOLOGIST KENNETH SCHNEIDER

FOR A TIME, energy policy was Topic A in the U.S. media. From 1973, when Arab oil producers launched their first boycott, until the early 1980s when crude oil prices spiked as high as forty dollars a barrel, it was a subject on everyone's lips. The earth was running out of oil, automobiles were grinding to a halt, and prices were going up, up, up—to fifty dollars a barrel, to seventy-five dollars, eventually to one hundred dollars or more.

But then came the unexpected. Beginning in 1982–83, prices dropped. Instead of shortages, energy markets found themselves swamped with excess petroleum. For free-market economists, it was a singular moment of triumph. Unfettered capitalism, they declared, had proved itself. By deregulating energy, Western governments had triggered a chain reaction in which rising prices led to a redoubled search for oil, which in turn led to new finds and sources. Rather than heading ever upward, prices reversed direction under the pressure of rising inventory levels and plunged. The markets, to quote the mantra of the day, had worked. Indeed, with oil producers from Texas to the Middle East singing the blues over what was by now a deepening oil glut, the Reagan administration dispatched Vice President George Bush to Saudi Arabia in 1986 to find some way of talking energy prices back up, an effort that was only partly successful.[1] Meanwhile, except for the occasional hand-wringing editorial in the *New York Times* about America's growing dependence on foreign oil, all talk of an energy crisis ceased. Gas lines, fistfights at the pump, skyrocketing prices—all vanished down the great American memory hole.

But were things really so simple? There is no question that free-marketeers were correct in arguing that a resource such as oil had to be understood not just geologically but in economic terms as well. As prices rose, people modified the way they used petroleum, the way they searched for it, and the way they extracted it. With consumers willing to pay higher prices for gasoline, drillers found it worthwhile to revisit underground nooks and crannies previously regarded as unprofitable. Crude that had once gone untapped was now brought to the surface. Geologically speaking, nothing had changed. Yet, in a very real sense, *available* petroleum supplies had expanded. Contrary to doom-and-gloom scenarios about a world bereft of energy, people wound up with more oil rather than less. Even when prices began creeping back up in the year 2000, in real terms they remained well below the levels of nineteen or twenty years earlier.

If neoclassical economics had demystified supply, however, they had remystified demand. The issue was not only why energy supplies were growing tighter and tighter in the 1970s but why demand was so high in the first place. It was a question that laissez-faire economists were not equipped to handle. They could only reply that if demand was high, it was because times were good and consumers had money to burn for cars, homes, and trips to the mall, all of which required greater and greater amounts of fuel. Demand was high, in other words, because demand was high. Circular reasoning of this sort reached something of a pinnacle in early 1996 when, following a slight uptick in gas prices, Bill Clinton fretted aloud at a Democratic fundraiser that if prices continued to go up, "there are not going to be as many people driving as far to do whatever it is they're going to do this summer."[2] A more perfect union required that Americans drive at least as far each summer as they drove the year before so they could sit in traffic among all the other Americans driving equally as far. More driving was leading to more congestion and hence more immobility, yet it was supremely important that Americans not get off the treadmill. Quantitative growth was the only thing that mattered. Quality was irrelevant.

But there was a problem: Quality was increasingly difficult to ignore for the simple reason that it was plunging so dramatically. As fuel consumption rose, pollution was intensifying, congestion was rising, while global warming was grabbing bigger and bigger headlines. If the *price* of driving was nearing an all-time low, the *cost* to society and the environment was shooting through the roof. The classic economic solution was to close the gap by "internalizing" such external costs in the price of driving. Since low prices at the pump sent a message that gas was abundant and could be used with abandon, the answer was to adjust prices so motorists would understand that driving was in fact expensive and should be approached with care. Motorists would have to pay more in the short run. But in the long run, nearly everyone would benefit—drivers who would be less likely to spend their time creeping along in stop-and-go traffic; pedestrians who would have to put up with less noise and fumes; suburbanites who would be less likely to be trapped by endless sprawl; and so on. By rationing through price, efficiency would be enhanced, allowing people and goods to move along at a lower overall cost.

But gasoline is not just any commodity such as breakfast cereal or powdered cocoa. In the homeland of Fordism, it is the ur-commodity, one whose price fluctuations are as politically sensitive as beef prices in Argentina, onions in India, or bread under the *ancien régime* in France. The price of gasoline is, without too much exaggeration, a *constitutional* question, one that touches on the most elemental issues having to do with the nature of freedom and the proper relationship between the individual, society, law, and the state. Instead of viewing driving as an isolated, private act, full-cost accounting, "internalizing the externalities," or whatever else one might call it would require its reclassification from an individual act to one that must be regulated and controlled for the benefit of larger society. Rather than categorizing it as a moral right, an individual freedom no less sacred than freedom of speech or worship, it would mean viewing it in strictly utilitarian terms as one component among many in a complex system of national transportation, one no more sacrosanct than, say, coastal shipping or interstate busing. Precisely because driving *is* such an ordinary, everyday occurrence, it would mean recognizing that democracy does not just involve large-scale issues such as international trade agreements or national health care. It would mean, rather, recognizing that the *demos* has an unqualified right to reach down into the microcosmic world of every last citizen and change it at will. Of course, in the modern era, government policies and economic forces are continually reshaping individual existence. But under the current American system, such changes are usually impersonal, indirect, or inadvertent. For "we the people" to *consciously* set about changing the fabric of everyday life would be nothing short of revolutionary.

Needless to say, change of this sort would put an end to Jeffersonian illusions about freedom as something to be achieved by withdrawing from larger society. It would instead imply a re-definition of freedom as something to be achieved through society—not a legacy from our forefathers that we are required to conserve and defend but something that "we the people" continually create anew. Instead of a concept of the individual and the mass as fundamentally antagonistic, it implies a relationship that is interconnected and mutually supportive. The individual gains nothing by defining his interests in opposition to those around him. Not only does he wind up impoverishing society, he winds up impoverishing himself.

Changing the price of gasoline also means changing a system of economics that is increasingly a victim of its own contradictions. A fundamental tenet of free-market economic theory is the notion that markets need better and better information in order to continually ratchet up efficiency to a higher level.[3] The more an individual economic actor knows about the costs of any given activity, the greater his ability to maximize the benefits. Yet the sort of atomistic viewpoint that arises when the individual is encouraged to think of himself as a being apart from society leads to information that is fragmentary and incomplete. The more the Fordist externalities pile up, the more partial and misleading such information becomes. The individual ends up knowing less and less not only about the costs he is imposing on others but about the costs he is imposing on himself. While he may be able to gain an edge on a competitor under such circumstances, the economic machinery of which he is a part functions more and more poorly. He may be able to afford a fancier and fancier car with which to drive to the Hamptons, yet he still winds up stuck for longer periods on the Long Island Expressway.

This is a process that free-market economics has served to obscure rather than to illuminate. To the extent that the free-marketeers can claim credit for alleviating the energy crisis of the 1970s and early 1980s, they must take blame for the gridlock that has followed. Rather than solving the energy crisis, they have merely succeeded in changing its shape.

. . . .

Some facts and figures concerning the dimensions of the new energy crisis:

Since 1925, the number of motor vehicles in the United States has been doubling every fifteen to twenty-five years, a rate of growth better than four times that of the general population.[4] Traffic volume, measured in total vehicle-miles per year, has also been increasing at roughly the same rate, meaning, among other things that as of the mid-1990s the total volume in the United States was roughly double what it was on the eve of the first Arab oil embargo in 1973.[5] But because highway capacity expanded by only about 3 percent during the same period, traffic congestion has risen dramatically.[6] Among the fifty biggest metropolitan areas in the United States, a study by the University of Texas found that forty-four saw double-digit increases in traffic delays between 1982 and 1994. Northeastern cities, such as New York and Boston, got off with increases of just 14 to 20 percent, no doubt because traffic was already at saturation levels. But other cities saw increases that were considerably greater. Estimated driver delays rose 25 percent in Chicago and Los Angeles, 32 percent in the San Francisco–Oakland area, 33 percent in Sacramento, 40 percent in Columbus, Ohio, and 49 percent in Salt Lake City. Worst of all was San Diego, where congestion rose a whopping 55 percent.[7]

There are many ways of wasting one's time, but crawling past an endless array of muffler shops, big-box stores, and diners while "shock jocks" scream and cackle on the radio is surely among the worst. Yet, thanks to deepening gridlock and ever widening sprawl, that is precisely how millions of Americans are spending their morning and evening commutes. In 1946, *Fortune* magazine declared that traffic congestion in Manhattan was "impenetrable" and "unbearable"; since then, the number of vehicles entering Manhattan each morning has more than doubled, from 390,000 to nearly a million.[8] In New Jersey, the state's largest newspaper complained in 1999 that an increase of some 5,000 cars per day over the year before was wreaking havoc on the Garden State Parkway: "What was once called the 'rush hour' could now be more accurately termed the 'rush four hours.' Bumper-to-bumper traffic is not uncommon as late as 8 p.m."[9] Yet traffic still continues to climb. In auto-ravaged Atlanta, where estimated traffic delays rose 40 percent between 1982 and

1994, the average commuter by the end of the decade was driving 36.5 miles back and forth each day to work, 7 miles more than in second-ranked Dallas and 15 miles more than in Los Angeles. "I always thought of Atlanta as a magical place," said one ex-resident who had bailed out for Chicago. "But it has lost its luster. You're just driving all the time there." In what the *Wall Street Journal* called "the shots . . . heard round sub-urban Atlanta," an exasperated motorist emptied a high-caliber handgun into a traffic light in 1997 where backups were approaching an hour a day. Yet widening the intersection was impossible because the Environmental Protection Agency had put a virtual freeze on highway construction due to deteriorating air quality.[10] Meanwhile, the Centers for Disease Control found that obesity in Georgia more than doubled between 1991 and 1998,[11] the result, at least in part, of spending too much time behind the wheel and not enough on foot.

Highway congestion is not just a matter of lost time, inconvenience, or ill health. It is also a matter of lost money. It can be measured in terms of added shipping costs, declining real-estate values, rising medical expenditures due to poor air quality and growing obesity, plus lost tax revenues due to businesses and individuals leaving town for less-congested parts of the country. Since the early 1980s, a small but thriving movement has sprung up among mass-transit activists and green-minded economists aimed at quantifying such externalities in order to come up with a total estimate of the true cost of driving. As a freelance Manhattan energy consultant named Charles Komanoff tells it, the effort arose out of the anti-nuclear-power movement of the 1970s and 1980s. Although one wing of the movement insisted on viewing nuclear power in strictly moral terms— nukes bad, solar power good, end of story—another tried to frame the debate in more sophisticated economic terms. It set out to analyze the economics of electricity production in hopes of answering two questions: why demand for electrical power had risen so strongly in the 1960s and 1970s and what the true long-range cost of nuclear power generation was likely to be in the 1980s and beyond. The result was a fascinating exercise in applied economics. Previously, both utilities and state regulators had viewed the problem in terms that were largely static. Electrical power was an unalloyed public good—always was, always would be. Therefore, it was the utilities' job to provide as much power as possible at the cheapest possible rate. In the case of nuclear power, a seemingly inexhaustible energy source, the aim was to bring those costs down so low that they would eventually approach zero. As a Westinghouse pamphlet put it, the goal was: "Power seemingly without end. Power to do everything man is destined to do. We have found what might be called *perpetual youth*."[12] But as economists like Komanoff, a Harvard graduate who became a stalwart of the antinuke movement, set out to prove, that goal was as spurious as any perpetual-motion scheme. Rather than falling, mounting capital costs, maintenance expenses, and safety provisions were combining in such a way as to insure that nuclear power would remain a high-cost option for decades to come. While nuclear power was not infinitely expensive as some antinuke activists liked to believe, its costs were such that it would remain uneconomical until far more was done to control demand, maximize the use of alternate energy sources such as solar, wind, and hydro, and stretch each watt out so that it could do maximum good. "The amount of energy required to provide a given service can . . . vary widely, depending upon the amounts of other resources used and the technology employed," noted Komanoff in 1979. "[T]he *productivity of energy* is not fixed but is susceptible to deliberate change."[13]

In the wake of the Three Mile Island disaster in 1979, ideas like these were all but irrefutable, which is why scores of nuclear-power projects were put on hold or halted midway through construction. Rather than a system designed to deliver maximum power at minimum price to the individual consumer, critics argued that it made much more sense to strive for electrical power at the lowest cost to society as a whole. Instead of an infinite public good in comparison to which all other considerations were secondary, it was more reasonable to regard electrical power as one good among many—important, but not more important, necessarily, than clean air or safety. So effective was this new way of thinking that Komanoff estimated that by the 1990s approximately two-thirds of the total social and environmental cost of electricity had been "internalized," which is to say incorporated into the rates charged to consumers and industrial users. However imperfect, it was still a vast improvement over the simplistic high-growth strategies of the 1950s, 1960s, and 1970s.[14]

. . . .

The parallels with transportation are obvious, which is why it was probably inevitable that economists like Komanoff would begin turning their attention to the problem of out-of-control highway transport once nuclear power began losing steam. Just as the gung-ho nuclear advocates of the 1950s and 1960s were obsessed with the goal of ultracheap electrical power to the exclusion of all other social and environmental considerations, gung-ho auto advocates were obsessed with the goal of ultracheap highway travel to the exclusion of all other considerations also. The idea was that Americans should be able to park where they want, fuel up when they want, and drive anywhere they want on toll-free state-of-the-art highways that would be gloriously empty twenty-four hours a day— all this, moreover, at only pennies a mile. But when gas prices are held to unrealistically low levels, several things happen. Demand rises, driving increases, and the United States finds itself more dependent on Persian Gulf oil than ever. When highways are toll free, traffic rises to fill the available space, which means that congestion grows accordingly. When parking is offered below cost, demand also rises, which means that the number of parking spaces continually expands. Asphalt spreads like petroleum from a beached supertanker. While clean technology can limit the pollution that each vehicle generates, it is no more than a stopgap measure as long as sources of pollution continue to proliferate. Global

warming continues to increase as long as sources of carbon dioxide proliferate as well.

The answer was obvious. Rather than building more highways, the
equivalent of constructing more power plants to satisfy an ever rising
demand curve, the solution was to take a page from the post–Three Mile
Island power industry and restructure rates so as to encourage conservation and restrain demand. Rather than ever lower prices leading to ever
greater gridlock, the answer was to price driving more realistically so that
demand would moderate and total costs would come down.

This is where quantification came in. In order to come up with a
more realistic rate structure, economic analysts needed to "cost out" such
items as highway congestion, unreimbursed road maintenance and construction, lost government revenue due to various auto tax breaks, and
other societal and environmental expenses. Detailed efforts were made to
compute the number of parking spaces that a typical motorist used each
day in the course of going to work, the supermarket, or McDonald's.
Ingenious stratagems were devised for gauging the economic impact of
traffic noise on nearby real-estate values. Despite the fragmented nature of
the highway bureaucracy—literally tens of thousands of government
agencies have a hand in transportation spending, everything from the U.S.
Department of Transportation to the local township road crew—efforts
were made to come up with a total bill for roadway construction, maintenance, and repair, plus ancillary highway services such as traffic cops, traffic courts, and emergency vehicles. The auto's very ubiquity added a
further layer of difficulty. Since the introduction of the Model T, the
motor vehicle has not only insinuated itself into every last corner of
American life but has transformed nearly every last aspect of American
existence. How was one to measure the environmental cost of covering a
landscape with an endless array of gas stations, used-car lots, and drive-
ins? It was like trying to measure the total environmental cost of coal
consumption during the Industrial Revolution. Still, if the problem was

staggering in its complexity, it was an indication that the costs were staggering as well.

The results of such studies varied. Despite supply-siders' blanket hostility to anything smacking of higher taxes, the feeling among mainstream economists, according to one journalistic survey, was that gasoline prices were indeed seriously out of line, although the increase that most thought necessary was only in the range of a dollar or so per gallon.[15] Based on 1996 levels of consumption, this would suggest that the U.S. auto deficit—the difference between what motorists were paying and the cost to larger society—was running at around $150 billion a year.[16] But environmental economists who aimed for a broader accounting wound up with even more serious numbers. In Washington, the World Resources Institute estimated in 1992 that the total societal and environmental deficit imposed by the automobile was running at $400 billion a year for the United States alone. In San Francisco, the Natural Resources Defense Council settled on a range of $378 billion to $629 billion, while in 1992 Charles Komanoff and Brian Ketcham, an environmental consultant in Brooklyn, came up with a total figure of $730 billion.[17] Rough as such estimates might be, the implications were dramatic. Adjusted for both inflation and increases in fuel consumption, they implied a deficit in year-2000 dollars of anywhere from $3.75 per gallon of highway fuel to nearly $7.

Since then, more data have accumulated. A 1994 study by the Clinton administration found that, because of incomplete insurance coverage, auto accidents were costing the public some $13.8 billion a year.[18] In 1996, Lawrence J. Korb, a former assistant secretary of defense, estimated that insuring an uninterrupted flow of oil from the Persian Gulf was costing the Pentagon at least $50 billion a year, the equivalent of about thirty-three cents per gallon of highway fuel.[19] The 1997 Texas study of highway congestion, ten years in the making, estimated that the average motorist was spending thirty-four hours a year in traffic tie-ups at a total cost to U.S. society of $51 billion.[20] Around the same time, a study by Mark A. Delucchi, a researcher at the University of California at Davis, boosted the estimate for all auto externalities, societal and environmental, to as much as $1.5 trillion a year (in year-2000 dollars), which is to say $10 per gallon or about 17 percent of gross domestic product.[21] Finally, based on a study by the European Union of highway transport along a 380-mile route from Frankfurt to Milan, the average passenger car was costing society roughly $1.50 a gallon over and above the $4 to $5 a gallon that German, Swiss, and Italian drivers were already paying for gasoline. These costs were for environmental costs and accidents only and did not include the cost of infrastructure maintenance, repair, and construction, which had they been included, would no doubt have pushed the total estimate considerably higher. Based on the same study, a fully loaded thirty- to forty-ton truck cost society an additional $17 a gallon in terms of accidents and environmental damage.[22]

If figures like these seem extreme, perhaps the best thing to do is to take a good look at a typical American landscape. There, as far as the eye can see, are gas stations, diners, drive-through banks, and shopping malls sitting in the middle of vast parking lots like islands in a tar-black sea. Out on the highway, the heavy metal vehicles creep along, nose to tail, like a line of slow-moving cattle. Sport utility vehicles, some getting less than fifteen miles per gallon, account for a growing portion of the traffic, as do huge eighteen-wheelers, the result of a growing reliance by malls and big-box stores on tractor-trailer deliveries.[23] Pedestrians are nowhere to be seen, if only due to a near-total absence of sidewalks. Bicycles, needless to say, are nowhere to be seen either; who, after all, would be crazy enough to venture on a two-wheeler into such thunderous traffic? Over in the nearby subdivisions, meanwhile, roads are built according to the "two fire-truck rule," meaning that they must be wide enough to accommodate two hook and ladders racing in opposite directions. Three-car garages are standard in many areas, while four-car garages are more and more common. (In Montauk, Long Island, designer Ralph Lauren reportedly set a local record in the 1990s with a six-door garage containing double rows of glistening Ferraris.[24]) Planners calculate that each home in a typical new development generates an average of 7.5 car trips per day, which perhaps explains why pedestrians and cyclists are less common here as well.[25] Kids bicycle less not only because their parents drive them wherever they want but because, thanks to ever rising traffic levels and ever growing sprawl, there are fewer places they can go under their own power. Not surprisingly, children's bike sales dropped better than 40 percent between 1987 and 1996 as a consequence. Said one bicycle company executive: "I had more freedom when I grew up in the Bronx than my son does today in Dayton, Ohio."[26]

With the number of motor vehicles in the United States now exceeding the number of adults (201.5 versus 187.4 million as of 1995), America has clearly paid an enormous price due to a national policy of induced traffic growth. Perhaps 17 percent of gross domestic product is not too far out of line after all.

· · · · · · · · · · · ·

But what is perhaps most significant about the effort to come up with a comprehensive economic analysis of the costs of driving is that it has taken so long in the first place. America prides itself on being the most businesslike of societies. But if "the chief business of the American people is business," as Calvin Coolidge put it in 1925, then, due to some curious dialectic, American society as a whole has felt obliged to conduct its affairs in a thoroughly unbusinesslike fashion so that the private business sector might grow. Where a corporation would be derelict were it to lose sight of costs and benefits for even a moment, the United States has decided as a matter of deep moral principle to ignore them as far as transportation is concerned for close to a century. Instead of analysis, American political leaders have preferred to serve up meaningless tautologies, such as the famous statement by George M. Humphrey, Eisenhower's archconservative treasury secretary: "America lives on wheels, and we have to provide the highways to keep America living on wheels and keep the kind and form of life we want."[27] Because America lives on wheels now, government must see to it that it lives on wheels forevermore. Having arrived at the best of all possible worlds, it is exceedingly important that the status quo continue indefinitely. Costs, therefore, are irrelevant.

This failure of analysis shapes and distorts all aspects of economic life. Take, for example, the blind worship of such standard economic indices as gross domestic product. Dissident economists have long complained that such economic measurements are misleading because they count all monetary transactions as positive economic contributions while making no attempt to distinguish between those that add to the well-being of society and those that detract. To quote Pigou:

> It is a paradox . . . that the frequent desecration of natural beauty through the hunt for coal or gold, or through the more blatant forms of commercial advertisement, must, on our definition, leave the national dividend intact, though, if it had been practical, as it is in some exceptional circumstances, to make a charge for viewing scenery, it would not have done so.[28]

An oversize billboard, in other words, counts as a positive contribution to GDP because it takes money to put one up, whereas an unspoiled landscape does not, because it is cost free. By the same token, a madman who takes a razor to the Mona Lisa can claim to be adding to the national economy because he is generating employment for art restorers, policemen, and court-appointed psychiatrists, while a suburban family that owns three cars can claim the same thing. After all, three cars mean more money for gas, tolls, repairs, and so forth, which means greater growth in terms of GDP. Pollution means greater growth to the degree that it leads to rising medical expenditures. A pedestrian who does not generate pollution is so much dead weight since all he does is walk.

Because indices like gross domestic product are used to shape and guide economic policy, features like these are not merely silly but destructive. This is why some economists have attempted to develop measures of their own that try to distinguish between positive and negative outcomes. A San Francisco think tank known as Redefining Progress, for example, has come up with a "genuine progress indicator" that aims to separate wealth-enhancing acts such as conservation of natural resources and unpaid housework from wealth-destroying ones that degrade the environment or generate unnecessary social costs. The result is a very different picture of U.S. economic performance. Where federal statistics show that, adjusted for inflation, disposable personal income rose 46 percent between 1973 and 1998, the "genuine progress indicator" shows that social well-being has declined 25 percent since peaking in the early 1970s. As mediocre as American economic performance has been according to the conventional indicators, its real performance has been worse.

One can take issue with such findings on any number of grounds. Redefining Progress's insistence on counting "family breakdown" as a cost, for instance, is debatable; while some family breakups are tragic, others benefit society by liberating individuals from oppressive living arrangements. While the "genuine progress indicator" counts the loss of old-growth forests as a cost, it is unclear why the loss of old-growth forests is any more significant than the loss, say, of old buildings or old neighborhoods, which it does not count. But criticisms like these are minor. Clearly, Redefining Progress is on the right track in arguing that economic measurements that make no effort to distinguish between costs and benefits are not only meaningless but are themselves sources of confusion and waste. A government determined to pump up GDP to ever higher levels is one that corrals its citizens into consuming just for the sake of consuming, with no thought to the impact on quality of life.

Indeed, one could take this critique a step further by arguing that not only should costs and benefits be carefully separated but that engaging in such distinctions is an essential democratic exercise. By distinguishing between what it classifies as costs and benefits, the demos defines itself and shapes society in a way that it wants it to be shaped. By the same token, not engaging in such distinctions means allowing economists to set the parameters in a vacuum, which means surrendering to the impoverished social and political ideas that underlie neoclassical economics.

Not only does this distort economic priorities, moreover, it distorts popular perceptions. Covert subsidies amounting to as much as $10 a gallon turn reality upside down by making costly activities seem cheap and cheap ones seem costly. Motorists may agree in some abstract sense that using a five-thousand-pound sports utility vehicle to fetch a carton of milk is the equivalent of using a sledgehammer to swat a fly. But when one is in a rush, who has time for such considerations? All one knows is that, because the nominal cost of operating an SUV is negligible, such a trip seems cost-effective. Indeed, when time, effort, and inconvenience are factored into the equation, running the same errand by bus seems many times more expensive. It means walking several blocks to a stop (assuming there is even one in the neighborhood), waiting for a bus that may never come, and then reversing the process on the way back. An unusually passionate environmentalist or mass-transit advocate might make the effort. But assuming he owns a car, why would anyone else bother? While those with time on their hands can afford the "luxury" of mass transit, those without must drive.

Subsidization thus leads to a form of Gresham's Law in which unsound practices drive out sound ones. Because motor vehicles benefit from rising subsidies, they force off the road modes that do not, even though they may in fact be more efficient. With society straining to accommodate a rising tide of traffic, minuscule items like sidewalks and bicycle paths become harder and harder to justify. Upscale communities can afford them, but hard-pressed ones cannot. Walking used to be something that poor people did to save money. But by artificially lowering the

price of driving, auto subsidies raise the effective cost of walking by causing distances to expand and subjecting the hapless pedestrian trudging
along the roadside to noise, pollution, and the threat of bodily injury from
passing motor vehicles. Under such circumstances, walking becomes a luxury as well, something for retirees to do in a protected environment such as
an indoor mall. "Normal" people, meanwhile, drive. If cities seem like
bottomless pits, absorbing more and more money in the form of welfare
payments and urban aid, it is because their economies are masked by an
Alice-in-Wonderland system that encourages energy consumption rather
than conservation. By obscuring their intrinsically greater rate of efficiency, the Fordist system sees to it that cities are deprived of business,
jobs, and tax revenue. True efficiency is the last thing a waste-addicted
economy can tolerate.

Covert auto subsidies also drive out social cohesion. A rigged economy makes it seem cost-effective to live in auto-centered communities in
which houses and other buildings are widely spaced so as to leave plenty
of room for roads, ramps, and parking. As land use grows ever more lavish, distances increase, and walking, cycling, and mass transit grow ever
more impractical—which is why suburbanites rarely leave home without
strapping themselves into a three-thousand-pound machine and why they
rarely encounter their fellow citizens face-to-face—unmediated by a wind-
shield—other than in the workplace or at the supermarket or mall. Aware
of the growing unpopularity of such living arrangements, the Disney
Corporation hired, beginning in the late 1980s, some of America's best-
known architects to design a model community in central Florida that
would have the look and feel of an old-fashioned small town, the kind of
place where kids could bike to the playground, people could sit on their
front porches and enjoy the night air, and residents could shop for groceries or take in a movie without having to turn on the ignition. But
despite intensive engineering and detailed regulations concerning what
color people could paint their houses and what decorations they could put

up—or, rather, *because* of such obsessive attention to detail—the result was a lifeless imitation of real communities that once arose nearly spontaneously. Because the underlying economics of everyday life are unchanged, the effort winds up being stilted and coercive.

Thus, society finds itself spending down more and more of its wealth in an increasingly desperate effort to insure that people drive rather than walk, waste rather than conserve, and meet as infrequently as possible face-to-face. In his widely cited study *Discipline and Punish,* the French literary theorist Michel Foucault described the elaborate measures that French royal authorities used to combat the spread of plague in the seventeenth century. Towns were closed off, homes were sealed, and residents were required to present themselves in front of their windows at a set time each day so that officials could make sure all were present and accounted for. Wooden contraptions were rigged up so that bread and wine could be delivered to each household without anyone having to meet. Ropes and pulleys were used to deliver meat, fish, and herbs. "If it is absolutely necessary to leave the homes," one official edict declared, "it will be done in turn, avoiding any meeting. Only the intendants, syndics, and guards will move about the streets."[29] Bizarre as such regulations may seem today, they at least represented an honest effort to deal with a public health crisis that French society at the time only dimly understood. The question for modern America is: What dangerous disease is it trying to contain by going to extraordinary lengths to see to it that its citizens remain quarantined from each other as well?

. . . .

Fordism required not just cars but environments in which cars could breed and multiply. The result has been immense outlays not only for roads and highways but for suburban housing and various kinds of housing-related services and infrastructure. Federal, state, and local governments appropriated money for sewage and water lines, firefighters, police, and public schools to serve new suburban communities while allowing older urban areas to run downhill. Journalists and various urban experts did their best to confuse matters by blaming the resultant urban decay on corrupt or incompetent politicians or an influx of racial minorities bringing with them the problems of poverty and crime. But factors like these were secondary at best. The real reason was a massive transfer of investment and financial support from the cities to the anticities springing up across the municipal lines.

The tax code, as we have seen, was the single most important lever for achieving this long-term economic shift. Its beginnings as an instrument of social engineering were modest. As late as 1948, the mortgage deduction and deduction for local real-estate taxes—the two most important home-owner tax subsidies—cost the federal government just $280 million a year. Yet by 1995, these and a handful of other home-owner tax subsidies were costing the government the equivalent of $94.5 *billion* a year in federal outlays, nearly four times the $24.1 billion that the federal government was spending for low-income housing.[30] Although a growing horde of conservative pundits did their best to persuade middle-class home owners that shiftless and lazy poor people were bleeding them dry, the reality was quite the opposite: The federal government was holding down low-income housing expenditures so that it could subsidize private housing for the middle class.

Not only do such tax deductions favor middle-class home owners over the poor but they favor upscale home owners over those who are merely middle-class. Because they have more surplus income, wealthy taxpayers are able to sink more money into real estate, leverage their investments more highly, and hence reap more tax benefits—which is why one study in the mid-1990s found that 44 percent of tax savings from the mortgage deduction was flowing to the top 5 percent of households in terms of income.[31] When all housing benefits were added together—public and private, direct government outlays and tax subsidies alike—another study found that 15 percent of the total was flowing to the bottom 20 percent of households, 5 percent to the second quintile, 6 percent to the third, and 16 percent to the fourth. Meanwhile, the top 20 percent wound up reaping 58 percent of the value of all subsidies and expenditures, an especially glaring example of "Robin Hood in reverse."[32]

This is what has led some housing critics to refer to the various home-owner tax deductions as "mansion subsidies." The bigger and more highly leveraged the home, the greater the payoff from the IRS. Thus, Senator John D. (Jay) Rockefeller of West Virginia was able in the early 1990s to reap an annual tax subsidy of $233,000 a year for a $15.3 million home he had purchased in Washington, D.C.[33] The upshot is not only a federal subsidy for oversized homes but for a wide range of conspicuous consumption—for two-thousand-square-foot kitchens, exercise rooms, entertainment centers, and twenty-four-foot cathedral ceilings, for heated pools, tennis courts, and so on. For creative-accounting types who, through the miracle of the second mortgage, are able to take advantage of such deductions to finance their credit-card purchases, it is a reward for all the possessions and accoutrements that go along with such fabulous digs—Sub-Zero refrigerators, Hi-Point professional stoves, deck furniture, seventy-two-inch television sets, and other items of that ilk. When former Secretary of Labor Robert Reich complained in 1992 that "America's symbolic analysts"—high-earning computer engineers, software designers, architects, physicians, lawyers, and the like—were "receding from the rest of society" into a private world of gated communities, air-conditioned cars, and verdant corporate campuses, he was zeroing in on an important social problem.[34] But what he neglected to mention was the degree to which the federal government was footing the bill. Rather than penalizing such antisocial behavior, the tax code was financing it.

Despite fine talk about integration and equal opportunity, tax expenditures also encourage growing racial segregation. The villain in this case is not just the mortgage deduction—which by disproportionately benefiting wealthy home owners exacerbates not just class differences but racial ones—it is also the IRS deduction for local real-estate taxes, a little-noticed but nonetheless important feature of the tax code that functions as a kind of matching-grants program for well-to-do suburbs. By permitting home owners to deduct local property taxes, the provision allows suburban municipalities composed largely or exclusively of home owners to tax themselves more heavily and thereby provide a greater array of local services than they would otherwise be able to do. Communities that open their doors to tenants—who tend to be poorer than home owners, are more likely to be nonwhite, and gravitate to apartments rather than single-family homes—find that they are less able to raise taxes to cover their growing costs. Once again, the effect is to reward exclusionary policies rather than to penalize them. If school integration declined in the 1990s (as, in fact, it did[35]), it was not because the federal government failed to enforce equal access laws more vigorously but because it actually paid for it to go down.

Tax subsidies also distort investment priorities—something that free-market economists would presumably criticize more vehemently if so many of them did not personally benefit from the current arrangement. Tax subsidies are inefficient from a neoclassical economic perspective because rather than maintaining a level playing field, they tilt it in favor of one type of investment over another. They favor certain sectors not because they are economically productive but because they are politically powerful. By channeling resources into private housing, the various home-owner deductions do nothing to improve America's trade balance or make American manufacturing more globally competitive. Oversize suburban homes are not exportable, yet still they soak up more and more funds. By 1994, investment in residential real estate thus exceeded total industrial investment in the United States by about 3 percent.[36] Money that should have gone into industry went instead into palaces for the well-to-do. The upshot was increasingly lavish surroundings for the topmost layer and lingering wage stagnation for the rest.

Not that tax subsidies are the entire story, of course—direct government outlays for water and sewage lines, reservoirs, and water-purification plants have also been important. Considering that the cost of a sewage line or water main is a direct function of its length, it is not surprising that it is far more expensive to extend such services to tony suburbs, where anything less than one-acre zoning is considered déclassé, than to more-compact communities. A 1974 study found that, even at three to five homes per acre, it cost nearly three times as much to provide sewer and water service per household ($19,369 versus $6,978 in current dollars) than in a high-density community composed 90 percent of apartments.[37] Federal expenditures for new sewer and water lines began in 1956 and peaked in 1980 at around $5 billion a year. Although this may not seem like much compared to subsidies such as the mortgage deduction, the multiplier effects are significant. Subsequent studies found that land served by sewage lines was worth two to four times land that was not.[38] It was yet another example of politicians using federal resources to seed land for developers while complaining bitterly about the greediness of the poor. If developers had to pay for such services themselves, presumably they would think twice before scattering homes over the landscape in such an uneconomical manner.

Finally, government subsidizes suburban home ownership by shutting its eyes to the environmental consequences. Suburban homes cost more to heat not only because they are bigger but because, unlike apartments that huddle together for warmth, they are exposed on all sides to the elements. Thus, a federal study found that while a typical single-family home consumed 240 million BTUs per year, a typical home in a high-density neighborhood composed of apartments, town houses, and only 10 percent single-family residences consumed just 140 million, more than 40 percent less.[39] The upshot is stepped-up consumption of heating oil, natural gas, and electric power, which means more pollution, more carbon-dioxide emissions, and more military expenditures in the Persian Gulf. Home owners do not pay for such expenditures. Rather, society does.

. . . .

For much of the twentieth century, however, Fordism did behave more or less as its designers had intended in at least one respect: It reduced the share of nominal income going to the topmost layer and boosted it among members of the broad middle class. Between 1900 and 1981, America's bottom 20 percent saw its share of aggregate family income decline slightly from 4.8 to 4.4 percent of the national total, a reduction of 8.3 percent. On the other hand, the top 20 percent saw its share of aggregate family income decline from 56 to 45.3 percent, a reduction of nearly 20 percent, while the top 5 percent saw its share drop even more precipitously from 35.7 to just 18.8 percent, a reduction of close to 50 percent. Meanwhile, the second, third, and fourth quintiles saw their shares fairly leap ahead by between 19 and 40 percent.[40]

The outcome was biased in favor of the upper middle class but still more egalitarian than what had previously prevailed. For a time, claims of having dulled the sharp edges of capitalism did not seem implausible on their face. Since then, however, the trend has reversed. The downward movement of the bottom 20 percent has accelerated—real family income for this group fell 5.2 percent between 1979 and 1995—while real family income for the second quintile fell slightly as well, down 1 percent. The third quintile saw real family income rise 3.9 percent, while the fourth saw a stronger increase of 11.4 percent. But the real story has been the top 5 percent, which saw its real family income rise an astonishing 45 percent in constant dollars between 1979 and 1994.[41] The United States thus exited the twentieth century with an income-distribution curve looking remarkably similar to the one it had when it entered.

Equally disturbing is the way income distribution in the United States has diverged from that of other industrial nations. Proportionally, America would seem to have the biggest middle class based on such traditional markers as private cars and single-family homes, yet in terms of income, it has one of the smallest. According to data compiled as part of the Luxembourg Income Study, an international effort at cross-border economic analysis, the United States was second from the bottom among nineteen First World nations in terms of the relative size of its middle-income population (defined for purposes of the study as those earning between 62.5 and 150 percent of the national median). With just 46.2 percent of its population in this category, the United States was far behind Finland (74.6 percent), Sweden (73.2 percent), Norway and Belgium (both 72.4 percent), Germany (64.0 percent), France (60.4 percent), and Canada (60.0 percent). Only Russia, at slightly better than 40 percent, was lower.[42] Although the United States likes to think of itself as a land of opportunity, a highly mobile society in which anyone with grit and determination can get ahead, international statistics by the 1990s showed that this was also not the case. A 1993 study by Greg J. Duncan of Northwestern University found that only 17 percent of American poor were able to lift themselves to a level 20 percent above the poverty line within the span of a year, whereas 44 percent were able to do so in the Netherlands, 37 percent in Sweden, 28 percent in France, and 25 percent in Ireland. For black Americans, the rate was even lower—a minuscule 8 percent. Another study found that of those in the bottom quintile in terms of income, 56 percent were still there five years later versus 52 percent in Germany. "Most economists simply can't believe that the U.S. has the same mobility as Germany," commented Richard Burkhauser, an economist at the University of Syracuse.[43] But it doesn't—America's is slightly worse.

Suburban subsidies are not the whole reason for polarization of this sort, but they are unquestionably a part. Fordist subsidies may have encouraged a certain leveling for a time, but once class conflict ceased to be a threat, they quickly turned into a force for the opposite. Moreover, when external costs are factored in—noise, pollution, the havoc caused by highway congestion, and so forth—the picture looks considerably worse. Whereas those with money are able to insulate themselves from such factors, those without are increasingly exposed. Instead of spacious, leafy communities, they are forced to live in traffic-clogged inner cities where asthma rates are rising or in cheaply constructed town houses grouped around great oval parking lots. While the rich, sequestered in high-priced real-estate zones such as the Hamptons, the upper reaches of Westchester County, or Silicon Valley, are able to corral an increasing portion of the benefits generated by the Fordist economic machine, those below are stuck with a growing share of the costs.

. . . .

If conservative social theorists like Charles Murray are to be believed, welfare is like an addictive drug: It confers a short-term benefit at a long-term cost. Instead of alleviating poverty, it deepens it by discouraging the development of such virtues as honesty, self-discipline, and thrift—character traits that, in the long run, are of far greater value to the poor than a monthly handout. The result is "a bounty on indolence and vice," to quote the British Poor Law Commission in 1834, one that worsens conditions for the supposed beneficiaries by deepening their dependence on the welfare system rather than providing them with the cultural tools needed to dig themselves out.[44]

There may actually be a grain of truth to this, which is why socialists have traditionally favored job programs rather than the dole. But leaving aside the chicken-and-egg question of whether poverty is a function of macroeconomic forces or individual moral failings, conservative analysis of this sort fairly demands the question of why, if welfare is impoverishing for the poor, it is not also impoverishing for the suburban middle class.

At first glance, the question seems absurd. After all, crack vials do not litter suburban streets, heroin addicts do not nod out in the doorways, and Ralph Lauren–clad teenagers do not mug little old ladies for their Social Security checks. These are examples of the sort of wealth-destroying behavior that welfare supposedly fosters but which are conspicuously absent in upscale suburban neighborhoods. Rather than beggars and the homeless, the suburbs are instead filled with people who go to work, pay their taxes, mow their lawns and putter around their gardens (although in affluent neighborhoods that is increasingly the job of low-paid immigrant workers), and on warm summer evenings, gather around the backyard grill. If anything, judging from employment data showing a lengthening workweek, they are filled with people who work too much rather than too little.

On closer inspection, however, certain parallels are evident. If middle-class suburbanites do not blow their money on drugs, they overinvest in real estate, which may ultimately prove more economically damaging. They drive far too much in oversize cars that impose a growing list of auto-generated costs on society and the environment. The national economy they participate in every day pumps out more carbon dioxide per capita than any other in the world, making them prime contributors to the problem of global warming. Rather than thrift, a combination of rising real estate and a stellar stock market was, by the late 1990s, fueling an ethos of carefree consumption—which explains why consumer savings in 1999 fell to a record low of just 2.4 percent per year.[45]

Could it be that suburban welfare undermines society no less than traditional welfare programs do? Or that the damage is even greater because the numbers involved are so much larger? As conservatives like Charles Murray might have predicted (if their analyses were not so egregiously one-sided), suburban welfare undermines conditions not only for society as a whole but, more immediately, for the recipients themselves. Between 1969 and 1987 statistics show that the number of hours an average American worker spent on the job rose by 9 percent. This means that the typical American worker lost 163 hours in leisure time per year, the equivalent of a four-week vacation.[46] But because rising auto subsidies encourage rising levels of traffic, the average American was also driving an additional 2,700 miles per year over the same period.[47] Based on an average speed of thirty miles an hour, this is the equivalent of an extra ninety hours behind the wheel. When we combine the two figures, we find that, by the late 1980s, Americans were spending an additional month and a half per year either at their jobs or working as unpaid chauffeurs. Income growth had slowed dramatically, yet the workload had increased. Is it any surprise, therefore, that family life has suffered, that members of the middle class find themselves more and more frazzled, or that time for simple activities like reading or gardening has decreased?

The supposed beneficiaries suffer in other ways also. The automobile is so inefficient as a form of transport that it imposes severe limits on the cultural facilities, both high and low, that a given community can afford. With so many social resources going to cars, parking lots, three-car garages, and the like, little is left over for cultural amenities ranging from taverns and ballparks to concert halls and zoos. With nearly twice as many people per square mile as the Netherlands, for example, Long Island is one of the more densely populated patches of real estate in the advanced industrial world. This in itself is far from a bad thing—high population densities, as we know from the Lower East Side, can lead to significant benefits. But with four times as many motor vehicles per square mile as the Netherlands, Long Island is also one of the most traffic-saturated places on earth, as anyone who has ever traveled on the Long Island Expressway can attest.[48] Traffic levels like these place an enormous strain not only on the environment but on what might be called the island's cultural carrying capacity, its ability to support a wide range of communal institutions. As Newsday columnist Robert Reno once pointed out, Long Island, in effect, is "a city of more than 2.5 million without a single comprehensive public library, no major seaport or international airport, no important concert hall or art museum, no public zoo or aquarium, no major league baseball stadium, and no major legitimate theater."[49] It has none of those things because it is too inefficient to afford them. If it is rich in malls, diners, and parking lots, it is poor in everything else.

In Chappaqua, New York, residents mobilized to block construction of a middle school because it would draw traffic, while in an upscale neighborhood in Fairfield, Connecticut, they mobilized to block construction of a softball field on the grounds that it would lead to, in the words of one home owner, "traffic and noise."[50] Real people suffer real consequences from such wasteful living arrangements—children who grow up without ever hearing a live musical performance, adults who never visit an art gallery, and so forth. Then there is the less tangible but still important demoralization that arises from subsidized waste. The astonishing success of Charles Murray's *Losing Ground* led to a bull market in old-fashioned morality, everything from William J. Bennett's best-selling *Book of Virtues* to neocon Gertrude Himmelfarb's *The De-Moralization of Society: From Victorian Virtues to Modern Values,* both published in 1995. Rather than making excuses for them, neo-Victorians like Himmelfarb argued that middle-class Americans should exhort the poor to learn the value of hard work and thrift so that they could then enter the middle class themselves. This is all well and good, but what values do middle-class welfare benefits *really* promote? Consider what a sales manager for a New Jersey auto dealership named Elio Principato told the *New York Times* in 1997 in explaining why he drives everywhere he goes:

> If I have to go to the 7-Eleven a half mile away, I'll take the car. It goes back a few years to when I had my '91 Mustang GT convertible. I was driving along. I was smoking a cigar. Top down, air conditioning blasting. My friend sitting next to me said, "You might as well throw dollars out the top." And so he went and did start throwing dollar bills out the top. And he yelled, "This is America. We are here to waste."[51]

Is this why the Pentagon spends $50 billion a year guarding the Persian Gulf—so that middle-class motorists can drive with the top down and the air conditioner on full blast? If one feels pity for children forced to grow up in the disorderly households of the poor, what does one feel for children forced to grow up in the oversize suburban homes in which waste is considered a virtue? If welfare encourages antisocial behavior among the poor, what does it encourage in the suburban middle class?

Maybe the real problem is not welfare per se so much as the nature of welfare as it had evolved over the *longue durée* of the twentieth century. By the 1990s, the American economic structure, thanks to an increasingly chaotic political system, was characterized by a spaghetti-like network of subsidies, income transfers, and welfare payments going every which way imaginable. Some benefited the corporations, others the individual consumer. Some transferred wealth from the rich to the poor; others from the poor to the rich. While some were originally designed to help the down-and-out, others had evolved over the years into classic soak-the-poor schemes enabling the affluent to buy more cars and bigger homes than they would otherwise be able. As the tangle has grown more complicated, the structure as a whole has grown more incomprehensible. For the individual citizen, the effect is like being trapped in a maze he can no longer understand. He feels lost and confused as he stumbles around searching for a way out. The more he struggles to hold fast to his own particular benefit, the more isolated and insecure he winds up feeling.

Of course, a dazed and baffled citizenry is not without advantages from a certain point of view. Where social conflict was all too simple from a bourgeois standpoint in the late nineteenth and early twentieth century, an ever more baroque array of cross-subsidies and benefit programs has since rendered it satisfactorily fragmented and confused. Instead of proletarians versus capitalists, it is now—what? Suburbanites versus developers, home owners versus low-income tenants, people who live on quarter-acre plots versus those who live on half-acre parcels, and so on ad infinitum. Rather than two nations going at one another like the Blues and the Grays in the Civil War, we are left with a thousand minibrawls erupting among ever more finely differentiated groups and subgroups—a form of limited chaos that, on one level at least, seems easier to manage and control.

But this is a delusion. The more waste accumulates, the more the social structure beneath it collapses and the more the people lose control of society as a whole. The thousands of journalists who descended on the upscale suburb of Littleton, Colorado, in the wake of the 1999 Columbine High School massacre reported back that students there lived in a world of labels. One group wore clothes by Tommy Hilfiger, another by Eddie Bauer, while the Trenchcoat Mafia dressed all in black à la Keanu Reeves in *The Matrix*. As the designers multiplied, the factions multiplied as well. In the absence of anything resembling a public square, students said they had no choice but to hang out at the local mall, absorbing its values and learning its language. In a postmodern consumer society, designer labels like these serve as signs and portents. People look to them for help in figuring out which group is trustworthy, which one is cool and hip, and which is potentially dangerous. But the better they grow at deciphering the code, the more they learn to adjust to a fundamentally irrational system. The more adept they become, the more lost they feel in the end.

Isolation and confusion reinforce the false logic of individualism. The more people despair of finding a democratic solution to the problems of society, the more the individual has no choice but to fall back on his or her own resources. As conditions deteriorate, the effective price of social amenities rises and the harder it becomes to find a nice home in a quiet community with good schools, low levels of crime, and a pleasant array of shops. The end result is what Cornell economist Robert H. Frank calls a "winner-take-all society" in which consumers push themselves to the breaking point in order to raise themselves up out of communities in which conditions are deteriorating. If the average American family in 1999 was carrying more than seven thousand dollars in credit-card debt and nearly one in seventy had filed for bankruptcy, it was not because people were spending merely in hopes of keeping up with the Joneses.[52] Rather, they were engaging in a high-stakes gambling strategy in order to avoid falling into the social void.

INTERNATIONALIZATION

Naked little urchins on the narrow streets of Bombay
dodge the rapidly moving cars. . . .
The slant-eyed natives of old China view with
interest or alarm the noiseless carriages that so quickly
pass by. The narrow jinrikisha *roads*
of the new Japan are being rebuilt. . . .

H. B. HARPER, FORD MOTOR COMPANY
EXECUTIVE, 1910

Paris must be adapted to the automobile even if
it means giving up a certain outmoded estheticism.

FRENCH PRIME MINISTER GEORGES POMPIDOU, 1971

RESHAM'S LAW, the notion that bad practices drive out good ones, also
holds true on an international scale. Bad national economies, those
that are socially and environmentally wasteful and regard individual
acquisitiveness as the supreme social good, drive out good ones, which is
to say those that regard waste as something to be avoided and individual
well-being as inseparable from that of society as a whole. This is especially
the case when the socially wasteful economy in question is as powerful as
the United States since World War II.

This is not unthinking cynicism of the sort that holds that the world is going to the dogs no matter what. In formulating his law, rather, the eponymous Sir Thomas Gresham, an English merchant who served as financial adviser to Queen Elizabeth I, was making a hard-nosed observation about the workings of a sixteenth-century national economy. When government tried to cut corners by reducing the gold or silver content in coins, the Elizabethan equivalent of printing money, Gresham noted that people quickly grew wise. Since there was no point using a gold sovereign where a brass one would do, they responded by taking the old coins out of circulation and melting them down for gold or jewelry. Old coins disappeared, consequently, while demand for adulterated new ones rose. Bad money, so to speak, drove out the good.

Similarly, when a country as powerful as the United States encourages individuals and corporations to discharge growing quantities of pollution, carbon dioxide, and the like into the environment without charging a penny in return, or when it provides an extensive public support system so that millions of motorists can drive ever more miles free of charge, it puts pressure on other capitalist economies to do the same. An economy that encourages externalization on such a scale enjoys a powerful competitive edge. Its profit margins appear larger because it is able to "socialize" a growing portion of the costs of production. Its goods seem cheaper because they are effectively subsidized. They seem strangely exciting because they promise something for nothing, i.e., the ability to race along an empty highway for just pennies a mile or the opportunity to live in a palatial suburban home and enjoy an enormous tax break to boot. Because they promise something for nothing, they represent freedom from the consequences of one's actions. Because they represent freedom, they represent "modernity," provided, that is, one defines modernity as the ever greater triumph of the individual over society. No matter how much other societies may disapprove of such policies, the pressure to emulate them in one way or another can only grow.

This is what made Americanization so irresistible in the first two or three decades after World War II. For the business sector, American corporations, with their aggressive advertising and global marketing campaigns, were clearly the wave of the future. As Jean Jacques Servan-Schreiber warned in his famous 1967 manifesto, *The American Challenge,* France's staid old business establishment ignored the new turbo-charged American corporate techniques at their peril; their only choice, he wrote, was to adapt or die. But meeting the American challenge meant emulating not only U.S. business methods but U.S. social policies. It meant "opening up" the social order to create room for motorways, parking lots, *hypermarchés,* and other Fordist accoutrements. If it didn't mean copying American-style suburbanization right down to the last backyard barbecue and cul-de-sac, it meant at the very least adapting aspects of it to the local environment.

This is not the place for a detailed exploration of Western Europe's intricate postwar pas de deux with American business and culture. Suffice it to say that America represented a knotty problem for all points on the political spectrum. America was both shockingly vulgar and shockingly successful. As much as French intellectuals loathed American manners and designs, they couldn't help but be overwhelmed by the sumptuousness of American daily life—the oversize cars, the oversize steaks, even the oversize bodies of movie stars like Jane Russell and Marilyn Monroe. America lacked all restraint, which is what made it both attractive and repellent. A 1961 film comedy, *La Belle Americaine,* a box-office hit in France that played briefly in the United States (where this writer caught it as a twelve-year-old in Stamford, Connecticut), made the point quite wittily. The movie, directed by Robert Dhery, depicts the riotous mishaps that befall a Parisian working-class couple when, through some fluke, they find themselves in possession of a brand-new Oldsmobile convertible, the "American beauty" of the title. The car is a rolling tribute to the short-term pleasures of overconsumption. It is so vast and luxurious that it makes everything French seem mean and stingy in comparison. As a historian named Kristin Ross pointed out in a lively 1995 study, *Fast Cars, Clean Bodies,* Parisian working-class life at this time was still small-scale and intimate. The film's protagonists live in an old-fashioned "artisanal" section that is

> almost a village within the city of Paris: what lies beyond their lively neighborhood is foreign turf. . . . Everything in the neighborhood is in immediate proximity; at the center is the café, with its elegant old, intermittently functional, coffee machine: the space of work (a bicycle-ride away for Marcel), relaxation, meals, and informal social contact interpenetrate effortlessly. . . . The *quartier* represents a multigenerational social cell more solid and intricate than the nuclear family, a kind of concentric representation of the world, with the "village" at the center and the café at the center of the village.[1]

In such an intimate, small-scale setting, an oversize Olds is the proverbial bull in a china shop. As Ross describes it, "the grotesque car fills the entire tiny square; neighbors gather around, children caress it."[2] Even though the car appears inanimate, the joke is that it seems to have a will of its own. It gets Marcel, the husband, fired from his factory job by making him late for work and triggers a series of calamities that reduce his wife to tears. The "too beautiful car" makes its owners do its bidding rather than the other way around. The servant becomes the master and vice versa.

This is as good a metaphor as any for the postwar Fordist invasion of European culture. All points on the European political spectrum had their own special reasons for loathing the United States. As the writer Claude Roy put it in 1972, poor Europeans loathed it because it was rich, rich Europeans because it was materialistic, leftists because it was imperialist, rightists "because it believed in progress, morality, and man's inherent goodness," and so on.[3] But the contrary was also the case: All points on the spectrum had their special reasons for allowing themselves to be seduced. The Stalinists remained hostile, certainly, but the anti-Stalinist left was attracted by American culture's irreverence and glorification of youth. Dismayed as it was by America's utter lack of a tragic sense, the right couldn't help but be entranced by a Fordist vision of a working class pacified by cars and consumer goods. To be sure, many things about France in particular, and Europe in general, served as obstacles to the Fordist advance. The urban tradition was far stronger than in the U.S., while the working-class left was immensely bigger and more powerful. As odd as it may seem to Americans, French shoppers were restrained by a tradition of anticommercial skepticism—the feeling that merchants were forever trying to put one over on unwary customers and that one should therefore hold onto one's money instead of throwing it away on worthless junk. But rather than stopping the American invasion, factors like these no more than slowed it. Touring a French bicycle factory shortly after the war, United Auto Workers President Walter Reuther listened patiently while a government official explained that not only did the factory provide jobs but, *mirabile dictu,* it paid such generous wages that workers could actually afford to purchase the fruits of their labor, which is to say the bicycles that they produced. Replied Reuther: "Well, if you pay bicycle wages, you get a bicycle economy. If you pay auto wages, you get an auto economy."[4] Whatever the immediate response, the point was not lost on European economic planners. The choice was either to surrender to the American invasion or develop a high-wage, high-consumption economy that would enable Europeans to compete on equal terms.

But the more Europeans tried to compete with Americans, the more like them they became. The result, among other things, was ever deeper motorization. Europeans started from a much lower point than the U.S. and in certain respects proceeded more cautiously. But, ultimately, the effects were the same. Car ownership rose, traffic multiplied, highway systems expanded almost magically, while jobs and business continued to bleed from the city center to the suburban outskirts. Particularly in former West Germany, the most motorized economy on the Continent, the consequences by the 1960s were the unmistakable beginnings of American-style blight—shuttered storefronts, trash-strewn streets, once-lively urban districts that were now quiet and empty. Not only did Hamburg lose 20 percent of its population between 1964 and 1986, for example, but even within the city it saw a steady outflow from the downtown portion to the outlying districts.[5] At its most elementary, the process was a simple matter of arithmetic. More people in cars meant fewer people on foot, which in turn meant fewer shops and neighborhoods geared to pedestrians. Where formerly distances were measured in meters and centimeters, they were now measured in kilometers or, worse, in minutes of driving time. The 1970s and 1980s did see a partial reversal, though. Impressive efforts were made to strengthen urban centers both large and small and to stem the loss of economic activity. Construction rules were tightened to rein in suburban sprawl, while a small army of planners and architects went to work on the old city centers, planting, buffing, and polishing them until they fairly gleamed. Crosswalks were redesigned to make them more pedestrian friendly, and auto-free malls were created in the oldest sections where the streets were narrowest and most crooked. Outdoor attractions such as public gardens, art shows, and markets acquired a new importance. Resources poured into the hitherto moribund rail sector, resulting in everything from high-speed TGV trains to the Paris RER. By the 1970s, transportation experts were talking of a "railroad renaissance," something that virtually no one would have predicted a decade or two earlier.

Still, the results were no more than mixed. On one hand, international tourist meccas such as Paris were more crowded than ever with people rediscovering (or, since they had never entirely forgotten them in Europe, reaffirming) such distinctly urban pleasures as strolling down a winding street, exploring a new neighborhood, or nursing a drink at a sidewalk café. It was a wonderful repudiation of all those posturban theorists who argued that the city was doomed to extinction. On the other hand, this mass reaffirmation of urban values was also accompanied by a certain narrowing of urban functions. The pre-Fordist city had had its pleasures, to be sure. But it had also been a place of conflict and drama. When Samuel Johnson declared that, "When a man is tired of London, he is tired of life; for there is in London all that life can afford," what he meant was that the city encompassed the totality of human experience: the good, the bad, and the indifferent. All were to be found in the city because the city was the focal point, the place where society was to be found in its most concentrated form. The well-scrubbed tourist city of the late twentieth century, by contrast, was less than three-dimensional. At least as far as its pricey downtown portions were concerned, it was filled with people eating, shopping, and museum going, but doing precious little else. Rather than reflecting the full scope of human activity, its functions were growing increasingly specialized. Once the oil shocks of the 1970s and early 1980s were out of the way, moreover, traffic levels out on the outskirts resumed their upward climb, an indication that, for the bulk of the population, the real business of work and family was still transpiring by car. The suburban fringe was where people went to buy what they needed, as one German planner put it, while the city, with its pedestrian malls and quaint boutiques, was where they went to buy what they didn't. Two decades of urban reinvestment had made the central city more beautiful, but also more peripheral. Rather than integrating work and play, the goal of urban planners since the 1960s, such policies had wound up reinforcing their separation.

Of course, this may be overstating things a bit. After all, an American can't help but be impressed by the general European level of commitment to its cities, the determination across the board to remain an urban society and prevent the entropy of suburban sprawl. From the vantage point of

America, where city-bashing is still a favorite national pastime, Europe's high level of urban consciousness is as astonishing as it is heartening. Nonetheless, beautification and enlightened planning are no substitute for a full frontal assault on a socioindustrial order that remains fundamentally antiurban. True urban revitalization, rather, entails at least three things: (1) exposing the essential artificiality of the auto-suburban mode, (2) demonstrating the greater efficiency of compact urban living once the full range of social and environmental costs are taken into account, and (3) showing that efficiency itself has to be understood not in limited business terms but in broader social terms so as to encompass the full range of human activities and concerns. If the city is to be understood as a machine for living, it must be shown that it is not only more economically productive in the narrow sense of the word, but more *humanly* productive, which is to say more conducive to the growth of culture and personality.

There is a scene in the 1953 movie *Roman Holiday*, high up on nearly everyone's list of favorite romantic comedies, in which a sheltered princess played by Audrey Hepburn steps out onto a crowded city street for the first time in her life. She is both startled and exhilarated. The street is filled with all manner of people doing all manner of things: women carrying groceries, children darting about underfoot, men on bicycles and motor scooters, bakers with trays of dough balanced on their heads, etc. What makes it all so exciting, especially for an AWOL member of a royal family, is the sense of democratic order, the fact that everyone is engaged in something different yet, in the final analysis, are all busily doing the same thing, which is utilizing the city as an arena and a tool. These are not tourists or museum goers. Neither are they environmentally conscientious citizens heeding the admonition of various green politicians to leave their cars at home and go about by foot. Rather, they are working people who live in the city simply because that is where the work is. They no more have to be reminded to use the city than a carpenter has to be reminded to use a hammer. The tragedy of Fordist development in the decades since *Roman*

Holiday is that it has taken the three-dimensional urban swirl and squashed it flat as a pancake. It has replaced lively crowds with slow-moving automobiles, the swirl of human voices with the roar of traffic, the varied odors of the city with the smell of exhaust. While the various urban revitalization efforts that began in the 1970s have stabilized conditions to a degree, they have no more than slowed the underlying process of decay. Full dimensionality has not been restored and *will* not be restored until the city is once again the focal point of society.

Until then, social impoverishment will continue. A small but telling example involves the village of Monétier-les-Bains, located in France's scenic Hautes-Alpes *département,* one of those heavenly spots where one can hike amid splashing streams and flower-strewn meadows by day and, provided one has the necessary cash reserves, dine splendidly by night. Yet in the summer of 1999, neither of the town's two main hotels served a single breakfast on their outdoor terraces. Regular visitors canceled their reservations and local businesses were forced to close. In the wake of a devastating fire that had killed more than forty people in a tunnel beneath Mont Blanc, truck traffic had been rerouted, sending a nonstop stream of thirty- and forty-ton tractor trailers rumbling through Monétier and other pristine Alpine villages. Bottles of aperitif rattled on the café shelves, children were afraid to walk to school, while pedestrians had to flatten themselves against the sides of buildings so that the monsters could pass. The mayor pronounced the social damage "incalculable," and passions reached the point where, in June 1999, representatives of Monétier and seven other hard-hit towns erected a forty-eight-hour roadblock to put a halt to traffic altogether. The blockade was "a final warning" to the government that "after twenty-five years of inertia," something had to be done to reduce the toll of traffic-borne destruction.[6]

By itself, Monétier's nightmare would be insignificant. But as an example of deepening decay across the whole of society, it is not. As uncounted costs mount, businesses suffer and jobs are lost, not only in the

Hautes-Alpes but throughout the entire French tourist industry, an economic sector whose importance in the twenty-first century is likely to increase. Rather than a sign of economic progress or modernization, truck traffic on this scale is a sign of economic and technological stagnation, an indication of society's inability to leave behind a system of transport whose costs are rapidly mounting and move on to something more efficient and up-to-date. Rather than fostering employment, industrial policies like these destroy it.

· · · · · · · · · · · · ·

As destructive as all this has been, however, the real calamity has taken place not in the First World but in the Third. In Europe, a comparative degree of social democracy in the postwar period forced even the most pro-auto politicians to pay lip service to pedestrian rights and the importance of preserving the urban fabric. No such restraints exist in kleptocratic Third World nations where the political elites hardly blink when speeding cars plow into peasants trudging along the sides of dimly lit roadways. Indeed, the only thing that has slowed the Fordist invasion since the 1950s and 1960s has been poverty itself—the fact that for decades after independence the only people who could afford cars were the local warlord and a shady "exporter" or two. Yet, in the end, such protections have proved meaningless. As the Fordist economy sought out every last remaining market no matter how remote, ownership rates began to rise. One Third World economy after another fell victim to a staggeringly uneven form of development in which a small number of cars, trucks, and buses were allowed to overwhelm an even smaller network of roads. As motorization swelled, the result was a degree of social immobility far greater than anything in the industrialized West. By the 1980s and 1990s, visitors to certain Third World "conurbations" were bringing back tales of a late capitalist hell in which motorists remained trapped in their stalled vehicles for hours on end amid the thickening fumes and rising heat of the shantytowns. Traffic moved more and more sluggishly, yet local officials continued to pursue policies all but designed to make conditions worse. With half as many people as New York City but twice as many cars (4.5 million motor vehicles versus 2.1), São Paulo, Brazil, was setting new records for traffic jams by the mid-1990s month after month. Yet local auto factories continued working around the clock so that roughly a thousand additional cars could be shoehorned onto the city's streets each day. In Rio de Janeiro, average rush-hour speeds fell from 19 miles per hour in 1994 to just 12 miles per hour a year later, while in Bangkok they fell to an average of 3.7 miles per hour, the speed of a brisk walk. With trips to the airport sometimes taking three to six hours, local entrepreneurs did a brisk business selling miniature toilets for use by stranded motorists. Lagos, Shanghai, and Jakarta, some of the fastest growing cities in the world, were even faster-growing traffic hot spots, while in Bombay and Calcutta traffic was doubling every five years.[7] In Nezahualcóyotl, a shantytown of two million people on the edge of Mexico City, residents had to travel for one or two hours in rickety buses through monstrous traffic jams and across unpaved roads merely to go to work.[8] Yet still the number of motor vehicles continued to climb.

The urban consequences are similar to those in America during the first years of Fordism, only vastly intensified. Simply because Third World cities are poorer and more crowded, a motorist venturing onto a congested city street imposes what are comparatively speaking far greater costs on a far greater number of people. Not only are the consequences death and injury from accidents but reduced urban access for those who need it most: peddlers, tradesmen, workers traveling by bus or jitney, peasants hurrying to market, and so forth. Adding insult to injury are misguided development policies that have led Third World cities to restrict bicycles, rickshaws, and pedicabs in order to make way for motor vehicles. Calcutta banned pedicabs in the 1990s, for example, while Delhi restricted their use—this despite the fact that pedicabs can transport anywhere from two and a half to five times as many people per mile of roadway as cars or taxis, without adding to atmospheric pollution.[9] In China, where auto ownership was expanding explosively by the 1990s, the mayor of Guangzhou, a city of 3.5 million people, banned bikes and motorcycles from the inner city in 1996 as part of an overall drive to reduce the bicycle's share of passenger traffic from 33 percent to just 13 percent by the year 2010.[10] More auto traffic would make Guangzhou seem more modern and up-to-date and hence more attractive to foreign investors. In Beijing, municipal authorities imposed a policy in the 1990s of limiting bicycles to overcrowded bike lanes separated from the rest of the roadway by nothing more than a white line. As a result, there was nothing to stop traffic-maddened motorists from darting into the lanes to get around some blockage or other. Indeed, officials closed off one street, the short but notoriously gridlocked Xisidong Avenue, to bicycles altogether. A highly efficient form of transportation had to be banned so that exhaust-spewing automobiles could occupy every last square inch. At traffic circles and street crossings, cyclists were forced to dismount and pick their way through four lanes of traffic before continuing on their way, a humiliating comedown for riders who were once king of the road.[11] In South Korea, where road construction rose from 47 to 61.5 percent of total transport investment between 1982 and 1993, traffic boomed, while mass transit, all too predictably, continued to pitch downhill.[12]

Policies like these are the modern equivalent of flogging peasants to make way for the royal coach. Meanwhile, pollution has added to the problem caused by paralyzing congestion. With few exceptions, Latin American cities by the 1990s were a hopeless mass of choking exhaust and blaring car horns from one end of the region to the other. In Mexico City, whose population now exceeds 20 million, traffic kicks up dust laden with bacteria and fungus from open garbage dumps and burning refuse, a phenomenon especially dangerous for children vulnerable to respiratory illness.[13] In a daring experiment, the Uruguayan writer Eduardo Galeano decided one afternoon to investigate traffic conditions in the Mexican capital on foot. "I walked for four hours amid groaning motors," he subsequently reported. "I survived. My friends gave me an effusive welcome, then they gave me the name of a good psychiatrist."[14]

In Asia, motor-vehicle ownership levels by the 1990s were still the lowest in the world: one for every 26 people versus one for every 3.7 in East and West Europe and one for every 1.3 in the U.S.[15] Yet pollution was far more severe thanks to high population densities. According to one UN study, the continent was thus home by the end of the millennium to thirteen of the fifteen cities with the worst air quality in the world. Thanks to leaded gasoline, blood lead levels in Shanghai were so high by the late 1990s it was estimated that as many as 65 percent of all children may have suffered brain damage as a consequence. In Bangkok, Delhi, and numerous other Asian cities, excessive levels of microscopic particulate matter were deemed responsible for an epidemic of childhood respiratory illness. When an English-educated university lecturer named Wichai Srirat brought his thirteen-month-old daughter, Alisa, home to Bangkok for the first time, the child quickly began gasping for air. He responded the only way a father could under the circumstances: by purchasing an air filter for his car so the child would be able to breathe freely whenever he took her for a ride. But this did nothing to protect the less affluent children who were forced to breathe the particulate matter that his automobile generated. Indeed, to the degree it lowered the real cost for him and his family, it may have added to the overall problem by allowing him to drive more freely, thereby adding to the cost for others. Meanwhile, respiratory illnesses, far deadlier in the less developed portion of the world, were by the 1990s the third leading cause of death worldwide after heart disease and cancer. By the year 2020, according to one study, they were projected to cause 2.47 million deaths per year.[16]

Finally, there is the question of roadway accidents, the most grievous social cost of all. In the United States, pedestrians and cyclists account for about one highway fatality in seven,[17] but in less developed countries in which only a small minority can afford a car, the proportion is far higher. Where even in advanced industrial countries, pedestrians and cyclists tend to be somewhat lower on the socioeconomic scale than motorists, in the Third World the economic gap between the two groups is comparatively enormous. It could be the difference between a government official hurrying to a dinner party and an illiterate peasant trudging behind a bullock-drawn cart or the difference between an international businessman and a naked child in a Calcutta slum whose only home is a square meter or two of sidewalk. Yet transportation policy across the less developed world dictates that hundreds of thousands of the poor sacrifice their lives each year so that the affluent can pretend they live in Los Angeles and drive with abandon.

The level of sacrifice is indeed horrifying. In India, annual roadway fatalities, estimated at 271,000 for the year 2000 according to one high-level study, were projected to rise to 546,000 by the year 2020. In China, over the same period, they were projected to rise from 267,000 to 409,000, while in Sub-Saharan Africa they were projected to rise from 211,000 to 479,000. For the world as a whole, annual highway fatalities were projected to go from 1.391 million in the year 2000 to 2.338 million by the year 2020—the equivalent of a Nazi Holocaust every two and a half years, a U.S. Civil War every three months, or a good-sized jumbo-jet crash every sixty minutes. Not only does carnage on this scale represent an immense wealth transfer from the poor to the rich but, given that the number of traffic victims aged fourteen years or younger is projected to rise from 279,000 to 358,000, it represents a generational transfer from the young to the old.[18] It is a toll that the liberal West would find intolerable were it to take place within its own borders, yet which it finds all too easy to ignore when it takes place somewhere else. As the urbanologist Paul Bairoch observed in the 1980s:

It would suffice to prohibit in five to ten years the use of all but electric vehicles and to impose speed limits of twenty to thirty kilometers per hour to make the city street once again what it should never have stopped being: a meeting place rather than the danger zone it is today. Each year, in the developed world alone, more than ten thousand children lose their lives crossing the streets. The number of those injured is ten times that figure. And the corresponding numbers for the elderly are twice as high again. Yet even this is the sort of drama only the rich have to deal with, trivial beside the drama in which the Third World is engaged.[19]

But, once again, it is important to emphasize the degree to which such conditions are not natural, inevitable, or homemade, but, rather, imposed on the Third World by the advanced industrial nations. They are costs that the developing world must shoulder so that the Fordist machinery can continue rolling forward.

. . . .

The effect of such development policies on the Third World cycle of boom and bust is not hard to discern. In a prescient article in *Foreign Affairs,* the MIT economist Paul Krugman pointed out in 1994 that the much ballyhooed "Asian Miracle" was based not on rising productivity but on the onetime mobilization of previously untapped economic resources. If Singapore was able to make a startling leap forward between 1966 and 1990 by doubling its proportion of jobholders, boosting the average level of education from near zero to a level approaching that of the industrialized West, and nearly quadrupling investment as a share of output, it was able to do so only on the basis of measures that, by definition, were unrepeatable.[20] Obviously, it could not go on doubling its proportion of jobholders every quarter century, just as it could not go on quadrupling the share of output devoted to investment. Instead, the only way it could continue growing would be to emulate more advanced economies by boosting productivity. Yet as far as anyone could tell, this was not taking place. Instead of raising efficiency, Singapore and the other Asian "tigers" were growing increasingly reliant on volatile short-term capital flows from the West.

The results were the global financial storms of 1997 and 1998. Krugman did not delve into the environmental issue in his article, but if he had, it would have made his argument even stronger. Allowing auto manufacturers to flood the streets with traffic and fill the air with pollution, as it turns out, was also a kind of onetime mobilization. Such policies were a gift to the business sector that by their very nature were unrepeatable as well. After allowing automakers to saturate local streets with cars once, Third World governments obviously could not allow them to do it again and again since there were no more streets to fill, just as they could not allow them to go on pouring more and more pollution into the atmosphere when people were already finding it difficult to breathe. The more they tried, the more likely the citizens would be to revolt and neighboring nations to complain. When a dense haze settled over much of Southeast Asia in 1998 because slash-and-burn farmers in Indonesia were setting fire to thousands of acres of woodlands, it was not just an environmental disaster but a financial one as well. Not only did it expose the hollowness of Indonesia's so-called modernization program but it was a sign that the government was losing control and that conditions were slipping backward. Already-nervous international investors grew even more jittery, and the financial panic accelerated. The underlying poverty of society was increasingly difficult to ignore beneath the surface glitz.

. . . .

And then there is global warming. The birth of the industrial revolution in the mid-eighteenth century meant the growth of steam power and an exponential increase in the use of coal. This in turn meant a growing volume of carbon-dioxide emissions, an inescapable by-product of combustion that is believed to be the chief factor in global warming. Carbon-dioxide levels rose slowly but steadily throughout the nineteenth century, accelerated significantly in the early twentieth, and then turned more violently upward in the 1950s as suburbanization took off in the United States and the auto culture spread to Europe and beyond. Where carbon-dioxide levels by the year 2000 were estimated to be 39 percent above the volumetric baseline of 277 parts per million that existed in 1750 on the eve of the industrial revolution, by the year 2050 they were projected to be as much as 100 percent higher, according to the UN's worst-case scenario, while by the year 2100 they were projected to be as much as triple or more. The result, according to the scientific consensus, was almost certain to be an ever more dramatic greenhouse effect in which average surface temperatures would rise as carbon dioxide trapped more and more sunlight and heat. In 1996, the UN's Intergovernmental Panel on Climate Change, composed of twenty-five hundred leading scientists and experts from around the globe, estimated that the hike in average global temperatures could be anywhere from two to six degrees, an estimate it subsequently hiked to eleven degrees Fahrenheit by the year 2100.[21] While the panel's report was necessarily cautious, replete with all sorts of hedges and qualifications, the implications were clear. A warmer atmosphere would almost certainly mean a wetter one, which in turn would likely mean "a more vigorous hydrological cycle" and "a possibility for more extreme rainfall events"—in other words, more violent storms leading to rising levels of wind damage and flooding.[22] In the first half of the 1990s, insurance companies throughout the world paid out more than $50 billion for various kinds of weather-related damage, more than triple what they had paid out in the entire previous decade. Yet as much as climatologists were loathe to attribute specific events to a long-term trend such as global warming, it was likely that in subsequent decades they would pay even more.[23] Similarly, although the effect might vary from place to place, a warmer atmosphere will obviously mean higher summertime temperatures across most of the Temperate Zone, where most of the globe's cities are located. If Manhattan, to cite just one example, was already a difficult place to be in July by the late 1990s, it was likely to grow even more sweltering in the years to come. The consequence would be higher levels of ozone, greater demand for electricity to run air conditioners during the summertime peak, and even more ovenlike sidewalks. The social gap between those with beachfront homes and those left gasping amid the asphalt and concrete would widen all the more.

Not that there is any need to exaggerate, of course. While one could imagine how global warming might trigger large-scale population transfers as people migrate from hotter to cooler climes, it is worth keeping in mind that the twenty-first century will almost certainly see large-scale population transfers regardless. Global population will continue churning whether the mercury rises or falls. Technology in the form of improved methods of flood control, more efficient air-conditioning, or new drugs to combat tropical diseases will likely take the edge off some of the pain. What's more, as conservatives delight in pointing out—when not trying to debunk global warming altogether—some effects might even be positive. If summers wound up more difficult, winters would be more benign. A warmer, wetter planet would be agriculturally more productive. Growing seasons would lengthen, and while crops in some areas might wilt in the heat, in other areas—the Canadian plains, for instance, or the Siberian taiga—they might blossom. Greenland might once again become the "green land" it perhaps was in the days of the Vikings. Viticulture might take root in southern England. Palm trees might sprout in southern Scotland.

Still, if a hotter and more humid planet is a more hospitable environment for crops, it is also more hospitable for microbes and disease-bearing insects. Thus, the UN's Intergovernmental Panel on Climate Change warned in 1996 that the portion of the world's population threatened by malaria could increase by 45 to 60 percent by the second half of the twenty-first century.[24] Rising sea levels—the UN panel predicts that the mean could rise by as much as thirty-seven inches by the year 2100—would threaten countless coastal areas with flooding, from Calcutta and much of Bangladesh to Jakarta, Tokyo, Lagos, and New Orleans, a major portion of which lies below sea level.[25] In China, a joint report by the World Bank, the UN Development Program, and the Chinese government's own National Environmental Protection Agency warned in 1995 that rising sea levels by the year 2050 could flood fourteen cities and counties along the vast Pearl River Delta, displacing some 76 million people.[26] Even a twelve-inch rise in sea levels, according to one Chinese government official, could have a devastating impact on coastal regions that are currently home to some 500 million people.[27] The Netherlands could see a repeat of the disastrous events of 1953 when high tides breached the dikes in the nation's southwest, resulting in massive flooding and some eighteen hundred deaths.

In Venice, perhaps the most vulnerable city of all, locals still talk about the *acqua alta* of 1966, in which the phases of the moon, a sharp drop in barometric pressure, and an unusual swell in the Adriatic combined to cause a rise in sea levels of nearly two meters. St. Mark's Place found itself under nearly four feet of water. According to a local newspaper, *Il Gazzettino:* "The air became unbreathable. Along with the carcasses of animals, the dead bodies from the cemetery floated through the streets and entered the houses." Although that flood is now classified as a once-in-eight-hundred-years occurrence, figures like these will have to be revised as the frequency and intensity of such events rises.[28] Although largely untouched by motorization during the twentieth century, Venice could find itself a prime victim in the twenty-first.

· · · · · · · · · · · ·

What is to be done? The solution is at once exceedingly simple and supremely difficult. Economically, the most efficient response would be to quantify the damage caused by each additional molecule of carbon dioxide and other greenhouse gases and then "internalize" the cost via a "green tax" on fossil fuels. Or, if this seems technically daunting, another method would be to work backward from the UN's goal of a 5.2 percent reduction in greenhouse-gas emissions from 1990 to 2012. This would mean calculating the dimensions of the economic disincentive per gallon of gasoline or pound of coal needed to reach such a goal, plugging it in via a carbon tax, and then readjusting the level from time to time depending on whether output is undershooting or overshooting the target. Based on studies at Stanford University and other institutions, a 20 percent reduction in emissions from 1990 levels—considerably more ambitious than what the UN has in mind—could be achieved surprisingly cheaply through a carbon tax equal to only about 45 cents per gallon of gasoline or 3.4 cents per kilowatt-hour of electricity.[29] At current levels of consumption, this works out to roughly twenty dollars more a month to fuel an average car and an extra twenty-five dollars a month on a typical residential utility bill. Costs like these are modest indeed, yet even the use of a term like *cost* in this context is misleading. While utility rates would rise, people would save money in the final analysis by avoiding the punishing long-term environmental consequences. Rather than going up, costs would ultimately go down.

Moreover, another school of thought holds that even that forecast is too pessimistic. By providing an incentive to both conserve energy and develop new forms of technology aimed at boosting energy efficiency overall, it argues that greenhouse-gas taxes could result in a net economic stimulus. Rather than a slower economy, the result could be an economy that is both cleaner and faster growing. According to a 1997 study by such environmental groups as the Alliance to Save Energy, the American Council for an Energy-Efficient Economy, and the Natural Resources Defense Council, the United States could cut emissions by 10 percent below 1990 levels, lower air pollution, and *still* save the average household $530 a year in expenditures for fuel and utilities by 2010. Another study, this one by the U.S. Energy Information Agency, found that reducing carbon-dioxide emissions 21 percent below 1990 levels could result in a net gain in GDP growth of 0.5 percent.[30]

Americans could thus have their cake and eat it, too. They could tax fossil fuels, reduce carbon-dioxide emissions, "grow" the economy, and find that they still had more money left in their pockets. In effect, it would mean recognizing that growing reliance on energy-wasting technology does not allow the economy to expand but in fact holds it back by preventing it from advancing to a new level of productivity. America's strength no longer lies in natural resources, which, after more than a century and a half of industrial development, are no longer so abundant. Rather, it lies in its intellectual and technical base: its college and university system—a Puritan legacy that is still the best such system in the world—its R&D network, and its highly educated workforce. The more technological development is in demand, the more the United States will be able to play to its strengths.

More ambitious goals, such as the 60 percent cut in carbon-dioxide output that atmospheric scientists say is needed to halt global warming in its tracks, would be more economically disruptive, of course, while the even deeper cuts needed to throw it into reverse would be even more so. But, ultimately, the question is akin to the one facing a young person who has been accepted into a prestigious medical school and is wondering whether or not to attend. Medical school is no joke. It means pressure, hard work, and a sharply curtailed social life. Yet, in the end, who can question whether it is worthwhile? Rather than a sacrifice, it is an investment, one that is almost certain to pay off. Similarly, the effort needed to halt or reverse global warming is not a sacrifice but an investment as well. It is an investment by society not in the environment but in itself—an investment in which the people of the world collectively decide that the purpose of economic growth is not to create a wilderness of *things* but to create a higher quality of life, and act accordingly.

So why doesn't it happen? Why doesn't the world embark on a concerted program of reductions in carbon-dioxide emissions immediately? The answer is political. While nearly everyone would ultimately gain if carbon-dioxide output is reduced, in the short run many, if not most, would suffer some degree of economic dislocation. The pain, moreover, would not be evenly distributed. Western Europe, with its densely populated cities and advanced rail network, might be able to weather the transition most easily. So might Japan. But an unstable giant like China, with its slowing growth rate, its widening economic gap between town and country, and its geriatric political leadership, could easily crack. India might crack as well, as could Pakistan, the oil exporters of the Middle East who would find themselves deprived of much of their revenue base, and so on.

And then there is the United States. America's carbon-dioxide output, like its energy consumption in general, is in a class by itself. At 19.88 metric tons per year, it produced twice as much carbon dioxide per capita in 1995 as Germany, Japan, and Great Britain, eight times as much as China, and twenty-three times as much as India.[31] Moreover, not only was it putting out more carbon dioxide per capita but, as the world's original Fordist economy, it had been doing so for a much longer time, making its aggregate contribution to the problem of global warming all the greater. Given all this, one might have assumed that the U.S. would be humble and contrite as its representatives traveled to Kyoto in December 1997 to attempt to hammer out an international agreement on global warming. In fact, it couldn't have been more obdurate. While the Clinton administration pushed for the most minimal program possible, Republican members of Congress demanded that the U.S. take no action at all until China, India, and other newly industrializing countries agreed to begin cutting back at the same time. The most powerful economy in the world was afraid to take a step for fear of losing advantage to the weakest.

While it was true that carbon-dioxide output was rising by the 1990s far faster in India and China than in the United States, three things were evident. One was that the trend was unlikely to continue. As the Chinese and Indian economies grow more sophisticated, energy usage will inevitably grow more sophisticated, which will make carbon-dioxide emissions easier to control. A second was that it was inconceivable that China and India would act without some initial sign of good faith on the part of the developed countries. As the chief contributors to the problem of carbon-dioxide buildup, the industrial nations and particularly the United States had to take the first step or the entire effort would be meaningless. The third thing that was apparent was that any talk of equal sacrifice on the part of First and Third World nations was absurd. At $28,600 as of 1996, U.S. GDP per person was ten times that of China and nearly eighteen times that of India. It was no fairer to expect all three countries to shoulder the burden equally than it would be to expect a grown man and a small child to equally shoulder a heavy weight.

．．．．．．．．．．．．．

In response to the 1997 Kyoto agreement, American industry immediately went on the offensive to block ratification in the U.S. Senate. The combatants read like a who's who of the auto-suburban complex: the American Automobile Manufacturers Association, the American Petroleum Institute, plus individual corporations such as Atlantic Richfield, Bethlehem Steel, Chrysler, Dow Chemical, General Motors, Goodyear Tire, Exxon, Mobil, Shell, and Texaco.[32] What these giants had in common was a shared devotion to the U.S. economy in its current form. They were committed to defending the status quo not in spite of the economy's growing inefficiency but because of it. Since their interests were bound up with one type of technology, they were determined to prevent the U.S.—and by extension, the world—from advancing to another. The result was a vast public-relations campaign aimed at advancing an argument to the effect that: (a) global warming doesn't exist; (b) even if it does exist, it's good for you; (c) even if it's not good for you, it is caused by natural rather than man-made forces; and (d) even if it is caused by man-made forces, it would be too costly to fix. When Bill Clinton gathered the press in the White House Rose Garden to discuss his response to global warming, he unveiled a grab bag of some fifty ideas to show his administration's level of commitment. They included everything from more-efficient household appliances to labeling automobile tires to let motorists know which treads contributed to better gasoline mileage. Such ideas were small-bore in the extreme, yet still they went almost nowhere. Congress blocked some, various federal agencies dragged their feet on others, while most of the rest proved ineffectual.[33] Although the U.S. had promised to hold emissions steady between 1990 and the year 2000, estimates were that by the end of the decade, they would be some 13 percent higher.[34] Even a fragmented, Lilliputian approach was beyond the American political system's capacity. A concerted response was out of the question.

"Protecting our environment is an honorable goal," declared a leading Republican congressman in 1997. "But we must ask ourselves an equally important question: Can we afford to destroy our children's economic future in the process?"[35] But this is a false dichotomy. A healthy economy is impossible without a healthy environment, just as, *pace* certain neo-Malthusian greens, a healthy environment in the modern era is impossible without a healthy economy. Sacrificing one to save the other was like sacrificing one's hand to save one's fingers.

· · · · · · · · · · · · ·

Global warming is a new kind of problem, one utterly without precedent. In the past, nations have succeeded at times in banding together to deal with international problems. Yet while these have sometimes led to intense bursts of activity, they have involved a relatively small number of countries for a relatively brief duration. Although fewer than a dozen countries engaged in serious fighting against the Axis in World War II, for example, it was all the combatants could do to prevent conflicts within the alliance from spinning out of control and blowing it apart. The United Nations, the successor to that wartime alliance, has proved more durable than the old League of Nations, yet it has always walked softly in the presence of the major powers, particularly those in the West. While the International Monetary Fund can be exceedingly tough on Third World governments whose social programs are deemed overly generous and whose finances are out of line, the idea that it would ever take a hard line with the U.S. is simply inconceivable. Unlike the problems of society and the automobile, there is no question in this instance as to who is the master and who is the servant.

Yet if the challenge of global warming is to be met, energy policy will have to be harmonized among some 180 nations, the technologically advanced and the newly industrializing alike. All will have to begin moving away from fossil fuels through a combination of conservation and a turn to solar, hydro, and other alternative energy sources. Tax policy will have to be harmonized so that the social costs of production and consumption are internalized while economic inequality is reduced. The temptation to cheat, to evade responsibility while loudly demanding that everyone else face up to theirs, will be almost irresistible. Nevertheless, effective yet equitable mechanisms will have to be put in place so that everyone falls into line. The 1997 Kyoto accords are well-nigh meaningless without ratification by the U.S. Senate—something that Republicans were still vowing to prevent as of the new millennium—but even if implemented, their all-too-modest goals would be no more than a starting point. A real attack on the problem would require deep changes in technology and economics, not to mention the political assumptions underlying them. Given that carbon dioxide remains in the atmosphere for a century or longer before breaking down, such changes would have to be put into effect not for years or even decades but for generations before the full effects would become apparent. The political leaders instituting such reforms would be lucky if their grandchildren lived to see the benefits.

Taxation and energy policy are core functions of the modern nation-state. Whether people travel by car, train, or bicycle, whether they live in cities or suburbs, whether government taxes the rich or the poor, commodities or income—these are some of the most basic ways that countries define themselves politically, socially, even philosophically. Internationalizing such functions means attacking not only the traditional prerogatives of the nation-state but the very idea of the nation-state itself. Moreover, it means attacking the biggest nation-state of them all, the United States—the nation-state that is most jealous of its own prerogatives and most dismissive of the rights of others. Not only is the U.S. the single greatest offender in terms of carbon-dioxide emissions, it is the one whose structure and mission, whose very makeup or *constitution,* are least open to reform.

This, admittedly, is a tough nut to crack. Practically speaking, a global policy shift is impossible if the global *hegemon* is opposed. Yet "practicality" of this sort is itself impractical in the face of a problem as potentially far-reaching as global warming. Not only has the global economic system grown ever more dynamic since the Industrial Revolution but the political system has grown ever more turbulent. Expectations have more than risen—they've accelerated. Since World War II, one region of the globe after another has been dragged into the mainstream of modern political development—China, India, and other areas that had slumbered for centuries and according to all the leading experts would go on slumbering for centuries more. For years, it was held to be axiomatic that such regions were incapable of progress. Yet, since 1945, such views have given way to the equal and opposite fear that vast portions of the globe would either modernize in a single great rush or collapse under the strain. Given this accelerating pattern of global development, it seems inconceivable that, in the face of global warming, the people of the world will go back to sleep as the conditions of their existence are progressively undermined. To the contrary, nearly everything since 1945 suggests that people will grow more impatient rather than less, and hence more demanding of reform.

This is not to say that a golden age of international cooperation is upon us. Indeed, the more the people of the world put their heads together to deal with common political problems, the more fractious global politics will become. Issues such as inequality of wealth and the meaning of international democracy will acquire a new centrality. They will become more irrepressible rather than less. There are any number of ways in which such a process could lead to disaster, but a more democratic global order contains within itself at least a kernel of possibility for success. While opportunities will be rife for demagogues to argue that global warming doesn't matter or that it is a hoax perpetrated by the Third World and its various green allies—an all-too-common theme in the looney-right editorial pages of the *Wall Street Journal*—a democratic framework is ultimately more favorable to those political forces that have analyzed the problem and have come up with rational plans of action. "Ultimately," of course, can cover a multitude of sins. Political democracy was ultimately successful from the seventeenth century to the twenty-first, but that didn't stop it from all but disappearing beneath the waves at any number of points. Still, if rationalism prevails, it will not be because people have suddenly laid aside their passions and prejudices. Rather, it will be because people will eventually realize that irrational means don't work and, indeed, only compound the problem by causing people to dig themselves in more deeply. As irrational solutions fail one by one, humanity will have to bring its rational faculties to bear—not because it wants to but because it has no choice.

Democracy—modern democracy, that is—is both rational and optimistic. This is not quite the perception in the United States where a long tradition of misanthropy going all the way back to the Founders holds that because people are inherently selfish, they can be counted on to do the wrong thing unless prevented by an immovable body of law. The more democratic society grows, the more selfishness and shortsightedness will become universal—or so Americans suppose. Rather than political realism, however, this is the opposite—a failure to comprehend that as new challenges arise, people must transform themselves in order to transform the society of which they are a part. Democracy means change, while a system that remains skeptical of the very possibility of change, that assumes that politics must remain frozen at an eighteenth-century level of development, is anything but democratic. Thanks to their immovable Constitution, Americans can't imagine anything higher up on the evolutionary scale than their own benighted Congress. They can't imagine a system in which politicians are willing to make tough decisions and voters are anything other than apathetic and uninvolved. The only world they can imagine is their own little corner writ large.

If this is all that democracy means, then the situation is indeed hopeless. Fortunately, however, it is not. Democratic theory has advanced beyond the archaic ideas propounded by the Founding Fathers in the 1780s. Rather than a process of endless horse-trading among ever more fragmented groups, democracy is now understood, at least in the more enlightened corners of the world, as a process by which people survey their situation as a whole and deal with it in as comprehensive a fashion as possible. It does not mean regarding society as the enemy of freedom but regarding it as potentially liberating. This is not to say that democracy never falls short—obviously, it does. But just as democrats recognize that the people will make mistakes, they also recognize that the people have a capacity to learn—indeed, that they can learn only if they have the freedom to make mistakes in the first place. As Marx wrote in 1842, efforts to deny the people the all-important freedom to err rest on the belief that

> true education consists in keeping a person wrapped up in a cradle throughout his life, for as soon as he learns to walk, he learns also to fall, and only by falling does he learn to walk. But if we all remain in swaddling clothes, who is to wrap us in

them? If we all remain in the cradle, who is to rock us? If we are all prisoners, who is to be the prison warder?[36]

Contrary to Jefferson, the most fundamental freedom of all is not the negative freedom to secede from society but the positive freedom to participate in society's struggle to adapt and grow. If it is the freedom to experiment and advance, it is also the freedom to fail, since experimentation is nothing without the ability to engage in trial and error. While the struggle against global warming will be filled with opportunities to fail, it will also be filled with opportunities to succeed. Power, in the final analysis, will flow to those parties that have analyzed the problem most thoroughly and have come up with the clearest programs in response.

10

THE SOLUTION

There was law in America, but
its benefits for the poor were accidental.

ANONYMOUS HUNGARIAN IMMIGRANT, 1907

ECONOMICALLY, there is no question as to what must be done. The negative externalities must be eliminated. Rather than turning a blind eye toward waste, society must adopt an ethos not only of individual but of collective responsibility. Rather than dealing with the problem in a piecemeal fashion, it must do so comprehensively. Among other things, this means that auto subsidies for the most part must be eliminated, either immediately or gradually, and that society must move toward a system in which motorists assume full economic responsibility the moment they avail themselves of public infrastructure, which they do the instant they leave their driveway. They must also assume full responsibility for the pollution they generate, the accidents they cause, the congestion they add to, and the global warming to which they contribute.

The scandalous subsidization of private real estate must cease. Tax subsidies for oversize mansions in the Hamptons or Beverly Hills are little short of criminal at a time when poor people are sleeping on sidewalks. These subsidies represent the private appropriation of public resources in such a way as to benefit an increasingly narrow stratum at the top. Rather than bringing housing prices down, tax subsidies such as the mortgage deduction drive them up by allowing builders to charge more than buyers would otherwise be willing to pay. While the resulting housing inflation profits those lucky enough to have bought into the market in the early stages of the postwar "long wave" of economic development, it does the opposite for would-be home owners who are trying to break into the market a half-century later. For this group, "starter" home prices are more and more out of reach, which is why the home-ownership rate in the United States for the thirty-five to forty-four year age group was 4 percent lower in 1996 than it was ten years earlier.[1] By diverting capital from industrial investment, a hypertrophied housing market undermines job growth. When officials fine a computer-chip company for the crime of generating too many jobs, something that officials in suburban Portland actually did to the Intel Corporation in mid-1999, it is a sign that something has gone seriously awry with a system that is so inefficient it fears each additional worker will send costs shooting through the roof.[2] As more and more resources go to consumption, production is crowded out. Work becomes an expense that affluent bedroom communities prefer to shunt off onto others. The result is a rentier economy intent on freezing society in place so that consumption and real-estate values can continue rising even as production tails off.

Could anything be more decadent? What, after all, is the point of rising real-estate values if employment does not grow, wages do not increase, and one's own children cannot find work? Overhousing leads to overconsumption of energy and land, while on a cultural and even spiritual level, it winds up undermining the very qualities it is supposed to enhance. In Britain, where the tax structure is far less favorable to home ownership, one study found that owners were less likely to see their home as a financial asset and more likely to see it as merely a home and nothing more.[3] Instead of an investment, it was simply a place to live. Moreover, to the degree that U.S.-style housing subsidies promote social atomization, they also encourage an increasingly antisocial concept of the home as not just a place of rest and repose but as a refuge from a society in a state of deepening breakdown. In his 1995 best-seller, *To Renew America*, Newt Gingrich indulged in an extended reverie in which a citizen of the future wakes up to a wall-size, high-definition television showing the surf off Maui, pours himself a cup of coffee, then works out on his own private exercise machine while checking his mail and reviewing the day's activities:

> Your home office is filled with communication devices, so you can ignore rush-hour traffic. . . . When you are sick, you sit in your diagnostic chair and communicate with the local health clinic. . . . You can write your own will, file your own adoption papers, form your own partnership or corporation— all with software programs available in your home. . . . Now imagine you want to learn something new, solve a personal problem, or enter some new profession. Do you have to go to night school or trek twenty-five miles to the nearest college? No, you simply enter the on-line learning system. . . .[4]

It is a picture of the suburban home as a self-contained universe, an existence in which an affluent suburbanite never has to set foot on a crowded street because he has everything that he could possibly need in his own government-subsidized home. Who needs society when one can lock oneself away watching television, playing video games, and surfing the Internet?

This vision of suburban isolationism is not just arid and futile but self-destructive. The more the middle class withdraws into a suburban fortress and pulls up the bridge behind it, the more it undermines the society of which it is a part. The more the social storms rage and beat outside the gate, the greater the likelihood that they will penetrate into their

cozy little sanctum. After watching suburbanites mobilize against a proposed new movie theater on the grounds that it might attract youth
gangs, a Dallas city councilman observed: "People right now are opposed
to any change, and that creates absolute instability as we go out and try to
promote economic development in the city."[5] The attempt to artificially
stabilize a tiny corner of the world is itself destabilizing.

This is what gives the suburbs their spooky subtext, the sense that
beneath that studied calm, dangerous forces are always welling up from
below. It is a subterranean vein of discontent that Hollywood has mined
repeatedly, from Nicholas Ray's *Rebel Without a Cause* (1955) to *American
Beauty* (1999). Moreover, Gingrich-style suburban autarchy fails on another
count as well. Amid all the hoopla over the Internet, people have lost sight
of the fact that not all the goods and services they order via the Web can be
downloaded—that some must be physically delivered. Rather than alleviating travel demand, communications advances from the telegraph and telephone forward have stimulated it, as Francis C. Moon, a professor of
mechanical engineering at Cornell, is fond of pointing out.[6] Other than its
Web site, what is Amazon.com but a warehouse and delivery system paying
its workers $7.50 an hour?[7] High-tech delivery services such as Kozmo.com
and Urbanfetch.com rely on a small army of bicycle couriers equipped with
two-way radios and data pagers, an example of late-twentieth-century
technology piggybacking on the technology of the late nineteenth.[8] Once
they leave cyberspace and enter the real world, such companies contribute
to highway overload as much as anyone else. Communications may grow
more efficient, but congestion will continue to worsen.

· · · · · · · · · · · ·

Indeed, by the turn of the millennium, it was apparent that the system
was approaching something like terminal gridlock. Sprawl had become
a dirty word, and regional newspapers from coast to coast were running
all-too-similar stories bemoaning the new kind of postindustrial ugliness

that was overspreading the landscape. To quote a list compiled by the *Buffalo News* in upstate New York, it was a random pastiche of uniformly distasteful elements:

> Traffic lights. Kentucky Fried popcorn chicken. Thruways. Eckerd's vitamin C. Chemlawn green. K-Mart blue. Satellite dishes. Wilson Farms Twist 'N Go cups. Endless rush hours. Auto Zone gas caps. Noise. The Rite Aid's drive-thru. Development. Noco peat moss. Split levels. Mobil self-service pumps. The Ames shoe department. School taxes. Burger King Whoppers. Sewer tax. Radar traps. Dairy Queen banana splits. Congestion. 7-Eleven Slurpies. Four-car families. Wendy's taco wraps. Soccer moms. Wal-Mart lawnmowers. Driveaholic dads. Mr. Oil Change lube jobs. Galleria teens. McDonald's Happy Meals.[9]

And so on ad infinitum, a list that would be little different were it compiled in Southern California, the outskirts of Lincoln, Nebraska, or central New Jersey. Between 1997 and 2000, twenty-two states passed various "smart growth" bills designed, supposedly, to rein in blight of this sort and encourage concentrated development better suited to mass transit.[10] The National Governors Association scrambled to get on board the new movement; so did innumerable local pols; and so, even, did Joel Garreau, author of the 1991 best-seller *Edge City: Life on the New Frontier*. Astonishing as it sounds, this book had celebrated glass-and-steel office-*cum*-shopping-center developments such as Tysons Corner, Virginia, as "the most purposeful attempt Americans have made since the days of the Founding Fathers . . . to create something like a new Eden," ignoring the awesome volume of traffic they generate. In 1999, Garreau announced that he was "picking up different vibes now." As he told one of the news magazines:

When I'm talking to people in Plano, Texas, or in Irvine, California, or any of these edge cities awash in money and jobs, and I ask people what's missing, I'm struck by how often the word "community" comes up. What it boils down to is a sense of loss about what people think they once had. That's why the issue has so much political juice.[11]

What had been lost was a social environment based on something other than cars, malls, and glass-and-steel office buildings with commanding views of traffic jams and parking lots.

Of course, the most famous antisprawl voice to emerge in fin de siècle America was that of Vice President Al Gore, whose 1992 book, *Earth in the Balance,* was a notably honest (for an American politician, that is) midlife meditation on the environmental issues facing the globe in the coming decades. During the 2000 presidential election, Gore came under intense pressure to rescind or at least downplay his earlier environmental views. His opponent, George W. Bush, a dutiful servant of Texas oil and gas interests, had never seen a gas station, SUV, or minimall that he didn't like. Moreover, the start of the campaign had coincided with a modest OPEC cut in oil production that, combined with America's gargantuan appetite for fossil fuels, had sent gas prices rising to two dollars or more per gallon—still low by the standards of the rest of the industrialized world, but the highest they had been in the United States in real terms in years. Yet Gore, to his credit, refused to back down even from his call for an international effort to phase out the internal combustion engine. Indeed, he told one Michigan audience that he had been wrong in writing in *Earth in the Balance* that the internal combustion engine could be phased out over twenty-five years: "I now see that we can do it in less than twenty-five years while preserving and creating new jobs."[12]

Statements like these took guts, but they also reflected opinion polls showing that American voters were not only concerned about the environment but, in the age of the Internet, were not especially alarmed by predictions that gasoline engines might someday give way to some new form of technology.[13] Simultaneously, however, the Gore campaign showed the American political system's fundamental inability to deal with issues like sprawl and gridlock in a serious way. Besides calling for a phase-out of the internal combustion engine, *Earth in the Balance* had also endorsed "higher taxes on fossil fuels" as "one of the logical first steps in changing our policies in a manner consistent with a more responsible approach to the environment." Where Gore had stood fast in regard to the first statement, he began backpedaling furiously in regard to the second—particularly when his opponent seized on it as evidence that Gore was unconcerned about rising prices at the pump.[14] Yet the original statement had been correct: A rational environmental policy was impossible without stepped-up fossil-fuel taxes to serve as a brake on demand, however much it ran counter to the conventional wisdom that the typical voter was so blinded by the state of his pocketbook that he or she would never agree to pay more now for some gain farther down the road. By June, Gore was talking about a massive effort to upgrade energy efficiency that was long on spending—$148 billion over ten years—but short on what policy analysts call revenue enhancement. The plan called for upgrading existing rail systems and building high-speed new ones in major transportation corridors, tax breaks for consumers and manufacturers who invest in energy-efficient homes, factories, vehicles, and appliances, and so on—all so that gasoline prices could remain at what, adjusted for inflation, were still historically low levels.[15]

"You deserve the independence to get in your car and drive anywhere you want to go—without emptying your wallet at every filling station," Gore told the voters. "You should also have the choice, if you want it, to park your car at a light-rail station and be moved swiftly into a newly thriving downtown."[16] This was cloud-cuckoo-land. Americans could *not* have it both ways. The choice was either subsidized motorization or some more-balanced form of development. Choosing one path meant not choosing another. A comprehensive new rail system would be unjustifiable in the absence of sufficient demand, yet demand would not rise to the necessary levels unless other forms of transportation were narrowed or closed off via desubsidization. Faceless federal bureaucrats could not force Americans out of their cars. But Americans could force *themselves* out by democratically choosing between the two. In the absence of such a shift, improved transportation efficiency would remain a pipe dream. Even if Gore's dream of a flashy new generation of electric cars came true, congestion and sprawl, two of the most rapidly rising costs associated with the automobile, would continue to cripple society unless the total volume of traffic, electric or gasoline-powered, were reduced. Not only would demand have to shift from auto to rail, but the very concept of mobility would have to be rethought. Rather than guaranteeing Americans "the independence to get in your car and drive anywhere you want to go," society would have to commit itself to the goal of providing Americans with the right *not* to get in their cars and, instead, stay put. American communities by the start of the twenty-first century were so ill arranged that they resembled homes with the stove at one end, the kitchen sink at another, the refrigerator in the basement, and the freezer in the attic. Rather than massive government investment in a new generation of high-tech gizmos designed to facilitate travel between such far-flung points, the first step was to tackle the layout and the endless trudging back and forth that it generated. This could not be done administratively by simply mandating more efficient designs if the economic system continued to send the opposite message. It could only be done by bringing the price of driving into line with the true social and environmental costs.

. . . .

The problem, therefore, is what to do about a network of subsidies and allowances that, rather than improving transportation and the quality of life, are undermining both. The answer is that nothing can be done, at least not under anything resembling current circumstances. American politics, as we have seen, are too fragmented and backward-looking to permit the people to mobilize so as to undertake such a dramatic feat of modernization. Indeed, not only does America's antiquated constitutional structure not permit such a mobilization, it was fairly designed to short-circuit such a process before it could begin. Not only does it fragment politics, it fragments consciousness. Not only does it prevent a comprehensive assault on society as a whole, it is so intellectually debilitating that it prevents people from thinking about American society in a comprehensive manner. As James Madison explained in the Federalist Papers, the Constitution was designed to create a series of firewalls so that "[a] rage for paper money, for an abolition of debts, for an equal division of property, or for any other improper or wicked project, will be less able to pervade the whole body of the Union than a particular member of it."[17] Madison's fear was that in a tightly organized, centralized structure, it would be all too easy for a dissident faction to seize center stage and draw the attention of the people as a whole. Therefore, he opted for a decentralized federation with plenty of checks and balances and separations of power in the belief that such a ramshackle structure would tend to muffle popular outbursts and prevent their spread from one section to the other. Madison wished to prevent the people from remaking society as a whole because he believed that they were more likely to do so for corrupt and selfish purposes than otherwise. He believed that the purpose of a strong constitution was to hold them back so that they would only be able to remake bits and parts.

But any attempt to artificially stabilize society through the creation of an immovable body of law is itself destabilizing. By seeking to prevent change, it deprives society of the oxygen it needs to breathe, thereby contributing to its own undoing. Under normal circumstances, there should be nothing terribly revolutionary about revamping housing and transportation policy. It is a project that any well-functioning democracy should be able to undertake in a mature, considered fashion. Yet America is so constitutionally inflexible after more than two centuries, its capacity for change is so limited, that even modest reform becomes more and more difficult without taking on the entire system. The situation is the opposite of what it was in the mid-nineteenth century when it was the Old World that seemed frozen. Now America must heave and strain to accomplish what other societies accomplish with relative ease. Cleaning up the mess created by nearly a century of Fordism is one of them.

· · · · · · · · · · · · ·

Nothing here is meant to suggest that subsidies per se must be eliminated. Obviously, no society that thinks of itself as progressive would want to cut off funding for art museums or public schools or impose admission fees on parks and playgrounds. However, not only must society determine which costs to "internalize" and which ones not to, but, even more fundamentally, the demos must define what constitutes a negative externality in the first place and what does not. From a conservative point of view, social atomization borne of hyper-motorization is a positive externality because it serves to break down society into an inert mass of consumers. When Margaret Thatcher declared in 1987 that "there is no such thing as society," only "individual men and women," what she meant is that her policies were designed to take what few shards of society remained in Britain and grind them into dust. From a left-wing perspective, similarly, social atomization is a negative externality because it prevents working-class people from connecting with one another on a political basis—which is why any left-wing government worth its salt would want to adopt policies aimed at promoting mass transit, urbanization, and the sort of "closely associated communities" that George W. Julian regarded as so vital during the Civil War. Surely, no socialist society—and in the final analysis, no coherent society can be anything other than socialist—would want to expend hundreds of billions of dollars a year so that a tiny layer can withdraw into a sumptuous world of private homes and cars. Only a society at war with itself, an antisociety, would be capable of anything so perverse.

What would a society look like in which the social and environmental costs of private transportation and housing were fully internalized? To begin with the most obvious, it would have less traffic, fewer motor vehicles, and fewer (and smaller) privately owned single-family homes. It is a technical question as to whether driving costs should be internalized via a gas tax alone or a variety of charges on everything from fuel and distance traveled (so as not to let electric vehicles completely off the hook) to time of travel (so as to reduce rush-hour delays). But regardless of the specific method, two things are apparent. One is that internalizing the full cost of driving would likely boost the price by as much as $10 a gallon or its equivalent over and above the current price of driving. The second is that such an increase would profoundly alter the economics of private transport and political geography. The immediate impact should not be exaggerated. At forty miles per gallon, well within reach of current technology, a $10 hike in the price of gasoline would mean raising driving costs by 25¢ a mile. As a result, a ten-mile trip back and forth to the mall would cost an additional $2.50 per vehicle, less than the cost of a round-trip on the New York City subways, while a two-hundred-mile weekend jaunt would cost an additional $50, the cost, approximately, of dinner for two at a budget restaurant. For most middle-class motorists in the U.S., this is less than crushing. Nevertheless, such an increase would unquestionably force motorists to keep one eye on the odometer the same way that a taxi rider keeps one eye on the meter. Over the long term, the cumulative effect would be to provide motorists with a potent incentive to walk, cycle, or use mass transit whenever possible, saving the car for mainly weekend travel when it could be put to its best use. No longer an everyday conveyance, the auto would become a special means of transport to be reserved for special occasions.

Altering the economics of transport would mean altering the economics of time and space. Instead of forcing people to live in far-flung
suburbs, the way the system does now, it would encourage them to live
within walking distance of shops, restaurants, and movie theaters. Instead
of providing people with an incentive to maximize the distance between
themselves and their neighbors, it would give them an incentive to cluster
together in compact communities. Rather than "nimby" (from "not in my
backyard") and "banana" ("build absolutely nothing anywhere near anything"), the guiding principles of today's suburban development, society
would once more have an incentive to squeeze tightly together. While
some might still wish to hold on to their cars, others would not. By its
very nature, a car encourages its driver to head out for the thinly settled
periphery where it has ample room to maneuver. It "seeks" the terrain to
which it is best suited. While this might appeal to those who wish to distance themselves from their fellow citizens, it would not appeal to others.
With dense-packed communities the new focus of society, most people
would prefer to burrow deeper into the center, where even a bicycle can
be a hindrance. Rather than holding on to their cars, they would prefer to
let them go. Rather than feeling less free as a consequence, they would
feel liberated by virtue of being better able to immerse themselves in the
life of the community. The more people free themselves in such a manner,
the more cities will be free to develop intensively so as to squeeze as many
activities as they can into a given amount of space.

Housing, for similar reasons, would shrink. With government subsidies no longer encouraging people to build gargantuan homes ever farther
out in the countryside, housing would acquire new shape and meaning as
it clustered around train stations, tramlines, ports, and other transit nodes.
While single-family housing might still have a place, more people would
undoubtedly prefer apartments. But even misanthropes who like to live
deep in the forest would find that glorious isolation could be found closer
at hand. The crude hut that Henry David Thoreau moved into on Walden

Pond in 1845 was less than two hundred yards from the Concord train station.[18] Yet two hundred yards were all Thoreau needed to effectively remove himself from civilization. A century and a half later, most Americans would have to fight their way through miles and miles of sprawl in order to find anything comparable. Rather than bringing nature closer, subsidized sprawl has pushed it farther away.

Given its economies of scale, rental housing would almost certainly increase relative to owning, while public ownership would undoubtedly expand also. While certain maximalists of the left would no doubt wish to abolish home ownership altogether, it is hard to see why privately owned homes are necessarily more problematic than privately owned shirts or sweaters. Private ownership would become one form of housing tenure among many, one with its own set of advantages and disadvantages. It might appeal to those who value long-term security or enjoy doing their own repairs, but not to those who wish to be unencumbered by possessions or who wish to do other things in their leisure time besides installing lighting fixtures or mowing the lawn. It is up to the people to decide, singly and collectively, which is more desirable. Meanwhile, subsidization not only obscures the true cost of home ownership, it obscures what may or may not be its true benefits. By artificially lowering the price of ownership, subsidization reduces consumer choice by forcing people to buy whether they want to or not. By reducing the ability to experiment with various forms, it prevents more efficient forms from emerging.

What would daily life be like under such a regimen? For a family living in a city apartment, life would revolve around the neighborhood, the subway, and, presumably, the tram. For the overwhelming majority of their transportation needs, urbanites would walk, bicycle, or take some kind of fixed-bed transit to some other point on the map where they would walk some more. With motorized traffic reduced or eliminated and crime, hopefully, brought under control, children would be free to walk or bike to school, the way city kids used to before the onslaught of the automobile.

They would be free to stop off on the way home to visit a candy store, to hang out with friends and play marbles, jacks, or stickball—not in the parks and playgrounds but on the sidewalks and streets where such activities belong. (Who knows—perhaps the more enterprising among them would land jobs running errands for the neighborhood bordello. . . .) In small towns and villages, the mix would be a bit different—less motorized transit and more walking and cycling. Because building heights would be lower in such communities, population densities would not be as great. But most people would still want to live close to a dense core of restaurants, movie theaters, and shops—not because some government *diktat* would require them to but because the economics of everyday life would make such proximity more logical and desirable. While some people might keep a car, few would use it for everyday tasks like running errands or going to work. Children would be free to play in the streets or in the woods and fields, which in a postsprawl era would be only a few steps away. The old walled city might even make a comeback, not for defensive purposes, obviously, but in order to create as clean a break as possible between town and country.

The goal is not the Manhattanization *du monde* but the creation of a wide variety of communities, from villages clustered around a single transit node to high-density cities resting on a complex mix of public infrastructure. Presumably, cities would benefit from economies of scale that permit them to offer more of everything—more services, more retail outlets, more job opportunities, even more kinds of people. But smaller communities would offer things that big cities could not: closer proximity to nature and agriculture, a slower pace, an atmosphere that is more neighborly and intimate. Still, the aim would not be to dictate what kind of community people should live in—the auto-suburban system does enough of that already. Rather, it would be to establish certain parameters that would allow them to try out a broad range of options.

People could experiment not only as to size, but as to the various ways that cities tackle the problems of urban management and space. Some might opt for low-rise solutions à la Paris or London; others, for high-rise ones à la New York. Some might prefer broad avenues, and others, winding alleyways, while some might strive for a mixture of both. Some might build themselves around water transport à la Venice or Hong Kong, and others, around land. Still, it is hard to imagine how twenty-first-century cities will be able to resist availing themselves of the possibilities inherent in vertical transport (aka the elevator). The more people who live and work on top of one another in high-rise apartments, office towers, or ateliers, the greater the value that can be created out of each hectare of land, kilometer of subway, or cubic meter of building space. Needless to say, there are also diseconomies inherent in hyper-urbanization of this sort, such as crowding and high construction costs. But urban values will rise to the degree such problems can be overcome.

Despite the horrors of the nineteenth-century slum, the industrial era saw a quantum leap in urban carrying capacity. From the Roman Empire until the industrial revolution, urban population densities in the West held relatively stable at between 20,000 and 40,000 people per square mile. Thereafter, they doubled and tripled, peaking at around 520,000 per square mile on Manhattan's Lower East Side between 1900 and 1910.[19] Reformers and agrarians were horrified at the consequences, but, then, reactionaries and agrarians were horrified by everything that industrial capitalism wrought—mass-produced goods, unions, strikes, the factory whistle, the train schedule, and so forth. They longed for a return to a world of thatched cottages and village handicrafts in which people told time by listening for the church bell or looking at the sun. But modernists recognize that, despite long hours, low pay, and abysmal working conditions, factories represented a great leap forward in human productive capacity. Modernists likewise recognized that the modern city, despite disease and overcrowding, did as well. Just as a steam-powered loom could produce many times more cloth than the old hand-driven variety, the metropolis could foster many times more human activity per square meter. It made people move more quickly, think more rapidly, and feel more engaged culturally, intellectually, and politically.

Perhaps the twenty-first century will see an equally dramatic advance in urban capacity, not just in quantitative terms but in qualitative ones also. The aim, after all, is not necessarily bigger cities but *better* cities, i.e., cities that provide more creative outlets and foster more of people's natural sociability. Not that a city should be a place of *forced* sociability, of course. In addition to opportunities to mix and mingle, the modern city should provide equally as many opportunities to be alone: art galleries in which one can lose oneself amid the paintings, park benches on which one can sit and read, bars in which one can drink and ponder. The growth of the great cities in the eighteenth and nineteenth centuries did not mean a closing off of human experience, but an opening up. Eighteenth-century London abounded in coffee shops, clubs, and magazines, while Jack London's descriptions in his semiautobiographical novel *Martin Eden* of tumultuous political meeting halls in turn-of-the-century San Francisco still crackle with excitement. Walt Whitman's urban poetry shows him to have been a tireless observer of human affairs, as it also shows him to have been something of a solitary observer, someone who studied the urban tableau without necessarily interacting. He was in the crowd, but never entirely of it. By virtue of its complexity and economies of scale, the city is able to accommodate and foster a complexity of modes of interaction.

Nevertheless, there is one mode that the pre-auto city was unable to accommodate and that the post-auto city presumably will be unable to as well: that of boredom. Suburbia, by contrast, is boring to its depths. One feels the enervation, the deep entropy, the moment one steps foot in a subdivision or mall. It is boring because it is inefficient. Where the pre-auto city fairly overflowed with politics, culture, and conflict, suburban society channels so much of its resources into private consumption that it has nothing left over for the communal. Not only is it left culturally impoverished as a consequence, but it is only able to stagger forward by impoverishing nearby cities that still have a few such communal institutions left to offer.

This is the suburb as a bottomless black hole that sucks up energy and wealth in order to sustain an increasingly uneconomical mode of existence. If ancient cities such as Rome drew parasitically off the countryside, the Fordist suburb draws parasitically off the cities. The purpose of re-urbanization is to put an end to such wasteful relationships. Its goal is not only to rediscover urban excitement but to rediscover urban efficiency, to create more economical designs for living so that society can once again afford the coffeehouses, clubs, theaters, and other cultural riches that cities once generated in abundance despite a far-lower level of industrial and scientific development.

Re-urbanization should not be understood in static terms. The idea is not simply to transfer resources from single-family homes to apartment buildings or from the auto sector to rail. Rather, the idea is to foster new types of technology that expand the pie at the same time that society redistributes the pieces. While dynamic in some respects, late-twentieth-century technological development has been static in others. Where the nineteenth century generated transportation revolutions seemingly every generation, the twentieth has given us just one: the automobile. This was the revolution to end all revolutions, which is why America has come to rely on motor vehicles for roughly 90 percent of its transportation needs.[20] Society has become overly dependent not because the auto is the last word in transportation but because, by overinvesting in Fordist technology, it has effectively closed off any alternatives.

. . . .

In biology and economics, this is what is known as "path dependency." Just as it makes sense in cross-country skiing to follow in the leader's

tracks rather than veering off into the deep snow, it makes sense in industry and technology to stick, whenever possible, to the path carved out by a
particular leader or pioneer. If Henry Ford has demonstrated that demand
for a cheap, mass-produced automobile is well-nigh insatiable, why pour
resources into the development of some alternative mode of transport,
whatever that may be? Why not follow up on Ford's success instead by
manufacturing a cheap, mass-produced car much like the one he made,
only a car that goes the master one better by being more stylish and fun?
Why not pull up closely behind him and then, when he falters, take advantage of his misstep and swing out ahead?

This is essentially what General Motors's legendary leader Alfred P.
Sloan Jr. did in the 1920s. Yet, rather than competition and development,
the result was a stop-and-go pattern of development in which periods of
breakthrough were followed by periods of slowing technology until everything at last came to a complete halt. In auto manufacturing, such a slowdown has been evident for years. As Sloan himself remarked in 1964:
"Great as have been the engineering advances since 1920, we have today
basically the same kind of machine that was created in the first twenty
years of the century"[21]—an observation that holds no less true some three
or four decades later. As different as a sleek new BMW may be from a
Model T, the two have more in common with each other than with either
the transportation technology that preceded the auto revolution or the
transportation that will undoubtedly follow. Although separated by the
better part of a century, the two automobiles are recognizably the same
species, or at least the same genus.

The problem with path dependency is that it is self-reinforcing. As
the path grows more crowded, the grooves grow deeper and deeper,
which makes it all the more difficult to set off on some alternative route.
The more problems pile up, the greater the temptation to attempt
to solve them within the existing framework despite mounting evidence
that the framework is itself the source of the trouble. Rail, as we have

seen, fostered an explosive form of urban concentration. Yet all attempts to solve the problem within a rail framework by building trolley lines and subways led to greater intensification than ever. Similarly, the automobile is responsible for everything from global warming to sprawl. Yet, while manufacturers have poured immense sums into antipollution technology, enhanced fuel efficiency, and various kinds of "smart technology" to enable drivers to steer clear of congestion, such auto-based solutions either have failed or will fail because they ignore the degree to which the auto itself is the cause of the trouble. By lowering driving costs, enhanced fuel efficiency encourages more people to drive longer distances, thereby adding to traffic. By allowing highways to accommodate more cars with less congestion, "smart technology" will enable more people to take to the road, which will, among other things, add to global warming. While it is hard to take issue with things like catalytic converters and lead-free gasoline, it is worth noting that, according to the Environmental Protection Agency, visibility in metropolitan areas has nonetheless been declining since 1980 due to growing levels of traffic.[22] Individually, cars may be cleaner. But collectively, they are dirtier simply because there are more of them.

Then there is the problem of what might be called, for lack of a better word, rampant "uglification"—the tendency of automobiles to foster an epidemic of parking lots, gas stations, shopping centers, and drive-through banks—that spreads itself across the landscape like some kind of gruesome rash. All efforts at resolving this problem within an auto framework have only made things worse. Environmentally sensitive housing developments with lots of open space, shopping malls designed to look like New England villages, environmentally sensitive corporate parks filled with ponds, picnic tables, and jogging trails—when not making a mockery of the very thing they are seeking to emulate, such attempts at Fordism-with-a-human-face compound the problem due to their increasingly profligate use of land. Since it is impossible within an auto framework to eliminate noise, fumes, and highway detritus, the most common response is to try to escape such noxious by-products by removing oneself as far as possible from the source. If the local highway strip is a raucous cantata of muffler shops and fast-food joints, then the answer is to locate an upscale new office park on hundreds of acres of verdant countryside on some as-yet-unspoiled country road several miles away. If parents want their children to be free to bicycle on old-fashioned, traffic-free streets, then the answer is to locate a development far out amid the greenery where the traffic jams have not yet penetrated.

But as such solutions multiply, distances balloon, auto dependency rises, and sprawl in fact accelerates. Corporate parks that are more spacious mean corporate parks that are farther apart. Far-flung housing developments mean an overall pattern of development that is too thinly settled to support mass transit, leaving residents no choice but to go about by car. The more people use the automobile to try to outrun the problems of the automobile, the faster those problems spread in the form of traffic, pollution, noise, and highway clutter. In such an auto-bound environment, one no longer uses a car to go anywhere because increasingly there is nowhere to go—nowhere at the end of the highway, that is, except more highways and more highway detritus. The very idea of "destination" loses its meaning as driving becomes a closed loop, a solipsistic exercise in which the purpose of driving is to drive some more—and more and more.

. . . .

Rather than sticking to the existing path by building a better trolley or locomotive, Henry Ford's great breakthrough was to build a better automobile, thereby enabling his customers to bypass the rail system altogether. Where the existing framework was helpless in the face of rising levels of urban concentration, the Model T dissolved cities as effortlessly as a glass of tea dissolves a lump of sugar. Rather than leading to the mass society whose growth seemed so inexorable, mass motorization triggered a chain reaction that led to something wholly unexpected: a new concept of the mass market and mass individualism. In what is shaping up to be the auto age's long and painful denouement, the question facing society is: What is the next stage of technology that will dissolve the automobile's growing list of problems as effortlessly as the auto dissolved rail's?

The very concept of the automobile provides a clue. The word *automobile* is a Latin-Greek neologism that translates, roughly, as "self-moving." The essence of a car is thus its self-propelling nature as a vehicle that moves from one point to another under its own power and the driver's own direction. But we also know that self-propulsion is a myth since drivers would be helpless—literally stuck in the mud—if society had not committed itself to a vast collective effort to enable them to go from here to there. Fuel had to be extracted and refined, the world's most elaborate highway system had to be built, a variety of highway services had to be provided nearly free of charge, while innocent bystanders had to be made to accept a range of social and environmental consequences that would otherwise have had them rising in revolt—all so that the motorist could continue in the belief that he was moving forward under his own steam. Lincoln thus had it wrong. If you can't fool all of the people all of the time, the people are perfectly capable of fooling themselves decade after decade as to the real relationship between society and the individual.

The more society conceives of mobility in individual terms, the more gridlocked both society and the individual become. Therefore, whatever technological form the next stage of transportation takes, one thing seems certain: It will entail a rejection of this spurious Fordist concept of automobility. Rather than viewing individual mobility as something to be achieved *apart* from society, it will recognize it as something to be achieved *through* society. This means a return to what we now know as mass transit. Since the antithesis of a self-steering, self-propelling mechanism is transportation that is driven by others along on a fixed track or bed, the result could be either a move toward a souped-up version of rail such as the high-speed TGV *("très grande vitesse")* or the German ICE technology or a departure from the old "steel wheels" approach and a turn toward something entirely new.

Indeed, the next new thing may already be upon us. Since the 1960s, engineers have been working on a revolutionary form of transport that abandons wheels altogether for lightweight "trains" that float several inches above a magnetized guideway. Known as maglev—short for magnetic levitation—this technology is not some flying-carpet fantasy but an accomplished fact. By the late 1990s, two maglev systems were in operation, the "Transrapid" that a consortium of engineering firms—including Daimler Benz, Siemens, and Thyssen—had developed on a nineteen-mile test track in northern Germany and a rival system developed by the Japanese Ministry of Transportation on a twenty-six-mile track west of Tokyo. Although the two systems vary in important respects—the Japanese system takes advantage of the latest developments in high-temperature superconductivity while the German system does not—both offer compelling advantages over current technology. Because a maglev train does not propel itself forward in the manner of a car or conventional train but is, in fact, propelled forward by a magnetic pulse moving along the guideway, there is no onboard engine. As a result, a maglev train is between one-half and two-thirds lighter than a steel-wheeled train, which makes it cheaper to run, build, and maintain. The absence of an onboard engine means that there is no need for an onboard engine crew, which translates into lower labor costs. The absence of wheels means reduced friction and significantly higher speeds.[23] Where current rail technology appears to be topping out at about 200 miles per hour, the maglev system under development in Otsuko, Japan, hit a speed of 550 kilometers per hour (330 mph) in 1997, nearly two-thirds higher. Given that such technology is still in its infancy, even greater speeds are likely farther down the road, especially if wind resistance is eliminated by enclosing the maglev track in an evacuated airtight tube, as some experts already propose.

The implications are remarkable. Three-hundred-plus miles per hour means New York to Chicago in three hours or less, not via far-flung airports, which can add hours to a journey on either end, but downtown to downtown. Five hundred miles per hour means New York to Los Angeles in six hours or so, approximately the time it now takes to go by air but eventually at far lower cost. Airlines would be rendered uncompetitive on all but the longest routes, while cars would be competitive only on the shortest. After all, who would want to drive from, say, New Haven to New York when another Japanese maglev system under development, the HSST, designed to maneuver through crowded, built-up metropolitan regions at a tortoiselike 120 miles an hour, could make the same journey in a half hour or less?[24] Who would want to spend hours trapped on the Long Island Expressway when other maglev systems could whisk one to the Hamptons in just twenty minutes?

The automobile's great advantage is that it delivers motorized transport right to one's doorstep. Unfortunately, it delivers the *problems* of motorized transport right to one's doorstep also. Fixed-bed transportation does not. By its very nature, it terminates in population centers where its potential customer base is concentrated. Since the technology will not go to the passenger, the passenger must go to the technology, which means that, rather than encouraging users to scatter themselves over the landscape, it encourages them to cluster around stations and terminals in order to maximize access. The greater the system's advantages over rival modes, the more important access becomes and the more pronounced the clustering. If maglev were to fulfill the fondest hopes of its enthusiasts by taking off the way rail did in the 1830s and 1840s, the result would be a return to a pre-auto mode of development in which the city would once again serve as a powerful magnet drawing population in toward the center rather than driving it away. Once again, the city would become the focal point.

Maglev does have at least two significant disadvantages: noise and capital costs. The first is not insurmountable. At high speeds, a maglev train is substantially quieter than a TGV—although, considering the immense noise generated by a high-speed train, this is not saying a great deal.[25] Still, shielding could alleviate much of the problem, particularly on the approach to population centers, while enclosing the guideway in an airtight tube would essentially eliminate it. But the other problem—money—is not so easily resolved. According to a 1993 study by the Argonne National Laboratory, an elevated maglev system would cost approximately $17.9 million per mile.[26] According to German projections, the Transrapid could cost as much as $50 million.[27] Adjusted for inflation, this could mean as much as $45 billion for a line stretching from New York to Chicago, $115 billion for one running from Chicago to Los Angeles, plus as much as $25 billion or so for a high-speed express serving the lucrative travel market between Washington, D.C., and Boston. Needless to say, such figures are highly tentative. But as daunting as they may seem, they are far from crushing in the context of a $9 trillion economy that thinks little of spending $2 billion for a single bat-winged B-2 bomber. Moreover, investments such as these must be viewed dynamically. While critics may argue that, with minor adjustments, America will be able to meet its transportation needs well into the twenty-first century with a system based largely on cars, trucks, and airlines, this is akin to arguing in the 1830s that America would be able to meet its transportation needs with a system based on wagons, canals, and steamboats. It could—provided traffic levels remained essentially static. But the introduction of the railroad insured that they would not. The purpose of maglev would similarly be to stimulate transportation growth by lowering the true social and environmental cost. In so doing, it would seek to "grow" the economy, and society with it. Given the low nominal cost of highway travel in the U.S., maglev is indeed difficult to justify under present circumstances. But when broader social and environmental factors are taken into account, it is evident that the current system is far more costly than officially acknowledged, which makes maglev less expensive by comparison.

. . . .

Rather than more of the same, the result could thus be something completely different—a completely different pattern of social development
resting on a completely different technological base. Still, the whole point
of this study has been to emphasize the political and economic over the
merely technological. From time to time, maglev projects have been
floated in the United States, most recently in New Orleans, the Atlanta-
Chattanooga corridor, and the heavily traveled route between Baltimore
and Washington.[28] Yet it is obvious that in the absence of two all-important
prerequisites—a public funding commitment and a new set of taxes and
fees aimed at internalizing the full cost of existing transport—such projects will go nowhere. Even with gas approaching two dollars a gallon, it is
impossible to justify spending billions and billions to link urban centers
that are increasingly specialized and depopulated. The idea makes so little
sense on its face that any such project will likely backfire by making
maglev seem like a boondoggle while making the old downtowns seem
more inefficient than ever. Yet in fact, it is American society that is growing more and more inefficient. In the 1830s, Americans were among the
first out of the gate in the international race to develop rail. Yet so deeply
is the U.S. committed to auto transport some 170 years later that it is
already decades behind the Europeans and Japanese in terms of high-
speed rail and will undoubtedly be last out of the starting gate when more
advanced technology comes on-line.

Unclogging transportation is thus one of an increasingly long list of
things that America cannot do in its present condition, right up there
with cleaning up political corruption or reducing economic inequality.
Since the barriers are primarily political, the remedy must be political as
well. This does not mean signing petitions and lobbying Congress for
funds but a mobilization of comparable depth and seriousness to the
mobilization that accompanied the development of the Model T. Just as

America's propertied classes embraced Fordism as a way of remaking society in its own image, some other part of society must embrace some new form of technology as a way of remaking society along different lines.

Obviously, that new force cannot be the middle class, which by its nature is atomized and conservative. Rather, it must be the working class, the same people who have suffered the most from de-urbanization and technological stagnation and who therefore have the most to gain from political and economic change. The political mobilization of the working class in turn means its transformation. Organized labor, to the degree it can be said to speak for American workers, has rarely advanced beyond Samuel Gompers's famous philosophy of "more"—more money, more cars, more consumer goods. Whatever the benefits of such a strategy during the so-called golden age of capitalism between 1945 and 1973,[29] it has backfired royally in the decades since as growth rates have slowed, cities have deteriorated, and a voracious shopping-mall culture has left working-class families clinging to the rooftops amid a rising tide of junk. Even if labor were able to return to the glory days of the 1960s when the UAW wrung bigger and bigger wage hikes out of the Big Three automakers—which it cannot—it would not begin to make up for all that has been lost.

Instead, the working class must broaden its field of vision. Rather than merely more of the same, it must strive for qualitative change. This means workers who don't just vote and lobby and occasionally go on strike, but workers who think and act as a *class* and thus as a force for the transformation of the whole of society. The very idea of class is subversive in the United States. Prior to 1877, as the nineteenth-century journalist E. L. Godkin once noted in the *Nation*, the middle class was secure in the belief that America had "solved the problem of enabling capital and labor to live together in political harmony."[30] After the Great Rail Strike of 1877, Americans were no longer so sure, which is why U.S. social policy since the late nineteenth century has amounted to one long attempt to do away with the very idea of class by turning urban proletarians into docile property-owning Jeffersonians.

A revitalized working-class movement would mean a return to the idea of class, not on the grounds that class is *not* anti-American, but on the grounds that it *is*—at least insofar as America is presently constituted—and hence a force for its political transformation. As the Hungarian Marxist philosopher Georg Lukacs once noted, the essence of working-class political consciousness is its totalizing worldview.[31] Rather than striving for a New Deal for organized labor within the existing constitutional structure, it means recognizing that it is impossible to change part of society without changing the whole. Thus, it is impossible to have high-tech mass transit, revitalized cities, and an end to gridlock and sprawl while worshipping at the same old Jeffersonian shrines, just as it is impossible to put an end to America's debilitating "civil religion" without addressing the social problems it has caused.

. . . .

A reinvigorated workers' movement will have to come to grips with the U.S. Constitution, the basis not only of American politics and law but of American consciousness. The Constitution can be understood in many ways—as an attempt to subordinate politics to an unchangeable body of law, as an effort to limit the unlimited power of a sovereign people, and so forth. But it can also be understood as an effort to regulate change. The ill-fated Articles of Confederation, America's first constitution, sought to banish change by requiring that even the slightest constitutional modification be approved by all thirteen states, a requirement that everyone knew would be all but impossible to meet. The Articles fell apart in a few short years as a consequence, which is why, during the second go-around in 1787, the Framers were careful to include an amending clause that would at least admit the possibility of constitutional evolution.

They did so only grudgingly, however. While not barring change entirely, the new document put it on the defensive by requiring it to submit to the elaborate amending procedure set forth in Article V, in which even the smallest constitutional change would require approval by two-thirds of each house and three-fourths of the states. The goal was to regulate change in perpetuity by admitting it only in dribs and drabs. Indeed, once the Bill of Rights was adopted and the Eleventh and Twelfth Amendments ratified between 1792 and 1804, the constitutional door slammed shut once again. For the next sixty years, the new Constitution would prove no less resistant to change than the old Articles of Confederation, which is why the United States would once again disintegrate in 1860–61.

Contrary to the cult of the Founders as a race of giants towering over all succeeding generations, the Framers were actually a group of provincial politicians living both on the edge of the civilized world and on the verge of the modern era. Politically speaking, they were children of England's "Glorious Revolution" of 1688–89, a thinly veiled coup d'état in which King James II was forced to resign the throne and the dual monarchy of William and Mary was allowed to take power. What distinguished the Glorious Revolution from other revolutions was its horror of extremism, either the unbridled monarchism of James II or the radical republicanism of Oliver Cromwell some forty years earlier. The generation that rose to power in its wake was therefore obsessed with delicate balances, limited government, and iron-clad constitutional guarantees of the rights of the individual vis-à-vis the power of the majority, especially where private property was concerned. These were all mechanisms designed to keep society in place and prevent it from being tossed this way and that by new political storms. As a voluminous body of historical scholarship has shown, the Anglo-American school of thought that the Glorious Revolution gave rise to—known variously as the Old Whig, True Whig, or Country party—conceived of freedom not as something to be fashioned

anew but as something to be achieved by holding fast to ancient principles. Sturdy old ways were the best—old-fashioned country ways, old-
fashioned religious ways, the old-fashioned balance of power between
Parliament and the crown that pertained before Cromwell, James II, and
other hotheads upset the applecart.[32]

When it came time, consequently, for the Continental Congress to
issue its indictment of George III exactly four score and seven years after
the Glorious Revolution, it accused him of seeking to establish "an
absolute Tyranny over these States" by, among other things, "taking away
our Charters, abolishing our most valuable Laws, and altering fundamentally the Forms of our Government"—in other words, seeking to enslave
Americans by depriving them of their ancient representative institutions.
Freedom was thus something the Americans already possessed but which
others were now trying to snatch away. In 1842, one of the last survivors of
the Battle of Concord, a certain Captain Preston, denied in an interview
that the uprising had had anything to do with the tea tax, the stamp tax,
or any of the other outrages supposedly visited on Americans by the
crown. When pressed as to why he had taken up arms, Captain Preston
replied: "Young man, what we meant in going for those redcoats was this:
we always had governed ourselves, and we always meant to. They didn't
mean we should."[33]

No matter how brave or freedom-loving the embattled farmers of
Massachusetts may have been, their revolt in certain respects was thus a
conservative one. In its defense of ancient ways in which "we always had
governed ourselves," it was closer in spirit to the Glorious Revolution
than to the French Revolution a few years later, which, rather than defending existing institutions, strove for something completely new. It was a
product of the *ancien régime* rather than the modern era. Although the
Constitution of 1787 was not without its progressive elements, it, too,
was closer to the spirit of 1688. Rather than a vehicle for carrying the
American people forward, it offered itself as an anchor against the forces of

change. Since change according to a country squire like Jefferson meant decay, enervation, and a fall from grace, the duty of all freedom-loving patriots was to turn their backs on modern corruption and hold fast to sturdy old republican ways.

. . . .

More than two centuries later, America's ancient Constitution has never been more conservative or less democratic. Where four states representing as little as 10 percent of the population were sufficient to block a constitutional amendment in 1790, today, thanks to the growing disparity in state populations, thirteen states representing just 4.5 percent of the population are enough to do the same. Indeed, when the day ever comes to reorganize the increasingly unrepresentative U.S. Senate on the basis of one-person–one-vote, Americans will discover that the situation is even worse. Thanks to an obscure clause in Article V stipulating that "no State, without its consent, shall be deprived of its equal suffrage in the Senate," all fifty states must agree if there is to be any deviation from the principle of equal state representation whatsoever. The disparity between California (population: 33 million) and a lily-white "rotten borough" like Wyoming (population: 525,000) will continue to mount, yet Americans will be powerless to do anything about it as long as just one state representing as little as 0.5 percent of the population says no.

As averse to change as the United States was in the eighteenth century, it is even more so in the twenty-first. Individually, Americans have never been freer to speak their minds, to express themselves artistically or sexually, or to worship whatever strange gods they may wish. But, collectively, they have never been more limited in their ability to restructure society as they would like rather than as the Founders wished it to be. This is a contradiction that sooner or later will make itself felt. Ironically, America finds itself in the same boat as eighteenth-century Britain when, due to the notorious "rotten borough" system, virtual ghost towns continued to send members to the House of Commons while a burgeoning metropolis like Manchester or, for that matter, Boston and Philadelphia, did not. When at last that notoriously corrupt system was overthrown with the passage of the Reform Act in 1832, the door was opened for the first time to class politics. The result a few short years later was the Chartist Movement, Britain's first working-class political party. Presumably—hopefully—the struggle to overthrow America's system of rotten-borough politics will at last open the door to class politics in the United States.

If the lament for a lost urban way of life is, in the final analysis, a lament for a lost system of politics, then the only way to create a new urban way of life is to create a new system of politics. Or, rather, considering the hollowed-out nature of American society, it means the creation of a system of politics where today there is none.

Of course, who would have thought that the most lackluster presidential campaign in memory would have given way to the most riveting constitutional crisis since Franklin D. Roosevelt's showdown with the Supreme Court in 1937? Although it ended with a judicial coup d'etat that has saddled America with a couple of Texas oil men as president and vice president, it is nonetheless a sign that the constitutional ice is beginning to crack. As another radical once said in the midst of a similar deep freeze, "O Wind, if Winter comes, can Spring be far behind?"

NOTES

I N T R O D U C T I O N

1. Janet Maslin, "A Scorsese Devil Hunt," *New York Times,* 22 October 1999, sec. E, p. 1.

2. Fred Siegel and Joel Kotkin, "Urban Renaissance? Not Yet," *Wall Street Journal,* 6 November 1997, sec. A, p. 22.

3. Michael M. Phillips, "Welfare's Urban Poor Need a Lift—to Suburban Jobs," *Wall Street Journal,* 12 June 1997, sec. B, p. 1; Kim Phillips-Fein, "You're Either On the Bus. . . ," *Baffler* 10 (1997): 87–95.

4. "In a Once-Booming Downtown, Merchants Wonder Where the Customers Went," *New York Times,* 11 May 1997, p. 28.

5. Barbara Tuchman, *A Distant Mirror: The Calamitous Fourteenth Century* (New York: Ballantine Books, 1978), p. 238.

C H A P T E R 1

1. Nathaniel Macon, the antebellum Southern spokesman, quoted in Arthur M. Schlesinger Jr., *The Age of Jackson* (Boston: Little, Brown, 1945), p. 310.

2. David Hackett Fischer, *Albion's Seed: Four British Folkways in America* (Oxford: Oxford Univ. Press, 1989), p. 30.

3. Edmund S. Morgan, *The Puritan Family: Religion and Domestic Relations in Seventeenth-Century New England* (Westport, Conn.: Greenwood Press, 1980), p. 3.

4. Ibid., p. 181.

5. Henry Steele Commager, ed., *Documents of American History,* 8th ed. (New York: Appleton-Century-Crofts, 1968), 1:23.

6. Alden T. Vaughan, ed., *The Puritan Tradition in America, 1620–1730* (Columbia, S.C.: Univ. of South Carolina Press, 1972), pp. 195–8.

7. Darrett B. Rutman, *Winthrop's Boston: Portrait of a Puritan Town, 1630–1649* (Chapel Hill: Univ. of North Carolina Press, 1965), pp. 202–40.

8. Jane Holtz Kay, *Lost Boston* (Boston: Houghton Mifflin, 1980), pp. 25, 49.

9. Christopher Hill, *The Century of Revolution, 1603–1714* (New York: W. W. Norton, 1966), pp. 142, 167–8.

10. Joseph E. Illick, *Colonial Pennsylvania: A History* (New York: Scribner's, 1976), p. 30.

11. Witold Rybczynski, *City Life: Urban Expectations in a New World* (New York: Scribner's, 1995), pp. 73–4.

12. D. W. Meinig, *The Shaping of America: A Geographical Perspective on 500 Years of History* (New Haven: Yale Univ. Press, 1986), 1:154.

13. Fischer, *Albion's Seed*, p. 416.

14. James Truslow Adams, *Provincial Society 1690–1763* (New York: Macmillan, 1927), p. 205.

15. Fischer, *Albion's Seed*, p. 390.

16. Meinig, *Shaping of America*, 1:154–5.

17. Ibid., 1:148.

18. David R. Goldfield, "Pears on the Coast and Lights in the Forest: The Colonial South," in *The Making of Urban America*, ed. Raymond A. Mohl (Wilmington, Del.: Scholarly Resources, 1988), p. 14.

19. Meinig, *Shaping of America*, 1:156.

20. Willard Sterne Randall, *Thomas Jefferson: A Life* (New York: Henry Holt, 1993), p. 324.

21. Ibid., p. 141.

22. Paul Leicester Ford, *The Works of Thomas Jefferson* (New York: Putnam, 1904), 4:85.

23. Nathan Schachner, *Thomas Jefferson: A Biography* (New York: Appleton-Century-Crofts, 1951), 2:642.

24. Thomas Fleming, "Jefferson or Mussolini?" *Chronicles*, November 1998, p. 12.

25. Ford, *Works of Thomas Jefferson*, 2:64, 81.

26. Ibid., 11:346–7; 12:8–9.

27. Jefferson, *Notes on the State of Virginia*, in Ford, *Works of Thomas Jefferson*, 4:20.

28. Ford, *Works of Thomas Jefferson*, 11:265.

29. Ibid., 12:11.

30. Ibid., 12:251.

31. Ibid., 12:420.

32. Clinton Rossiter, ed., *The Federalist Papers* (New York: New American Library, 1961), p. 35.

33. Harold C. Syrett, ed., *The Papers of Alexander Hamilton*, 27 vols. (New York: Columbia Univ. Press, 1961–87) 10:270.

34. Ford, *Works of Thomas Jefferson*, 8:432.

35. Ibid., 11:348.

36. Ibid., 22:447–9.

37. Syrett, *The Papers of Alexander Hamilton*, 1:89–90.

38. Clinton Rossiter, *Alexander Hamilton and the Constitution* (New York: Harcourt Brace and World, 1964), p. 161.

39. R. R. Palmer, *The Age of Democratic Revolution: A Political History of Europe and America, 1760–1800,* 2 vols. (Princeton: Princeton Univ. Press, 1959–64), 2:26–7.

40. Joyce Appleby, *Liberalism and Republicanism in the Historical Imagination* (Cambridge, Mass.: Harvard Univ. Press, 1992), pp. 185–6.

41. Frances Trollope, *Domestic Manners of the Americans* (London: Penguin Classic, 1997), p. 172.

42. Stanley Lebergott, *The Americans: An Economic Record* (New York: W. W. Norton, 1984), pp. 108–10.

43. Meinig, *Shaping of America*, 2:268.

44. Barrington Moore Jr., *Social Origins of Dictatorship and Democracy: Lord and Peasant in the Making of the Modern World* (Boston: Beacon Press, 1966), p. 128.

CHAPTER 2

1. John Drayton, quoted in Kay, *Lost Boston*, p. 41.

2. Ibid., p. 42.

3. Lewis Mumford, *The City in History: Its Origins, Its Transformations, and Its Prospects* (New York: Harcourt, Brace and World, 1961), pp. 378–90.

4. Rutman, *Winthrop's Boston*, p. 159.

5. Carl Bridenbaugh, *Cities in the Wilderness: The First Century of Urban Life in America, 1625–1742* (New York: Knopf, 1960), p. 72; Rutman, *Winthrop's Boston*, pp. 188–90.

6. Rutman, *Winthrop's Boston*, pp. 200–1.

7. Carl Seaburg, *Boston Observed* (Boston: Beacon Press, 1971), p. 82.

8. Rutman, *Winthrop's Boston*, p. 10.

9. Larzer Ziff, *Puritanism in America: New Culture in a New World* (New York: Viking, 1973), pp. 83, 86–7; Fischer, *Albion's Seed*, pp. 28–30.

10. Kay, *Lost Boston*, p. 41.

11. Bridenbaugh, *Cities in the Wilderness*, p. 256.

12. Ibid., p. 292.

13. G. B. Warden, "Town Meeting Politics in Colonial and Revolutionary Boston," in *Boston 1700–1800: The Evolution of Urban Politics*, ed. Ronald P. Formisano and Constance K. Burns (Westport, Conn.: Greenwood Press, 1984), p. 22.

14. Gary B. Nash, *The Urban Crucible: Social Change, Political Consciousness, and the Crisis of the American Revolution* (Cambridge, Mass.: Harvard Univ. Press, 1979), p. vii.

15. Bridenbaugh, *Cities in the Wilderness*, pp. 43, 303, 308.

16. Henry Adams, *History of the United States During the Administrations of Thomas Jefferson* (New York: Library of America, 1986), p. 107.

17. Ibid., pp. 41, 48.

18. Daniel Feller, *The Jacksonian Promise: America, 1815–1840* (Baltimore: Johns Hopkins Univ. Press, 1995), p. 4.

19. Adna Ferris Weber, *The Growth of Cities in the Nineteenth Century* (Ithaca: Cornell Univ. Press, 1962), p. 24.

20. James M. McPherson, *The Battle Cry of Freedom: The Civil War Era* (New York: Oxford Univ. Press, 1988), p. 9.

21. Meinig, *Shaping of America*, 2:333.

22. Charles Sellers, *The Market Revolution: Jacksonian America, 1815–1846* (New York: Oxford Univ. Press, 1991), p. 394.

23. Schlesinger, *Age of Jackson*, p. 247.

24. Sellers, *Market Revolution*, p. 127; Michael Goldfield, *The Color of Politics: Race and the Mainsprings of American Politics* (New York: New Press, 1997), pp. 90–1.

25. Schlesinger, *Age of Jackson*, p. 424.

26. McPherson, *Battle Cry of Freedom*, p. 196.

27. Ibid., p. 197.

28. Ibid.

29. Ibid., p. 28.

30. Lebergott, *Americans*, p. 163.

31. Sellers, *Market Revolution*, p. 394.

32. Michael Mann, *The Sources of Social Power* vol. 1 (Cambridge: Cambridge Univ. Press, 1986), 136.

33. McPherson, *Battle Cry of Freedom*, p. 11.

34. Lebergott, *Americans*, pp. 108–10.

35. Arthur Charles Cole, *The Irrepressible Conflict, 1850–1865* (New York: Macmillan, 1934), p. 18.

36. Meinig, *Shaping of America*, 2:283.

37. Patrick O'Donnell, "Industrial Capitalism and the Rise of the Modern American Cities," *Kapitalistate* 6 (fall 1977): 109–10.

38. Meinig, *Shaping of America*, 2:159.

39. McPherson, *Battle Cry of Freedom*, pp. 19–20.

40. Ibid., pp. 202–33.

41. Moore, *Social Origins of Dictatorship and Democracy*, p. 150.

42. Louis M. Hacker, *The Triumph of Capitalism in America* (New York: Simon and Schuster, 1940), p. 352.

43. Sidney George Fisher, *The Trial of the Constitution* (New York: Negro Univ. Press, 1969), pp. 41, 62.

44. McPherson, *Battle Cry of Freedom*, p. 19.

45. Ibid., p. 95.

46. Allan Nevins, *The Emergence of Modern America, 1865–1878* (New York: Macmillan, 1927), p. 32.

47. The words are actually those of Julian's daughter summing up her father's views. Hacker, *Triumph of Capitalism in America*, p. 368.

CHAPTER 3

1. Weber, *Growth of Cities in the Nineteenth Century*, p. 24.

2. Sean Dennis Cashman, *America in the Age of the Titans: The Progressives and World War I* (New York: New York Univ. Press, 1988), p. 198; Robert L. Heilbroner and Aaron Singer, *The Economic Transformation of America: 1600 to the Present* (San Diego: Harcourt Brace Jovanovich, 1984), p. 225.

3. Bureau of the Census, *Historical Statistics of the United States, Colonial Times to 1970*, vol. 1 (Washington, D.C.: U.S. Govt. Printing Office, 1975), p. 106.

4. Melvyn Dubofsky, *Industrialism and the American Worker, 1865–1920*, 2nd ed. (Arlington Heights, Ill.: Harlan Davidson, 1985), pp. 10–11.

5. Brooks Adams, *The Law of Civilization and Decay* (New York: Macmillan, 1895), p. 324.

6. T. J. Jackson Lears, *No Place of Grace: Antimodernism and the Transformation of American Culture, 1880–1920* (New York: Pantheon, 1981), p. 133.

7. Roy Lubove, *The Progressives and the Slums: Tenement House Reform in New York City, 1890–1917* (Pittsburgh: Univ. of Pittsburgh Press, 1962), p. 54.

8. Josiah Strong, *Our Country: Its Possible Future and Its Present Crisis* (New York: American Home Missionary Society, 1885), pp. 143–4.

9. Heilbroner and Singer, *Economic Transformation of America,* p. 99.

10. Samuel P. Hays, *The Response to Industrialism 1885–1914* (Chicago: Univ. of Chicago Press, 1995), p. 11.

11. McPherson, *Battle Cry of Freedom,* p. 95.

12. Nevins, *Emergence of Modern America,* pp. 50–1; Heilbroner and Singer, *Economic Transformation of America,* p. 153.

13. Gilbert C. Fite and Jim E. Reese, *An Economic History of the United States* (Boston: Houghton Mifflin, 1973), p. 310.

14. H. Adams, *Education of Henry Adams,* p. 240.

15. Nevins, *Emergence of Modern America,* p. 69.

16. Allan Nevins, *Ford: The Times, the Man, the Company* (New York: Scribner's, 1954), p. 18.

17. Lebergott, *Americans,* p. 11.

18. Nevins, *Emergence of Modern America,* p. 400.

19. Gabriel Kolko, *The Triumph of Conservatism: A Reinterpretation of American History, 1900–1916* (New York: Free Press, 1963), pp. 26, 40–2, 140–1.

20. Clay McShane, *Down the Asphalt Path: The Automobile and the American City* (New York: Columbia Univ. Press, 1994), p. 120.

21. Glenn Yago, *The Decline of Transit: Urban Transportation in German and U.S. Cities, 1900–1970* (Cambridge: Cambridge Univ. Press, 1984), pp. 89–93.

22. Brooks Adams, *The Theory of Social Revolutions* (New York: Macmillan, 1913), p. 204.

23. H. Adams, *Education of Henry Adams,* p. 499.

24. E. J. Hobsbawm, *The Age of Revolution, 1789–1848* (New York: New American Library, 1962), p. 242.

25. Lubove, *Progressives and the Slums,* p. 53.

26. Dubofsky, *Industrialism and the American Worker,* p. 19.

27. Ibid., p. 21.

28. Cole, *Irrepressible Conflict,* pp. 362–3.

29. Ibid., p. 44.

30. Samuel Eliot Morison, *The Oxford History of the American People* (New York: New American Library, 1972), 3:81.

31. Robert M. Fogelson, *America's Armories: Architecture, Society, and Public Order* (Cambridge, Mass.: Harvard Univ. Press, 1989), pp. 20–1.

32. Dubofsky, *Industrialism and the American Worker*, p. 44.

33. Fogelson, *America's Armories*, p. 19.

34. Carl Smith, *Urban Disorder and the Shape of Belief: The Great Chicago Fire, the Haymarket Bomb, and the Model Town of Pullman* (Chicago: Univ. of Chicago, 1995), p. 107.

35. Michael Harrington, *Socialism* (New York: Saturday Review Press, 1972), p. 121.

36. H. W. Brands, *The Reckless Decade: America in the 1890s* (New York: St. Martin's, 1995), p. 147.

37. Smith, *Urban Disorder*, p. 198.

38. Ibid., p. 207.

39. Brands, *Reckless Decade*, p. 154.

40. "Women in the Strike," *Chicago Tribune*, 9 July 1894, p. 3.

41. "Day of Riot and Disorder," *New York Times*, 6 July 1894, p. 1.

42. Smith, *Urban Disorder*, p. 258.

43. Gen. Nelson A. Miles, "The Lesson of the Recent Strikes," *North American Review* 453 (August 1894): 181, 185, 188.

44. McAlister Coleman, *Eugene V. Debs: A Man Unafraid* (New York: Greenberg, 1930), p. 210 n.

45. Stanley Buder, *Pullman: An Experiment in Industrial Order and Community Planning, 1880–1930* (New York: Oxford Univ. Press, 1967), p. 182.

46. Smith, *Urban Disorder*, p. 260.

47. Gustave Le Bon, *The Crowd: A Study of the Popular Mind* (orig. "La Psychologie des Foules") (New York: Viking, 1960), p. 14; emphasis in the original.

48. Ibid., pp. 30, 32.

49. Ibid., pp. 18, 110, 121.

50. Arno J. Mayer, *The Persistence of the Old Regime: Europe to the Great War* (New York: Pantheon, 1981), p. 291.

51. Jaap van Ginneken, *Crowds, Psychology, and Politics, 1871–1899* (Cambridge: Cambridge Univ. Press, 1992), pp. 185–7.

52. Ibid., p. 17.

53. Mayer, *Persistence of the Old Regime*, p. 277.

54. Charles H. Cooley, "The Theory of Transportation," *Publications of the American Economic Association* 9 (1894): 92.

55. Weber, *Growth of Cities in the Nineteenth Century*, pp. 461–2.

56. Irving Howe, *World of Our Fathers* (New York: Harcourt Brace Jovanovich, 1976), pp. 149–50.

57. Strong, *Our Country*, p. 128.

58. Lewis F. Fried, *Makers of the City* (Amherst: Univ. of Massachusetts Press, 1990), pp. 31–2.

59. Hays, *The Response to Industrialism*, p. 138.

60. Jacob Riis, *How the Other Half Lives: Studies Among the Tenements of New York* (New York: Sagamore Press, 1957), p. 60; Riis, *The Battle With the Slum* (New York: Macmillan, 1902), p. 214.

61. Fried, *Makers of the City*, p. 20.

62. Riis, *How the Other Half Lives*, p. 207.

63. Ibid., p. 55.

64. Ibid., pp. 44–5.

65. Ibid., pp. 70–5.

66. Ibid., pp. 22, 43, 46.

67. Ibid., p. 204.

68. Ibid., p. 15.

69. Riis, *Battle With the Slum*, p. 216.

70. Fried, *Makers of the City*, pp. 59–60.

71. Ibid., pp. 60–1.

CHAPTER 4

1. Thomas Hine, *Populuxe* (New York: Knopf, 1986), pp. 3, 23.

2. Walter E. Weyl, *The New Democracy: An Essay on Certain Political and Economic Tendencies in the United States* (New York: Macmillan, 1913), p. 219.

3. See Richard Hofstadter, *The Paranoid Style in American Politics, and Other Essays* (New York: Knopf, 1965), Michael Kazin, *The Populist Persuasion: An American History* (New York: HarperCollins, 1995), and Lawrence Goodwyn, *Democratic Promise: The Populist Moment in America* (New York: Oxford Univ. Press, 1976).

4. Alexis de Tocqueville, *Democracy in America* (New York: Random House, 1990), 2:157.

5. Jefferson to Thomas Ritchie, 25 December 1820, in Ford, *Works of Thomas Jefferson*, 12:177.

6. Richard Hofstadter, "North America," in *Populism: Its Meaning and National Characteristics,* ed. Ghita Ionescu and Ernest Gellner (London: Weidenfeld and Nicolson, 1969), p. 13.

7. Leland D. Baldwin, *The Stream of American History* (New York: American Book Co., 1957), 2:28.

8. Goodwyn, *Democratic Promise,* pp. 264–5.

9. Hofstadter, "North America," p. 12.

10. Merrill D. Peterson, *The Jefferson Image in the American Mind* (New York: Oxford Univ. Press, 1962), p. 257.

11. Harold C. Syrett, ed., *American Historical Documents* (New York: Barnes and Noble, 1960), p. 305.

12. Walter T. K. Nugent, *The Tolerant Populists: Kansas Populism and the Nation* (Chicago: Univ. of Chicago Press, 1963), p. 115.

13. Bruce Palmer, "The Southern Populist Creed," in *Major Problems in the Gilded Age and the Progressive Era,* ed. Leon Fink (Lexington, Mass.: D. C. Heath, 1993), p. 198.

14. Ignatius Donnelly, *Caesar's Column: A Story of the Twentieth Century* (Cambridge, Mass.: Belknap Press, 1960), pp. 295–310.

15. Oscar Handlin, "American View of the Jew at the Opening of the Twentieth Century," in *Antisemitism in the United States,* ed. Leonard Dinnerstein (New York: Holt, Rinehart and Winston, 1971), p. 56.

16. Paolo E. Coletta, *William Jennings Bryan* (Lincoln: Univ. of Nebraska Press, 1964), 1:140.

17. Ibid., 1:139.

18. James Livingston, *Pragmatism and the Political Economy of Cultural Revolution, 1850–1940* (Chapel Hill: Univ. of North Carolina Press, 1994), p. 100.

19. Ibid.

20. Arthur Meier Schlesinger, *The Rise of the City, 1878–1898* (New York: Macmillan, 1933), pp. 357–8.

21. Paul Boyer, *Urban Masses and Moral Order in America, 1820–1920* (Cambridge, Mass.: Harvard Univ. Press, 1978), pp. 205–15.

22. Ibid., p. 208.

23. Jon M. Kingsdale, "The 'Poor Man's Club': Special Functions of the Urban Working-Class Saloon," in Mohl, *Making of Urban America,* pp. 120–33.

24. Strong, *Our Country,* pp. 84–5.

25. Richard Jensen, *The Winning of the Midwest: Social and Political Conflict, 1888–1896* (Chicago: Univ. of Chicago Press, 1971), p. 183.

26. Henry Adams, *History of the United States During the Administrations of James Madison* (New York: Library of America, 1986), p. 377.

27. Boyer, *Urban Masses,* p. 262.

28. Herbert Croly, *The Promise of American Life* (New York: Macmillan, 1909), p. 145.

29. Harold Underwood Faulkner, *The Quest for Social Justice 1898–1914,* (New York: Macmillan, 1931), p. 88.

30. George E. Mowry, *The California Progressives* (Berkeley: Univ. of California Press, 1951), p. 88.

31. Ibid., pp. 50–1.

32. Ibid., pp. 51–154.

33. Peter Schrag, *Paradise Lost: California's Experience, America's Future* (New York: New Press, 1998), p. 191–2.

34. Robert B. Westbrook, "Politics as Consumption," in *The Culture of Consumption: Critical Essays in American History, 1880–1980,* ed. Richard Wightman Fox and T. J. Jackson Lears (New York: Pantheon, 1983), p. 154.

35. Faulkner, *Quest for Social Justice,* pp. 157–8.

36. Lubove, *Progressives and the Slums,* pp. 91–2.

37. Ibid., pp. 131–2.

38. Christine Holbo, "Eugenic America: Hygiene, Habitation and Americanization, 1880–1920," *Stanford Humanities Review* 5 (1996), p. 66.

39. Ibid., p. 180.

40. Boyer, *Urban Masses,* p. 269.

41. Benjamin C. Marsh, *Lobbyist for the People: A Record of Fifty Years* (Washington, D.C.: Public Affairs Press, 1953), pp. 11, 31.

42. Lubove, *Progressives and the Slums,* pp. 233–4.

43. John Nolen, *Twenty Years of City Planning Progress in the United States* (National Conference on City Planning, 1927), p. 12.

44. Mark S. Foster, *From Streetcar to Superhighway: American City Planners and Urban Transportation, 1900–1940* (Philadelphia: Temple Univ. Press, 1981), p. 143.

45. Gordon Whitnall, "History of Zoning," *The Annals of the American Academy of Political and Social Science* 155, no. 2 (May 1931): 8.

46. Seymour I. Toll, *Zoned America* (New York: Grossman, 1969), p. 115.

47. Ibid., p. 151.

48. Ibid., pp. 158–9.

49. Ibid., p. 173.

50. M. Christine Boyer, *Dreaming the Rational City: The Myth of American City Planning* (Cambridge, Mass.: MIT Press, 1983), p. 95.

51. Ibid., p. 164.

52. W. L. Pollard, "Outline of the Law of Zoning in the United States," *The Annals of the American Academy of Political and Social Science* 155, no. 2 (May 1931), pp. 15–6; Toll, *Zoned America,* p. 262; Boyer, *Dreaming the Rational City,* p. 167.

53. Boyer, *Dreaming the Rational City*, p. 167.

54. David Nasaw, *Children of the City: At Work and At Play* (Garden City, N.Y.: Anchor/Doubleday, 1985), pp. 139–40.

55. Howe, *World of Our Fathers*, p. 256.

56. Nasaw, *Children of the City*, pp. 147–9.

57. Jane Addams, *The Spirit of Youth and the City Streets* (New York: Macmillan, 1910), pp. 87–8, 92–3.

58. Boyer, *Urban Masses*, pp. 243–4.

59. Nasaw, *Children of the City*, p. 36.

60. Ibid., pp. 167–83.

61. Boyer, *Urban Masses*, p. 192.

62. Faulkner, *Quest for Social Justice*, p. 93.

63. Michael Gold, *Jews Without Money* (New York: Carroll and Graf, 1930), p. 15.

64. Faulkner, *Quest for Social Justice*, p. 160.

65. Boyer, *Urban Masses*, p. 194.

66. Mann, *Sources of Social Power*, 2:481.

67. Boyer, *Urban Masses*, p. 235.

68. Ibid., p. 209.

69. Faulkner, *Quest for Social Justice*, p. 160.

70. Ibid., p. 206.

71. Ibid., pp. 207–17.

72. Mayer, *Persistence of the Old Regime*, p. 300.

73. Walter Lippmann, *A Preface to Politics* (New York: Mitchell Kennerley, 1914), p. 63.

74. Christopher Hill, *The English Bible and the Seventeenth-Century Revolution* (London: Penguin Books, 1994), p. 21.

75. Lippmann, *Preface to Politics*, p. 127.

76. Ibid., pp. 127–8.

CHAPTER 5

1. Cooley, "Theory of Transportation," p. 296.

2. A. F. Weber, *Growth of Cities in the Nineteenth Century*, p. 228.

3. London ended *The Iron Heel*, his 1907 tale of the American fascism that might have been, with a vision of urban upheaval not unlike Ignatius Donnelly's in

Caesar's Column. In *The Time Machine* (1895), H. G. Wells speculates that workers and the middle class would grow so far apart that they would evolve into different species. Anatole France ended his wonderful 1908 satire, *Penguin Island,* with a vision of modern Paris torn apart by civil war.

4. "Mr. Ford's Page," *Dearborn (Michigan) Independent,* 7 June 1924, p. 7.

5. Peter Collier and David Horowitz, *The Fords: An American Epic* (New York: Summit Books, 1987), p. 70.

6. Booth Tarkington, *The Magnificent Ambersons* (New York: Scribner's, 1921), p. 275.

7. Ibid., p. 11.

8. Ibid., p. 259.

9. Ibid., p. 260.

10. Ibid., p. 394.

11. Ibid., pp. 391–2.

12. Ibid., p. 261.

13. Heilbroner and Singer, *Economic Transformation of America,* pp. 261–2.

14. McShane, *Down the Asphalt Path,* p. 175.

15. Ibid., pp. 176, 189.

16. Ibid., pp. 215–6.

17. Ibid., pp. 216–8.

18. *Municipal Journal and Engineer* 23 (20 November 1907), p. 577; quoted in McShane, *Down the Asphalt Path,* p. 217.

19. McShane, *Down the Asphalt Path,* pp. 193–7.

20. Ibid., p. 199.

21. Joseph Interrante, "The Road to Autopia," in *The Automobile and American Culture,* ed. David L. Lewis and Laurence Goldstein (Ann Arbor: Univ. of Michigan Press, 1983), p. 95.

22. New York City Department of Transportation, *Spanning the Twenty-first Century: Reconstructing a World Class Bridge Program,* 1988, p. 15.

23. Elliot G. Sander, New York City Commissioner of Transportation, "New York City Case Study: A Transit-Dependent Core of an Auto-Oriented Region," 23 November 1995, p. 19.

24. Paul Barrett, *The Automobile and Urban Mass Transit: The Formation of Public Policy in Chicago, 1900–1930* (Philadelphia: Temple Univ. Press, 1983), p. 57.

25. James J. Flink, *The Car Culture* (Cambridge: MIT Press, 1975), p. 40.

26. Cashman, *America in the Age of the Titans,* p. 282.

27. Ibid., pp. 50–2.

28. Collier and Horowitz, *The Fords,* pp. 152–5.

29. Ibid., p. 161.

30. Henry Ford, *My Life and Work* (Garden City, N.Y.: Doubleday, Page, 1926), p. 103.

31. Robert Lacey, *Ford, the Man and the Machine* (Boston: Little, Brown, 1986), p. 143.

32. "Flashes of Fact Across America," *Dearborn (Michigan) Independent,* 8 November 1919, p. 6.

33. "Germany's Reaction Against the Jew," *Dearborn (Michigan) Independent,* 29 May 1920, p. 2.

34. "Jewish Power and America's Money Famine," *Dearborn (Michigan) Independent,* 16 July 1921, p. 8.

35. " 'Jew York' Always Gets Money," *Dearborn (Michigan) Independent,* 16 July 1921, p. 9.

36. Hugh C. Mitchell, "The City Beautiful—A Modern Development," *Dearborn (Michigan) Independent,* 13 September 1924, p. 9.

37. Ibid.

38. "Mr. Ford's Page," *Dearborn (Michigan) Independent,* 1 May 1920, p. 5.

39. Ibid., 21 May 1921, p. 5.

40. Ibid., 16 September 1922, p. 5.

41. Ibid., 4 February 1922, p. 5.

42. H. Ford, *My Life and Work,* pp. 248–9.

43. Ibid., p. 253.

44. "Mr. Ford's Page," *Dearborn (Michigan) Independent,* 21 May and 25 June 1921, p. 5.

45. Lacey, *Ford, the Man and the Machine,* p. 228.

46. Frederick Engels, *The Condition of the Working-Class in England,* in *Collected Works,* Karl Marx and Frederick Engels (London: Lawrence and Wishart, 1975), 4:418.

47. David Brody, *Workers in Industrial America: Essays on the Twentieth Century Struggle* (New York: Oxford Univ. Press, 1980), p 11.

48. Ibid., p. 13.

49. Kenneth T. Jackson, *Crabgrass Frontier: The Suburbanization of the United States* (New York: Oxford Univ. Press, 1985), p. 231.

CHAPTER 6

1. Jackson, *Crabgrass Frontier,* pp. 274–5.

2. Kenneth T. Jackson, "Gentlemen's Agreement: Discrimination in Metropolitan America," in *Reflections on Regionalism,* ed. Bruce Katz (Washington, D.C.: Brookings Institution Press, 2000), pp. 185–217.

3. Richard Averill Walker, "The Suburban Solution: Urban Geography and Urban Reform in the Capitalist Development of the United States" (Ph.D. thesis, Baltimore: Johns Hopkins Univ., 1977), p. 477.

4. Martha L. Olney, *Buy Now, Pay Later: Advertising, Credit, and Consumer Durables in the 1920s* (Chapel Hill: Univ. of North Carolina Press, 1991), p. 47.

5. Robert W. Westbrook, "Politics as Consumption," in *Culture of Consumption*, ed. Fox and Lears, p. 147; *Dubious Democracy 1998* (Takoma Park, Md.: Center for Voting and Democracy, 1999).

6. Bureau of the Census, *Historical Statistics of the United States,* 1:646; Boyer, *Dreaming the Rational City,* p. 106.

7. Weyl, *New Democracy,* p. 220.

8. Herbert Hoover, *American Individualism* (Garden City, N.Y.: Doubleday, Page, 1922), p. 24.

9. Ellis W. Hawley, untitled essay in *Herbert Hoover and the Crisis of American Capitalism,* J. Joseph Huthmacher and Warren I. Susman (Cambridge, Mass.: Schenkman Publishing, 1973), p. 10.

10. Yago, *Decline of Transit,* p. 11.

11. Foster, *From Streetcar to Superhighway,* p. 55.

12. Rosalyn Baxandall and Elizabeth Ewen, *Picture Windows: How the Suburbs Happened* (New York: Basic Books, 2000), p. 39.

13. Gail Radford, *Modern Housing for America: Policy Struggles in the New Deal Era* (Chicago: Univ. of Chicago Press, 1996), pp. 14, 22.

14. Joseph Arnold, quoted in Walker, "Suburban Solution," p. 466.

15. Ronald Tobey, Charles Wetherell, and Jay Brigham, "Moving Out and Settling In," *American Historical Review* 95 (December 1990), p. 1414.

16. Lewis Mumford, *The Highway and the City* (New York: Harcourt Brace, 1963), p. 246.

17. Referring to the preindustrial weavers of the eighteenth century, Engels wrote: "They could rarely read and far more rarely write; went regularly to church, never talked politics, never conspired, never thought, delighted in physical exercise, listened with inherited reverence when the Bible was read, and were, in their unquestioning humility, exceedingly well-disposed toward the 'superior' classes. But intellectually, they were dead." Marx and Engels, *Collected Works,* 4:309.

18. Lewis Mumford, *The Culture of Cities* (New York: Harcourt Brace, 1938), p. 266.

19. Ibid., p. 249.

20. Ibid., p. 255.

21. Ibid., pp. 239–77.

22. Mumford, *Highway and the City,* pp. 238, 243, 246, 245.

23. Mumford, "The Intolerable City: Must It Keep Growing?" *Harper's,* February 1926, p. 292.

24. Mumford, *Highway and the City*, p. 242.

25. Doug Saunders, "Citizen Jane," *The Globe and Mail*, 11 October 1997, sec. C, p. 1.

26. Jane Jacobs, *The Death and Life of Great American Cities* (New York: Random House, 1961), p. 55.

27. Ibid., p. 153.

28. Ibid., p. 376.

29. Ibid., p. 374.

30. Ibid., pp. 18–9.

31. Ibid., p. 40.

32. Ibid., pp. 99–100.

33. Ibid., p. 158.

34. Ibid., pp. 205–6.

35. Lewis Mumford, "The Skyline: Mother Jacobs' Home Remedies," *New Yorker*, 1 December 1962, p. 168.

36. Donald L. Miller, *Lewis Mumford: A Life* (New York: Weidenfeld and Nicolson, 1989), p. 496.

37. Jacobs, *Death and Life*, p. 21.

38. Ibid., p. 171.

39. Walker, "Suburban Solution," p. 510.

40. Ibid., p. 566.

41. Foster, *From Streetcar to Superhighway*, p. 166; Walker, "Suburban Solution," p. 596.

42. Jackson, *Crabgrass Frontier*, pp. 190, 195.

43. Dixon Wecter, *The Age of the Great Depression, 1929–1941* (New York: Macmillan, 1948), pp. 226–7.

44. Daniel R. Fusfeld, *The Economic Thought of Franklin D. Roosevelt and the Origins of the New Deal* (New York: Columbia Univ. Press, 1956), p. 84; Joseph L. Arnold, *The New Deal in the Suburbs: A History of the Greenbelt Town Program, 1935–1954* (Columbus: Ohio State Univ. Press, 1971), p. 27; Reynold M. Wik, *Henry Ford and Grass-Roots America* (Ann Arbor: Univ. of Michigan Press, 1972), pp. 192–5.

45. Peterson, *Jefferson Image in the American Mind*, p. 352.

46. Fusfeld, *Economic Thought of Franklin D. Roosevelt*, p. 86.

47. Peterson, *Jefferson Image in the American Mind*, p. 332.

48. Ibid., p. 355.

49. Ibid., p. 361.

50. Ibid., p. 363.

51. Radford, *Modern Housing for America,* p. 88.

52. Jackson, *Crabgrass Frontier,* pp. 195–6.

53. Ibid., pp. 205–6.

54. Tobey, Wetherell, and Brigham, "Moving Out and Settling In," p. 1,414.

55. Jackson, *Crabgrass Frontier,* pp. 194, 197–218.

CHAPTER 7

1. Lacey, *Ford, the Man and the Machine,* pp. 386–7.

2. Adolf Hitler, *Mein Kampf* (Boston: Houghton Mifflin, 1971), p. 27.

3. Yago, *Decline of Transit,* p. 112.

4. Hitler, *Mein Kampf,* p. 138.

5. Ibid., p. 36.

6. Yago, *Decline of Transit,* pp. 33–42; Walter Henry Nelson, *Small Wonder: The Amazing Story of the Volkswagen* (Boston: Little, Brown, 1965), p. 29.

7. R. J. Overy, "Cars, Roads, and Economic Recovery in Germany, 1932–8," *Economic History Review* 28, no. 3 (August 1975): 469; R. J. Overy, *The Nazi Economic Recovery 1932–1938,* 2nd ed. (Cambridge: Cambridge Univ. Press, 1996), pp. 46–7.

8. Henry Ford, *365 of Henry Ford's Sayings* (Grymes Hill, N.Y.: P. M. Martin, 1923), p. 13.

9. Arnold R. Silverman, "Defense and Deconcentration," in *Suburbia Re-examined,* Barbara M. Kelly (New York: Greenwood Press, 1989), pp. 158–9.

10. Graham Romeyn Taylor, *Satellite Cities: A Study of Industrial Suburbs* (New York: D. Appleton, 1915), p. 23.

11. Bureau of the Census, *Historical Statistics of the United States,* 1:300.

12. Kevin Phillips, *Boiling Point: Republicans, Democrats, and the Decline of Middle-Class Prosperity* (New York: Random House, 1993), p. 15.

13. Fox and Lears, eds., *Culture of Consumption,* p. ix.

14. Alan Thein Durning, *How Much Is Enough: The Consumer Society and the Future of the Earth* (New York: Norton, 1992, pp. 21–2; quoted in Richard Smith, "Creative Destruction," *New Left Review* 222 (March/April 1997), p. 14. Originally quoted in Vance Packard, *The Waste Makers* (New York: D. McKay, 1960).

15. Fox and Lears, *Culture of Consumption,* p. x.

16. Jackson, *Crabgrass Frontier,* p. 249.

17. Hine, *Populuxe,* p. 3.

18. David Gross, "Space, Time, and Modern Culture," *Telos* 50 (winter 1981–2), p. 73.

19. Ibid., p. 71.

20. The Slits, quoted in *Wall Street: How it Works and for Whom*, Doug Henwood (London: Verso, 1997), pp. 228, 244.

21. Steven A. Holmes, "Leaving the Suburbs for Rural Areas," *New York Times*, 19 October 1997, p. 34.

22. James T. Patterson, *Grand Expectations: The United States, 1945–1974* (New York: Oxford Univ. Press, 1996), p. 345.

23. John Kenneth Galbraith, *The Affluent Society* (Boston: Houghton Mifflin, 1984), p. xxiv.

24. Ibid. (1958), pp. 253, 257.

25. Department of Commerce, *Highway Statistics 1958* (Washington, D.C., 1960), p. 25; American Automobile Manufacturers Association, *Motor Vehicle Facts and Figures 1997* (Detroit, 1997), p. 64.

26. A. C. Pigou, *The Economics of Welfare* (London: Macmillan, 1924), p. 33.

27. A. C. Pigou, *Socialism versus Capitalism* (London: Macmillan, 1964).

28. *Report of the National Advisory Commission on Civil Disorders* (Washington, D.C.: U.S. Govt. Printing Office, 1968), pp. 218–9, 224–5.

29. Lebergott, *Americans*, p. 359.

30. Charles Murray, *Losing Ground: American Social Policy, 1950–1980* (New York: Basic Books, 1984), p. 186.

31. George H. Hildebrand, quoted in Kelly, *Suburbia Re-Examined*, p. xii.

32. Stephen E. Ambrose, *Eisenhower* (New York: Simon and Schuster, 1984), 2:543.

33. Ibid., pp. 547–8.

34. Jurgen Habermas, *Legitimation Crisis* (Boston: Beacon Press, 1975), p. 39.

35. Louis Menand, "Inside the Billway," *New York Review of Books*, 14 August 1997, p. 4.

36. Schrag, *Paradise Lost*, p. 8.

37. Ibid., pp. 113, 116.

38. Robert Kuttner, *Revolt of the Haves: Tax Rebellions and Hard Times* (New York: Simon and Schuster, 1980), pp. 48–9.

39. Schrag, *Paradise Lost*, pp. 162–3.

40. Isaac Kramnick, *Republicanism and Bourgeois Radicalism: Political Ideology in Late Eighteenth-Century England and America* (Ithaca, N.Y.: Cornell Univ. Press, 1990), p. 263.

41. Walter Lippmann, *Public Opinion* (New York: Macmillan, 1961), pp. 269–70.

CHAPTER 8

1. Karen Tumulty and Eleanor Clift, "U.S. Losing Ability to Explore for Oil," *Los Angeles Times,* 5 April 1986, p. 1.

2. Editorial, "Gas Prices, Gas Politics," *New York Times,* 6 May 1996, sec. A, p. 18.

3. For a sophisticated free-market discussion of the economic role of information, see Friedrich A. von Hayek, "The Use of Knowledge in Society," in *The Essential Hayek,* ed. Chiaka Nishiyama and Kurt R. Leube (Stanford: Hoover Institution Press, 1984), pp. 211–24.

4. Bureau of the Census, *Historical Statistics of the United States,* 2:716; U.S. Environmental Information Agency, *Annual Energy Review,* table 2.8 available @ www.eia.doe.gov/aer; Matthew L. Wald, "Number of Cars Is Growing Faster Than Human Population," *New York Times,* 21 September 1997, p. 35.

5. American Automobile Manufacturers Association, *Motor Vehicle Facts and Figures 1997* (Washington, D.C.), p. 64.

6. Bureau of the Census, *Statistical Abstract of the United States: 1998,* 118th ed., (Washington, D.C., 1998), p. 642; *Statistical Abstract of the United States: 1975,* 96th ed., p. 564.

7. Texas Department of Transportation, *Urban Roadway Congestion–1982 to 1994,* (Austin, 1997), pp. 12, 19, 23, 32.

8. Anthony R. Ameruso, Commissioner, New York City Department of Transportation, "Memorandum: Traffic Improvements and Strategies," (22 March 1982), p. 1; James Rutenberg, "Gridlock Grinds Traffic to a Halt," *(New York) Daily News,* 22 June 1998, pp. 2–3.

9. Paul Mulshine, "If California's too crowded, then how about New Jersey?" *(Newark) Star-Ledger,* 18 April 1999, sec. 10, p. 3.

10. Greg Jaffe, "Is Traffic-Clogged Atlanta the New Los Angeles?" *Wall Street Journal,* 18 June 1998, sec. B, p. 1; Texas Department of Transportation, *Urban Roadway Congestion,* p. 12.

11. Ali H. Mokdad, et al., "The Spread of the Obesity Epidemic in the United States, 1991–1998," *Journal of the American Medical Association,* 27 October 1999, p. 1522.

12. Steven Mark Cohn, *Too Cheap to Meter: An Economic and Philosophical Analysis of the Nuclear Dream* (Albany, N.Y.: SUNY Press, 1997), p. 19.

13. Charles Komanoff, "Doing Without Nuclear Power," *New York Review of Books,* 17 May 1979, p. 15.

14. Telephone interview with author, 6 May 1999.

15. Jackie Calmes and Christopher Georges, "Economists Say Gasoline Tax Is Too Low," *Wall Street Journal,* 7 May 1996, sec. A, p. 2.

16. Federal Highway Administration, *1996 Highway Statistics,* table MF-21 (updated periodically), available @ www.fedstats.gov.

17. James MacKenzie, Roger Dower, and Donald Chen, "The Going Rate: What It Really Costs To Drive," World Resources Institute, Washington, D.C., 1992; John Moffett, "The Price of Mobility," Natural Resources Defense Council, San Francisco, 1991; and Brian Ketcham and Charles Komanoff, "Win-Win Transportation," Komanoff Energy Associates, New York, 1992. In addition, Todd Litman, "Transportation Cost Survey," 113 Decatur, Olympia, Washington, 1992, put the total cost at $513 billion, while Michael Voorhees, "The True Costs of the Automobile to Society," 3131 Bell Dr., Boulder, Colorado, 1992, arrived at a bottom-line figure of $631 billion. For a comparative analysis, see John Holtzclaw, "America's Autos on Welfare: A Summary of Studies," *Transportopia Bulletin,* winter 1993, p. 11. Between 1992 and early 2000, the consumer price index rose a total of 21 percent, while highway fuel consumption rose about 16 percent.

18. National Highway Traffic Safety Administration, "The Economic Cost of Motor Vehicle Crashes, 1994" (Washington, D.C., 1996), p. 2.

19. Lawrence J. Korb, "Holding the Bag In the Gulf," *New York Times,* 18 September 1996, sec. A, p. 21.

20. Texas Department of Transportation, *Urban Roadway Congestion,* p. 19.

21. Mark A. Delucchi, "Total Cost of Motor-Vehicle Use," *Access* 8 (spring 1996), p. 12.

22. Andrea Ricci and Sigurd Weinreich, "QUITS—Quality Indicators of Transport Systems," in *Social Costs and Sustainable Mobility: Strategies and Experience in Europe and the United States,* ed. K. Rennings, O. Hohmeyer, and R. L. Ottinger (Mannheim, Germany: Center for European Economic Research, 2000), pp. 23–53.

23. Keith Bradsher, "Auto Makers Seeking to Avoid Fines Over Mileage Rules," *New York Times,* 2 April 1998, sec. A, p. 18; Agis Salpukas, "What's Next, Tail Fins?" *New York Times,* 15 February 1996, sec. D, p. 1; Keith Bradsher, "Light Trucks Have Passed Cars on the Retail Sales Road," *New York Times,* 4 December 1997, sec. D, p. 4; Anne Wilde Mathews, "More Trucks Shake Residential America," *Wall Street Journal,* 29 April 1997, sec. B, p. 1.

24. Stephen Willliams, "The Grit and the Glory: Help From the Home Doctor," *New York Times,* 25 September 1997, sec. F, p. 16.

25. "Making the Connection," 1000 Friends of Oregon (Portland, Oregon, 1997), p. 9.

26. Neal Templin, "The Bicycle Loses Ground as a Symbol of Childhood Liberty," *Wall Street Journal,* 10 September 1996, sec. A, p. 1.

27. Davies, *Age of Asphalt,* p. 4.

28. Pigou, *Economics of Welfare,* p. 33.

29. Michel Foucault, *Discipline and Punish: The Birth of the Prison* (New York: Random House, 1979), p. 195.

30. Howard, *Hidden Welfare State,* pp. 21–6.

31. G. Pascal Zachary, "Mortgage Deduction Comes Under Fire," *Wall Street Journal*, 15 August 1995, sec. A, p. 2.

32. National Low Income Housing Coalition, Washington, D.C. Data are for fiscal year 1991.

33. Peter Dreier and John Atlas, "Deductio Ad Absurdum," *Washington (D.C.) Monthly*, February 1990, p. 19.

34. Robert B. Reich, *The Work of Nations: Preparing Ourselves for Twenty-first Century Capitalism* (New York: Random House, 1992), p. 252.

35. Jeffrey Rosen, "The Lost Promise of School Integration," *New York Times*, 2 April 2000, sec. 4, p. 1.

36. G. Pascal Zachary, "Mortgage Deduction Comes Under Fire," *Wall Street Journal*, 15 August 1995, sec. A, p. 2.

37. Brian J. O'Connell, "The Federal Role in the Suburban Boom," in Kelly, *Suburbia Re-Examined*, p. 189.

38. O'Connell, "Federal Role in the Suburban Boom," p. 188.

39. John P. J. Madden, "Energy," in *The Suburban Economic Network: Economic Activity, Resource Use, and the Great Sprawl*, ed. John E. Ullmann (New York: Praeger, 1977), p. 87.

40. Lebergott, *Americans*, p. 498.

41. William Wolman and Anne Colamosca, *The Judas Economy: The Triumph of Capital and the Betrayal of Work* (Reading, Mass.: Addison-Wesley, 1997), pp. 170–1.

42. Doug Henwood, "Producing Poverty," *Left Business Observer* 89 (27 April 1999), p. 5. Income classes were defined relative to the national median after taxes and government transfer payments.

43. Aaron Bernstein, "Is America Becoming More of a Class Society?" *Business Week*, 26 February 1996, p. 90.

44. British Poor Law Commission of 1834, quoted in Charles Murray, *Losing Ground*, p. 16.

45. "Consumers Kept Spending In December," *New York Times*, 1 February 2000, sec. C, p. 2.

46. Juliet B. Schor, *The Overworked American: The Unexpected Decline of Leisure* (New York: Basic Books, 1991), p. 35.

47. American Automobile Manufacturers Association, *Motor Vehicle Facts and Figures 1997*, p. 65.

48. Brian Ketcham, "Price It Right! End Roadway Entitlements," presented at "Long Island, A New Vision: A Conference on the Economy, Jobs, and the Environment," Hofstra University, 4 December 1992, p. 10.

49. Quoted in John E. Ullmann, "Problems, Prospects, and Obstacles," in *Suburban Economic Network*, ed. Ullmann, pp. 231–2.

50. David M. Herszenhorn, "Now It's 'Nothing in My Backyard,'" *New York Times,* 16 April 2000, p. 35.

51. N. R. Kleinfield, "Born to Drive," *New York Times,* 25 September 1997, sec. B, p. 1.

52. Robert H. Frank, "The Victimless Income Gap?" *New York Times,* 12 April 1999, sec. A, p. 25.

CHAPTER 9

1. Kristin Ross, *Fast Cars, Clean Bodies: Decolonization and the Reordering of French Culture* (Cambridge, Mass.: MIT Press, 1995), p. 51.

2. Ibid., p. 50.

3. Quoted in Serge Guilbaut, *How New York Stole the Idea of Modern Art: Abstract Expressionism, Freedom, and the Cold War* (Chicago: Univ. of Chicago Press, 1983), p. 101.

4. David E. Cole and Sean P. McAlinden, "We Can't Fight Japan," *New York Newsday,* 2 February 1992, p. 28.

5. Statistisches Landesamt Hamburg, "Bevölkerungsentwicklung Hamburgs in den letzten 125 Jahren" (Hamburg, 1991).

6. Roland-Pierre Paringaux, "Crushed by the juggernaut invasion," (*London*) *Guardian Weekly,* 28 October–3 November 1999, p. 30; reprinted from *Le Monde,* 14 October 1999.

7. Keith Bradsher, "In the Biggest, Booming Cities, A Car Population Problem," *New York Times,* 11 May 1997, sec. 4, p. 4; "The Car Trap," *World Press Review,* December 1996, p. 6; "Around the Globe, Big Worries and Small Signs of Progress," *New York Times,* 1 December 1997, sec. F, p. 9.

8. Thomas Angotti, "The Latin American Metropolis and the Growth of Inequality," *NACLA Report on the Americas* 28, no. 4 (January–February 1995), p. 13.

9. Walter Hook and Matteo Martignoni, "The Cycle Rickshaw can save the Taj Mahal; the Taj Mahal can save the Cycle Rickshaw," *Sustainable Transport* 7 (winter 1997), pp. 8–9.

10. Walter Hook, "Will China Forsake the Bicycle?" *World Press Review,* December 1996, p. 7; Smith, "Creative Destruction," p. 33.

11. Elisabeth Rosenthal, "Tide of Traffic Turns Against the Sea of Bicycles," *New York Times,* 3 November 1998, sec. A, p. 4.

12. Samjin Lee, "Fighting for the 'Seoul' of Transport in Korea," *Sustainable Transport* 7, p. 10.

13. Angotti, "Latin American Metropolis," p. 17.

14. Eduardo Galeano, "Autocracy: An Invisible Dictatorship," *NACLA Report on the Americas* 28, no. 4, p. 27.

15. American Automobile Manufacturers Association, *Motor Vehicle Facts and Figures 1997*, pp. 45–7.

16. Nicholas D. Kristof, "Across Asia, a Pollution Disaster Hovers," *New York Times*, 28 November 1997, sec. A, p. 1; Christopher J. L. Murray and Alan D. Lopez, *The Global Burden of Disease* (Cambridge, Mass.: Harvard Univ. Press, 1996), 1:362.

17. American Automobile Manufacturers Association, *Motor Vehicle Facts and Figures 1997*, p. 86.

18. Murray and Lopez, *Global Burden of Disease*, 1:624–7, 628–31, 636–9, 648–51, 768–71, 772–5, 780–3, 792–5.

19. Paul Bairoch, *Cities and Economic Development: From the Dawn of History to the Present* (Chicago: Univ. of Chicago Press, 1988), p. 517.

20. Paul Krugman, "The Myth of Asia's Miracle," *Foreign Affairs*, November 1994, pp. 70–1.

21. Richard Smith, *New Left Review* 222, p. 16.

22. Stephen J. DeCanio, *The Economics of Climate Change* (San Francisco: Redefining Progress, 1997), p. 4.

23. Ross Gelbspan, "A Global Warning," *The American Prospect*, March–April 1997, p. 37.

24. DeCanio, *Economics of Climate Change*, pp. 7–8.

25. "Excerpts from Report on Warming's Impact," *New York Times*, 1 December 1997, sec. F, p. 4.

26. Smith, "Creative Destruction," pp. 16–7.

27. Gelbspan, "A Global Warning," p. 37

28. Paul Betts, "Rising tide of defiance," *Financial Times*, 30 January 1999, sec. 2, p. 1.

29. Estimates of the size of a carbon tax needed to achieve a 20 percent reduction below 1990 levels average around $170 per metric ton of carbon. A 1997 federal study found that a tax of $100 per metric ton works out to twenty-six cents per gallon of gas and two cents per kilowatt-hour. See DeCanio, *Economics of Climate Change*, pp. 17–8.

30. Ibid., p. 23.

31. Margaret Kriz, "Different Ways to Measure Pollution," *National Journal*, 15 November 1997, p. 2,293.

32. "Big Biz slates PR blitz to kill global warming treaty," *O'Dwyer's PR Services Report*, February 1998, p. 1.

33. John H. Cushman Jr., "Why the U.S. Fell Short of Ambitious Goals for Reducing Greenhouse Gases," *New York Times*, 20 October 1997, sec. A, p. 15.

34. John H. Cushman Jr., "U.S. Says Its Greenhouse Gas Emissions Are at Highest Rate in Years," *New York Times*, 21 October 1997, sec. A, p. 22.

35. Eric Schmitt, "Congress, the Kibbitzer at the Climate Table, Waits for Its Turn," *New York Times,* 1 December 1997, sec. F, p. 6.

36. Marx and Engels, *Collected Works,* 1:153.

CHAPTER 10

1. Bureau of the Census, *Statistical Abstract of the United States: 1997,* 117th ed. (Washington, D.C., 1997), p. 725.

2. Sam Howe Verhovek, "Fighting Sprawl, Oregon County Makes Deal With Intel to Limit Job Growth," *New York Times,* 9 June 1999, sec. A, p. 18.

3. J. Kemeny, *The Myth of Home-Ownership: Private Versus Public Choices in Housing Tenure* (London: Routledge and Kegan Paul, 1981), p. 11.

4. Newt Gingrich, *To Renew America* (New York: HarperCollins, 1995), pp. 55–6.

5. Scott McCartney, "Communities, Fearful of Importing Crime, Bar Routine Businesses," *Wall Street Journal,* 15 March 1994, sec. A, p. 1.

6. Interview with author, Ithaca, N.Y., 11 May 1999.

7. Joseph Gerth, "Amazon.com puts town back to work," *Detroit News,* 15 February 2000, sec. A, p. 1.

8. Glenn Collins, "Selling Online, Delivering on Bikes," *New York Times,* 24 December 1999, sec. B, p. 1.

9. Anthony Violanti, "Life in Sprawl Land," *Buffalo News,* 2 July 2000, sec. M, p. 6.

10. Haya El Nasser, "Development bursting seams of sprawl laws," *USA Today,* 11 July 2000, sec. A, p. 3.

11. Jodie T. Allen, "Sprawl, from here to eternity," *U.S. News and World Report,* 6 September 1999, p. 22.

12. "Campaign Briefing," *New York Times,* 22 April 2000, sec. A, p. 9.

13. Robin Toner, "Reissue of Gore Book May Be a Two-Edged Sword," *New York Times,* 14 April 2000, sec. A, p. 26.

14. Frank Bruni, "Bush Suggests Gore Supports Higher Gas Prices," *New York Times,* 24 June 2000, sec. A, p. 10.

15. Ceci Connolly, "Gas Prices, Surplus Fuel, a Gore Proposal," *Washington Post,* 28 June 2000, sec. A, p. 7.

16. Bonnie Harris, "Gore Offers $25 Billion for Energy Efficient Transit," *Los Angeles Times,* 30 June 2000, sec. A, part 1, p. 23.

17. Rossiter, ed., *Federalist Papers,* p. 84.

18. McShane, *Down the Asphalt Path,* p. 14.

19. Boris S. Pushkarev and Jeffrey M. Zupan, *Public Transportation and Land Use Policy* (Bloomington: Univ. of Indiana Press, 1977), p. 5.

20. U.S. Department of Transportation, *Transportation in the United States: A Review* (Washington, D.C.: 1987), p. 5.

21. Jean-Pierre Bardou, Jean-Jacques Chanaron, Patrick Fridenson, and James M. Laux, *The Automobile Revolution: The Impact of an Industry* (Chapel Hill: Univ. of North Carolina Press, 1982), p. 208.

22. U.S. Environmental Protection Agency, *Brochure on National Air Quality: Statistics and Trends*. Available @ www.epa.gov.

23. Donald M. Rote, "Comparison of High-Speed Rail and Maglev System Costs," Argonne National Laboratory, p. 4 (undated).

24. Hiroyuki Ohsaki, "Linear Drive Systems for Urban Transportation in Japan," Department of Electrical Engineering, University of Tokyo, p. 3 (undated).

25. Francis C. Moon, *Superconducting Levitation: Applications to Bearings and Magnetic Transportation* (New York: John Wiley, 1994), p. 253.

26. Rote, "Comparison of High-Speed Rail and Maglev System Costs," p. 4.

27. Moon, *Superconducting Levitation*, p. 235.

28. Paula Purpura, "High Speed Train Planning Gets New Grant," *(New Orleans) Times-Picayune*, 5 March 2000, sec. A, p. 26; Gita M. Smith, "Floating train gains momentum," *Atlanta Constitution*, 17 October 1999, sec. H, p. 2; Alan Sipress, "High-Speed Rail Makes Stride," *Washington Post*, 22 May 1999, sec. B, p. 2.

29. See Stephen A. Marglin and Juliet B. Schor, eds., *The Golden Age of Capitalism: Reinterpreting the Postwar Experience* (Oxford: Clarendon Press, 1990).

30. Fogelson, *America's Armories*, p. 21.

31. Georg Lukacs, *History and Class Consciousness: Studies in Marxist Dialectics* (Cambridge: MIT Press, 1971), p. 69.

32. The literature on the eighteenth-century Country opposition is by now enormous. See, for example, Bernard Bailyn, *The Ideological Origins of the American Revolution* (Cambridge, Mass.: Harvard Univ. Press, 1967); J. G. A. Pocock, *The Machiavellian Moment: Florentine Political Thought and the American Republican Tradition* (Princeton: Princeton Univ. Press, 1975); Isaac Kramnick, *Bolingbroke and His Circle: The Politics of Nostalgia in the Age of Walpole* (Cambridge, Mass.: Harvard Univ. Press, 1968); John Brewer, *The Sinews of Power: War, Money, and the English State, 1688–1783* (Boston: Unwin Hyman, 1989); and J. G. A. Pocock, ed., *Three British Revolutions, 1641, 1688, 1776* (Princeton: Princeton Univ. Press, 1980).

33. Morison, *Oxford History of the American People*, pp. 212–3.

BIBLIOGRAPHY

FOLLOWING IS A LIST OF THE BOOKS AND MAJOR
ARTICLES USED IN THE PREPARATION OF THIS STUDY:

Abu-Lughod, Janet L. *Before European Hegemony: The World System A.D. 1250–1350*.
New York: Oxford Univ. Press, 1989.

Adams, Brooks. *The Theory of Social Revolutions*. New York: Macmillan, 1913.

———. *The Law of Civilization and Decay*. New York: Macmillan, 1895.

Adams, Henry. *History of the United States During the Administrations of James
Madison*. New York: Library of America, 1986.

———. *History of the United States During the Administrations of Thomas Jefferson*.
New York: Library of America, 1986.

———. *The Education of Henry Adams*. Boston: Houghton Mifflin, 1973.

Adams, James Truslow. *Provincial Society 1690–1763*. New York: Macmillan, 1927.

Addams, Jane. *The Spirit of Youth and the City Streets*. New York: Macmillan, 1910.

Aglietta, Michel. *A Theory of Capitalist Regulation: The U.S. Experience*. London:
New Left Books, 1979.

Ambrose, Stephen E. *Eisenhower*. 2 vols. New York: Simon and Schuster, 1983–84.

Angotti, Thomas. "The Latin American Metropolis and the Growth of Inequality."
NACLA Report on the Americas 28, no. 4 (January–February 1995).

Appleby, Joyce. *Liberalism and Republicanism in the Historical Imagination*.
Cambridge, Mass.: Harvard Univ. Press, 1992.

Arnold, Joseph L. *The New Deal in the Suburbs: A History of the Greenbelt Town
Program, 1935–1954*. Columbus: Ohio State Univ. Press, 1971.

Bailyn, Bernard. *The Ideological Origins of the American Revolution*. Cambridge,
Mass.: Harvard Univ. Press, 1967.

Bairoch, Paul. *Cities and Economic Development: From the Dawn of History to the Present.* Chicago: Univ. of Chicago Press, 1988.

Baldwin, Leland D. *The Stream of American History.* 2 vols. New York: American Book Co., 1957.

Bardou, Jean-Pierre, Jean-Jacques Chanaron, Patrick Fridenson, and James M. Laux. *The Automobile Revolution: The Impact of an Industry.* Chapel Hill: Univ. of North Carolina Press, 1982.

Barrett, Paul. *The Automobile and Urban Mass Transit: The Formation of Public Policy in Chicago, 1900–1930.* Philadelphia: Temple Univ. Press, 1983.

Baxandall, Rosalyn, and Elizabeth Ewen. *Picture Windows: How the Suburbs Happened.* New York: Basic Books, 2000.

Boyer, M. Christine. *Dreaming the Rational City: The Myth of American City Planning.* Cambridge, Mass.: MIT Press, 1983.

Boyer, Paul. *Urban Masses and Moral Order in America, 1820–1920.* Cambridge, Mass.: Harvard Univ. Press, 1978.

Boyer, Robert. *The Regulation School: A Critical Interpretation.* New York: Columbia Univ. Press, 1990.

Brands, H. W. *The Reckless Decade: America in the 1890s.* New York: St. Martin's, 1995.

Brewer, John. *The Sinews of Power: War, Money, and the English State, 1688–1783.* Boston: Unwin Hyman, 1989.

Bridenbaugh, Carl. *Cities in the Wilderness: The First Century of Urban Life in America, 1625–1742.* New York: Knopf, 1960.

Brody, David. *Workers in Industrial America: Essays on the Twentieth Century Struggle.* New York: Oxford Univ. Press, 1980.

Brooks, Michael W. *Subway City: Riding the Trains, Reading New York.* New Brunswick, N.J.: Rutgers Univ. Press, 1997.

Buder, Stanley. *Pullman: An Experiment in Industrial Order and Community Planning, 1880–1930.* New York: Oxford Univ. Press, 1967.

Burke, Edmund. *Reflections on the Revolution in France.* London: Penguin, 1986.

Cashman, Sean Dennis. *America in the Age of the Titans: The Progressives and World War I.* New York: New York Univ. Press, 1988.

Castells, Manuel. *The Urban Question: A Marxist Approach.* Cambridge, Mass.: MIT Press, 1977.

Center for Voting and Democracy. *Dubious Democracy 1998.* Takoma Park, Md.: Center for Voting and Democracy, 1999.

Chevigny, Paul. *Edge of the Knife: Police Violence in the Americas.* New York: New Press, 1995.

Cohn, Steven Mark. *Too Cheap to Meter: An Economic and Philosophical Analysis of the Nuclear Dream.* Albany, N.Y.: SUNY Press, 1997.

Cole, Arthur Charles. *The Irrepressible Conflict, 1850–1865.* New York: Macmillan, 1934.

Coleman, McAlister. *Eugene V. Debs: A Man Unafraid.* New York: Greenberg, 1930.

Coletta, Paolo E. *William Jennings Bryan.* 2 vols. Lincoln: Univ. of Nebraska Press, 1964.

Collier, Peter, and David Horowitz. *The Fords: An American Epic.* New York: Summit Books, 1987.

Commager, Henry Steele, ed. *Documents of American History.* 8th ed. New York: Appleton-Century-Crofts, 1968.

Cooley, Charles H. "The Theory of Transportation." *Publications of the American Economic Association* 9 (1894).

Cranmer, H. Jerome. *New Jersey in the Automobile Age: A History of Transportation.* Princeton: Van Nostrand, 1964.

Croly, Herbert. *The Promise of American Life.* New York: Macmillan, 1909.

Davies, Richard O. *The Age of Asphalt: The Automobile, the Freeway, and the Condition of Metropolitan America.* Philadelphia: J. P. Lippincott, 1975.

Davis, Mike. *Prisoners of the American Dream: Politics and Economy in the History of the U.S. Working Class.* London: Verso, 1986.

DeCanio, Stephen J. *The Economics of Climate Change.* San Francisco: Redefining Progress, 1997.

Delucchi, Mark A. "Total Coat of Motor-Vehicle Use." *Access* 8 (spring 1996).

Dinnerstein, Leonard, ed. *Antisemitism in the United States.* New York: Holt, Rinehart and Winston, 1971.

Donaldson, Scott. *The Suburban Myth.* New York: Columbia Univ. Press, 1969.

Donnelly, Ignatius. *Caesar's Column: A Story of the Twentieth Century.* Cambridge, Mass.: Belknap Press, 1960.

Dowd, Douglas. *The Waste of Nations: Dysfunction in the World Economy.* Boulder, Colo.: Westview Press, 1989.

Dreier, Peter, and John Atlas. "Deductio Ad Absurdum." *Washington (D.C.) Monthly,* February 1990.

Dubofsky, Melvyn. *Industrialism and the American Worker, 1865–1920.* 2nd ed. Arlington Heights, Ill.: Harlan Davidson, 1985.

Durning, Alan Thein. *How Much Is Enough: The Consumer Society and the Future of the Earth.* New York: Norton, 1992.

Faulkner, Harold Underwood. *The Quest for Social Justice, 1898–1914.* New York: Macmillan, 1931

Feller, Daniel. *The Jacksonian Promise: America, 1815–1840*. Baltimore: Johns Hopkins Univ. Press, 1995.

Fink, Leon, ed. *Major Problems in the Gilded Age and the Progressive Era*. Lexington, Mass.: D. C. Heath, 1993.

Fischer, David Hackett. *Albion's Seed: Four British Folkways in America*. Oxford: Oxford Univ. Press, 1989.

Fisher, Sidney George. *The Trial of the Constitution*. New York: Negro Univ. Press, 1969.

Fite, Gilbert C., and Jim E. Reese. *An Economic History of the United States*. Boston: Houghton Mifflin, 1973.

Flink, James J. *The Car Culture*. Cambridge, Mass.: MIT Press, 1975.

Fogelson, Robert M. *America's Armories: Architecture, Society, and Public Order*. Cambridge, Mass.: Harvard Univ. Press, 1989.

Ford, Henry. *My Life and Work*. Garden City, N.Y.: Doubleday, Page, 1926.

———. *365 of Henry Ford's Sayings*. Grymes Hill, N.Y.: P. M. Martin, 1923.

Ford, Paul Leicester, ed. *The Works of Thomas Jefferson*. 12 vols. New York: Putnam, 1904.

Formisano, Ronald P., and Constance K. Burns, eds. *Boston 1700–1800: The Evolution of Urban Politics*. Westport, Conn.: Greenwood Press, 1984.

Foster, Mark S. *From Streetcar to Superhighway: American City Planners and Urban Transportation, 1900–1940*. Philadelphia: Temple Univ. Press, 1981.

Foucault, Michel. *Discipline and Punish: The Birth of the Prison*. New York: Random House, 1979.

Fox, Richard Wightman, and T. J. Jackson Lears, eds. *The Culture of Consumption: Critical Essays in American History, 1880–1980*. New York: Pantheon, 1983.

Fried, Lewis F. *Makers of the City*. Amherst: Univ. of Massachusetts Press, 1990.

Friedman, Milton, and Anna Jacobson Schwartz. *A Monetary History of the United States, 1867–1960*. Princeton: Princeton Univ. Press, 1963.

Fuller, Graham E., and Ian D. Lesser. "Persian Gulf Myths." *Foreign Affairs* 76, no. 3 (May–June 1997).

Fusfeld, Daniel R. *The Economic Thought of Franklin D. Roosevelt and the Origins of the New Deal*. New York: Columbia Univ. Press, 1956.

Gaither, Gerald H. *Blacks and the Populist Revolt: Ballots and Bigotry in the 'New South.'* University, Ala.: Univ. of Alabama Press, 1977.

Galbraith, John Kenneth. *The Affluent Society*. Boston: Houghton Mifflin, 1984.

———. *The Affluent Society*. Boston: Houghton Mifflin, 1958.

Galeano, Eduardo. "Autocracy: An Invisible Dictatorship." *NACLA Report on the Americas* 28, no. 4 (January–February 1995).

Gelbspan, Ross. "A Global Warning." *The American Prospect*, March–April 1997.

Gilje, Paul A. *The Road to Mobocracy: Popular Disorder in New York City, 1763–1834.* Chapel Hill: Univ. of N. Carolina Press, 1987.

Gingrich, Newt. *To Renew America*. New York: HarperCollins, 1995.

Ginneken, Jaap van. *Crowds, Psychology, and Politics, 1871–1899.* Cambridge: Cambridge Univ. Press, 1992.

Goddard, Stephen B. *Getting There: The Epic Struggle Between Road and Rail in the American Century*. New York: Basic Books, 1994.

Gold, Michael. *Jews Without Money*. New York: Carroll and Graf, 1930.

Goldfield, Michael. *The Color of Politics: Race and the Mainsprings of American Politics*. New York: New Press, 1997.

Goldstein, Robert Justin. *Political Rights in Modern America: From 1870 to the Present*. Boston: G. K. Hall, 1976.

Goodwyn, Lawrence. *Democratic Promise: The Populist Moment in America*. New York: Oxford Univ. Press, 1976.

Gore, Al. *Earth in the Balance: Ecology and the Human Spirit*. Boston: Houghton Mifflin, 1992.

Greene, David L., and Danilo J. Santini. *Transportation and Global Climate Change*. Washington, D.C.: American Council for an Energy-Efficient Economy, 1993.

Gross, David. "Space, Time, and Modern Culture." *Telos* 50 (winter 1981–2).

Guilbaut, Serge. *How New York Stole the Idea of Modern Art: Abstract Expressionism, Freedom, and the Cold War*. Chicago: Univ. of Chicago Press, 1983.

Habermas, Jurgen. *Legitimation Crisis*. Boston: Beacon Press, 1975.

Hacker, Louis M. *The Triumph of Capitalism in America*. New York: Simon and Schuster, 1940.

——— and Helene Zahler. *The United States in the Twentieth Century*. New York: Appleton-Century, 1952.

Harrington, Michael. *Socialism*. New York: Saturday Review Press, 1972.

Harvey, David. *Consciousness and the Urban Experience: Studies in the History and Theory of Capitalist Urbanization*. Baltimore: Johns Hopkins Univ. Press, 1985.

Hays, Samuel P. *The Response to Industrialism 1885–1914*. Chicago: Univ. of Chicago Press, 1995.

Heilbroner, Robert L., and Aaron Singer. *The Economic Transformation of America: 1600 to the Present*. San Diego: Harcourt Brace Jovanovich, 1984.

Henwood, Doug. "Producing Poverty." *Left Business Observer* 89 (27 April 1999).

———. *Wall Street: How it Works and for Whom*. London: Verso, 1997.

Hill, Christopher. *The Century of Revolution, 1603–1714.* New York: W. W. Norton, 1966.

———. *The English Bible and the Seventeenth-Century Revolution.* London: Penguin Books, 1994.

Hine, Thomas. *Populuxe.* New York: Knopf, 1986.

Hitler, Adolf. *Mein Kampf.* Boston: Houghton Mifflin, 1971.

Hobsbawm, E. J. *The Age of Revolution, 1789–1848.* New York: New American Library, 1962.

Hofstadter, Richard. *The American Political Tradition—And the Men Who Made It.* New York: Knopf, 1948.

———. *The Paranoid Style in American Politics, and Other Essays.* New York: Knopf, 1965.

Holbo, Christine. "Eugenic America: Hygiene, Habitation and Americanization, 1880–1920." *Stanford Humanities Review* 5 (1996).

Holtzclaw, John. "America's Autos on Welfare: A Summary of Studies." *Transportopia Bulletin* (winter 1993).

Hook, Walter, and Matteo Martignoni. "The Cycle Rickshaw can save the Taj Mahal; the Taj Mahal can save the Cycle Rickshaw." *Sustainable Transport* 7 (winter 1997).

Hoover, Herbert. *American Individualism.* Garden City, N.Y.: Doubleday, Page, 1922.

Howard, Christopher. *The Hidden Welfare State: Tax Expenditure and Social Policy in the United States.* Princeton: Princeton Univ. Press, 1997.

Howe, Irving. *World of Our Fathers.* New York: Harcourt Brace Jovanovich, 1976.

Huthmacher, J. Joseph, and Warren I. Susman. *Herbert Hoover and the Crisis of American Capitalism.* Cambridge, Mass.: Schenkman Publishing, 1973.

Illick, Joseph E. *Colonial Pennsylvania: A History.* New York: Scribner's, 1976.

Ionescu, Ghita, and Ernest Gellner, eds. *Populism: Its Meaning and National Characteristics.* London: Weidenfeld and Nicolson, 1969.

Jackson, Kenneth T. *Crabgrass Frontier: The Suburbanization of the United States.* New York: Oxford Univ. Press, 1985.

Jacobs, Jane. *The Death and Life of Great American Cities.* New York: Random House, 1961.

Jensen, Richard. *The Winning of the Midwest: Social and Political Conflict, 1888–1896.* Chicago: Univ. of Chicago Press, 1971.

Jung, C. J. *Civilization in Transition.* 2nd ed. Princeton: Princeton Univ. Press, 1970.

Katz, Bruce, ed. *Reflections on Regionalism.* Washington, D.C.: Brookings Institution Press, 2000.

Kay, Jane Holtz. *Lost Boston*. Boston: Houghton Mifflin, 1980.

Kazin, Michael. *The Populist Persuasion: An American History*. New York: HarperCollins, 1995.

Kelly, Barbara M., ed. *Suburbia Re-examined*. New York: Greenwood Press, 1989.

Kemeny, J. *The Myth of Home-Ownership: Private Versus Public Choices in Housing Tenure*. London: Routledge and Kegan Paul, 1981.

Kolko, Gabriel. *Main Currents in Modern American History*. New York: Harper and Row, 1976.

———. *The Triumph of Conservatism: A Reinterpretation of American History, 1900–1916*. New York: Free Press, 1963.

Komanoff, Charles. "Doing Without Nuclear Power." *New York Review of Books,* 17 May 1979.

Kramnick, Isaac. *Bolingbroke and His Circle: The Politics of Nostalgia in the Age of Walpole*. Cambridge, Mass.: Harvard Univ. Press, 1968.

———. *Republicanism and Bourgeois Radicalism: Political Ideology in Late Eighteenth-Century England and America*. Ithaca, N.Y.: Cornell Univ. Press, 1990.

Krugman, Paul. "The Myth of Asia's Miracle." *Foreign Affairs,* November 1994, pp. 70–1.

Kuttner, Robert. *Revolt of the Haves: Tax Rebellions and Hard Times*. New York: Simon and Schuster, 1980.

Lacey, Robert. *Ford, the Man and the Machine*. Boston: Little, Brown, 1986.

Lasch, Christopher. *The Culture of Narcissism: American Life in the Age of Diminishing Expectations*. New York: Norton, 1978.

Lears, T. J. Jackson. *No Place of Grace: Antimodernism and the Transformation of American Culture, 1880–1920*. New York: Pantheon, 1981.

Leavitt, Helen. *Superhighway-Superhoax*. Garden City, N.Y.: Doubleday, 1970.

Lebergott, Stanley. *The Americans: An Economic Record*. New York: W. W. Norton, 1984.

Le Bon, Gustave. *The Crowd: A Study of the Popular Mind*. New York: Viking, 1960.

Lee, Samjin. "Fighting for the 'Seoul' of Transport in Korea." *Sustainable Transport 7* (winter 1997).

Lenin, V. I. *Imperialism: The Highest Stage of Capitalism*. New York: International, 1939.

Leonard, Jonathan Norman. *The Tragedy of Henry Ford*. New York: G. P. Putnam's Sons, 1932.

Lewis, David L., and Laurence Goldstein, eds. *The Automobile and American Culture*. Ann Arbor: Univ. of Michigan Press, 1983.

Lippmann, Walter. *A Preface to Politics.* New York: Mitchell Kennerley, 1914.

———. *Public Opinion.* New York: Macmillan, 1961.

Livingston, James. *Pragmatism and the Political Economy of Cultural Revolution, 1850–1940.* Chapel Hill: Univ. of North Carolina Press, 1994.

Lloyd, Brian. *Left Out: Pragmatism, Exceptionalism, and the Poverty of American Marxism, 1890–1922.* Baltimore: Johns Hopkins Univ. Press, 1997.

Lubove, Roy. *The Progressives and the Slums: Tenement House Reform in New York City, 1890–1917.* Pittsburgh: Univ. of Pittsburgh Press, 1962.

Lukacs, Georg. *History and Class Consciousness: Studies in Marxist Dialectics.* Cambridge: MIT Press, 1971.

Mann, Michael. *The Sources of Social Power.* 2 vols. Cambridge: Cambridge Univ. Press, 1986–93.

Marglin, Stephen A., and Juliet B. Schor, eds. *The Golden Age of Capitalism: Reinterpreting the Postwar Experience.* Oxford: Clarendon Press, 1990.

Markusen, Ann R. "Class and Urban Social Experience." *Kapitalstate* 4–5 (summer 1976).

Marsh, Benjamin C. *Lobbyist for the People: A Record of Fifty Years.* Washington, D.C.: Public Affairs Press, 1953.

Marx, Karl, and Frederick Engels, *Collected Works.* 47 vols. London: Lawrence and Wishart, 1975.

———. *Selected Correspondence.* Moscow: Foreign Language Publishing House, 1953.

Mayer, Arno J. *The Persistence of the Old Regime: Europe to the Great War.* New York: Pantheon, 1981.

McMath, Robert C. *American Populism: A Social History, 1877–1898.* New York: Hill and Wang, 1993.

McPherson, James M. *The Battle Cry of Freedom: The Civil War Era.* New York: Oxford Univ. Press, 1988.

McShane, Clay. *Down the Asphalt Path: The Automobile and the American City.* New York: Columbia Univ. Press, 1994.

Meinig, D. W. *The Shaping of America: A Geographical Perspective on 500 Years of History.* 2 vols. New Haven: Yale Univ. Press, 1986.

Menand, Louis. "Inside the Billway," *New York Review of Books,* 14 August 1997.

Miles, Gen. Nelson A. "The Lesson of the Recent Strikes," *North American Review* 453 (August 1894).

Miller, Donald L. *Lewis Mumford: A Life.* New York: Weidenfeld and Nicolson, 1989.

Mohl, Raymond A., ed. *The Making of Urban America.* Wilmington, Del.: Scholarly Resources, 1988.

Moon, Francis C. *Superconducting Levitation: Applications to Bearings and Magnetic Transportation.* New York: John Wiley, 1994.

Moore, Barrington Jr. *Social Origins of Dictatorship and Democracy: Lord and Peasant in the Making of the Modern World.* Boston: Beacon Press, 1966.

Morgan, Edmund S. *The Puritan Family: Religion and Domestic Relations in Seventeenth-Century New England.* Westport, Conn.: Greenwood Press, 1980.

Morison, Samuel Eliot. *The Oxford History of the American People.* New York: New American Library, 1972.

Mouffe, Chantal. "The End of Politics and the Rise of the Radical Right," *Dissent* (fall 1995).

Mowry, George E. *The California Progressives.* Berkeley: Univ. of California Press, 1951.

Mumford, Lewis. *The City in History: Its Origins, Its Transformations, and Its Prospects.* New York: Harcourt, Brace and World, 1961.

———. *The Culture of Cities.* New York: Harcourt Brace, 1938.

———. *The Highway and the City.* New York: Harcourt Brace, 1963.

———. "The Intolerable City: Must it Keep on Growing?" *Harper's,* February 1926.

———. "The Skyline: Mother Jacobs' Home Remedies," *New Yorker,* 1 December 1962.

Murray, Charles. *Losing Ground: American Social Policy, 1950–1980.* New York: Basic Books, 1984.

Murray, Christopher J. L. and Alan D. Lopez. *The Global Burden of Disease.* 2 vols. Cambridge, Mass: Harvard Univ. Press, 1996.

Nasaw, David. *Children of the City: At Work and At Play.* Garden City, N.Y.: Anchor/Doubleday, 1985.

Nash, Gary B. *The Urban Crucible: Social Change, Political Consciousness, and the Crisis of the American Revolution.* Cambridge, Mass.: Harvard Univ. Press, 1979.

Nelson, Walter Henry. *Small Wonder: The Amazing Story of the Volkswagen.* Boston: Little, Brown, 1965.

Nevins, Allan. *Ford: The Times, the Man, the Company.* New York: Scribner's, 1954.

———. *The Emergence of Modern America, 1865–1878.* New York: Macmillan, 1927.

Newman, Peter W. G., and Jeffrey R. Kenworthy. *Cities and Automobile Dependence: A Sourcebook.* Brookfield, Vt.: Gower Technical, 1989.

Nishiyama, Chiaka, and Kurt R. Leube, eds. *The Essential Hayek.* Stanford: Hoover Institution Press, 1984.

Nolen, John. *New Ideals in the Planning of Cities, Towns, and Villages* (New York: American City Bureau, 1919), p. 88.

———. *Twenty Years of City Planning Progress in the United States.* National Conference on City Planning, 1927.

Nugent, Walter T. K. *The Tolerant Populists: Kansas Populism and the Nation.* Chicago: Univ. of Chicago Press, 1963.

O'Connor, James. *Accumulation Crisis.* London: Basic Blackwell, 1984.

———. *The Fiscal Crisis of the State.* New York: St. Martin's, 1973.

O'Donnell, Patrick. "Industrial Capitalism and the Rise of the Modern American Cities." *Kapitalistate* 6 (fall 1977).

Ohsaki, Hiroyuki. "Linear Drive Systems for Urban Transportation in Japan." Department of Electrical Engineering, University of Tokyo (undated).

Olney, Martha L. *Buy Now, Pay Later: Advertising, Credit, and Consumer Durables in the 1920s.* Chapel Hill: Univ. of North Carolina Press, 1991.

Overy, R. J. "Cars, Roads, and Economic Recovery in Germany, 1932–8." *Economic History Review* 28, no. 3 (August 1975).

———. *The Nazi Economic Recovery 1932–1938.* 2nd ed. Cambridge: Cambridge Univ. Press, 1996.

Palmer, R. R. *The Age of Democratic Revolution: A Political History of Europe and America, 1760–1800,* 2 vols. Princeton: Princeton Univ. Press, 1959–64.

Patterson, James T. *Grand Expectations: The United States, 1945–1974.* New York: Oxford Univ. Press, 1996.

Peterson, Merrill D. *The Jefferson Image in the American Mind.* New York: Oxford Univ. Press, 1962.

Phillips, Kevin. *Boiling Point: Republicans, Democrats, and the Decline of Middle-Class Prosperity.* New York: Random House, 1993.

Phillips-Fein, Kim. "You're Either On the Bus. . . ." *Baffler* 10 (1997).

Pigou, A. C. *The Economics of Welfare.* London: Macmillan, 1924.

———. *Socialism versus Capitalism.* London: Macmillan, 1964.

Pocock, J. G. A. *The Machiavellian Moment: Florentine Political Thought and the American Republican Tradition.* Princeton: Princeton Univ. Press, 1975.

———, ed. *Three British Revolutions, 1641, 1688, 1776.* Princeton: Princeton Univ. Press, 1980.

Polanyi, Karl. *The Great Transformation.* Boston: Beacon Press, 1957.

Polenberg, Richard. *One Nation Divisible: Class, Race, and Ethnicity in the United States Since 1938.* New York: Viking, 1980.

Pollard, W. L. "Outline of the Law of Zoning in the United States." *The Annals of the American Academy of Political and Social Science* 155, no. 2 (May 1931).

Pushkarev, Boris S., and Jeffrey M. Zupan. *Public Transportation and Land Use Policy.* Bloomington: Univ. of Indiana Press, 1977.

Radford, Gail. *Modern Housing for America: Policy Struggles in the New Deal Era.* Chicago: Univ. of Chicago Press, 1996.

Randall, Willard Sterne. *Thomas Jefferson: A Life*. New York: Henry Holt, 1993.

Reich, Robert B. *Opposing the System*. New York: Crown, 1995.

———. *The Work of Nations: Preparing Ourselves for Twenty-first Century Capitalism*. New York: Random House, 1992.

Rennings, K., O. Hohmeyer and R. L. Ottinger, eds. *Social Costs and Sustainable Mobility: Strategies and Experience in Europe and the United States*. Mannheim, Germany: Center for European Economic Research, 2000.

Report of the National Advisory Commission on Civil Disorders. Washington, D.C.: U.S. Govt. Printing Office, 1968.

Riis, Jacob. *How the Other Half Lives: Studies Among the Tenements of New York*. New York: Sagamore Press, 1957.

———. *The Battle With the Slum*. New York: Macmillan, 1902.

Ross, Kristin. *Fast Cars, Clean Bodies: Decolonization and the Reordering of French Culture*. Cambridge, Mass.: MIT Press, 1995.

Rossiter, Clinton. *Alexander Hamilton and the Constitution*. New York: Harcourt Brace and World, 1964.

———, ed. *The Federalist Papers*. New York: New American Library, 1961.

Rote, Donald M. "Comparison of High-Speed Rail and Maglev Systems Costs." Argonne National Laboratory (undated).

Rutman, Darrett B. *Winthrop's Boston: Portrait of a Puritan Town, 1630–1649*. Chapel Hill: Univ. of North Carolina Press, 1965.

Rybczynski, Witold. *City Life: Urban Expectations in a New World*. New York: Scribner's, 1995.

Sachar, Howard M. *A History of Jews in America*. New York: Knopf, 1992.

Schachner, Nathan. *Thomas Jefferson: A Biography*. New York: Appleton-Century-Crofts, 1951.

Schlesinger, Arthur Meier. *The Rise of the City, 1878–1898*. New York: Macmillan, 1933.

Schlesinger, Arthur M. Jr. *The Age of Jackson*. Boston: Little Brown, 1945.

Schor, Juliet B. *The Overworked American: The Unexpected Decline of Leisure*. New York: Basic Books, 1991.

Schrag, Peter. *Paradise Lost: California's Experience, America's Future*. New York: New Press, 1998.

Seaburg, Carl. *Boston Observed*. Boston: Beacon Press, 1971.

Sellers, Charles. *The Market Revolution: Jacksonian America, 1815–1846*. New York: Oxford Univ. Press, 1991.

Sennett, Richard, ed. *Classic Essays on the Culture of Cities*. Englewood Cliffs, N.J.: Prentice-Hall, 1969.

Siegel, Fred. *The Future Once Happened Here: New York, D.C., L.A., and the Fate of America's Big Cities.* New York: Free Press, 1997.

Smith, Carl. *Urban Disorder and the Shape of Belief: The Great Chicago Fire, the Haymarket Bomb, and the Model Town of Pullman.* Chicago: Univ. of Chicago, 1995.

Smith, Richard. "Creative Destruction." *New Left Review* 222 (March/April 1997).

Sombart, Werner. *Why Is There No Socialism in the United States?* London: Macmillan, 1976.

Sorkin, Michael, ed. *Variations on a Theme Park: The New American City and the End of Public Space.* New York: Hill and Wang, 1992.

Strong, Josiah. *Our Country: Its Possible Future and Its Present Crisis.* New York: American Home Missionary Society, 1885.

Syrett, Harold C., ed. *American Historical Documents.* New York: Barnes and Noble, 1960.

———, ed. *The Papers of Alexander Hamilton.* 27 vols. New York: Columbia Univ. Press, 1961–87.

Tarbell, Ida M. *The Nationalizing of Business, 1878–1898.* New York: Macmillan, 1936.

Tarkington, Booth. *The Magnificent Ambersons.* New York: Scribner's, 1921.

Taylor, Graham Romeyn. *Satellite Cities: A Study of Industrial Suburbs.* New York: D. Appleton, 1915.

Thelen, David P. *Robert M. La Follette and the Insurgent Spirit.* Madison: Univ. of Wisconsin Press, 1985.

Thorns, David C. *Suburbia.* London: MacGibbon and Kee, 1972.

Tobey, Ronald, Charles Wetherell, and Jay Brigham. "Moving Out and Settling In." *American Historical Review* 95 (December 1990).

Tocqueville, Alexis de. *Democracy in America.* 2 vols. New York: Random House, 1990.

Toll, Seymour I. *Zoned America.* New York: Grossman, 1969.

Trollope, Frances. *Domestic Manners of the Americans.* London: Penguin Classic, 1997.

Tuchman, Barbara. *A Distant Mirror: The Calamitous Fourteenth Century.* New York: Ballantine Books, 1978.

Turner, Frederick Jackson. *The Frontier in American History.* New York: Henry Holt, 1920.

Ullmann, John E., ed. *The Suburban Economic Network: Economic Activity, Resource Use, and the Great Sprawl.* New York: Praeger, 1977.

Vaughan, Alden T., ed. *The Puritan Tradition in America, 1620–1730.* Columbia, S.C.: Univ. of South Carolina Press, 1972.

Walker, Richard Averill. "The Suburban Solution: Urban Geography and Urban Reform in the Capitalist Development of the United States." Ph.D. thesis, Baltimore: Johns Hopkins Univ., 1977.

Weber, Adna Ferris. *The Growth of Cities in the Nineteenth Century.* Ithaca: Cornell Univ. Press, 1962.

Weber, Max. *The City.* New York: Free Press, 1958.

Wecter, Dixon. *The Age of the Great Depression, 1929–1941.* New York: Macmillan, 1948.

Weyl, Walter E. *The New Democracy: An Essay on Certain Political and Economic Tendencies in the United States.* New York: Macmillan, 1913.

Whitnall, Gordon. "History of Zoning." *The Annals of the American Academy of Political and Social Science* 155, no. 2 (May 1931).

Wiebe, Robert H. *Self-Rule: A Cultural History of American Democracy.* Chicago: Univ. of Chicago Press, 1995.

Wik, Reynold M. *Henry Ford and Grass-Roots America.* Ann Arbor: Univ. of Michigan Press, 1972.

Wolman, William, and Anne Colamosca. *The Judas Economy: The Triumph of Capital and the Betrayal of Work.* Reading, Mass.: Addison-Wesley, 1997.

Wreszin, Michael. "Arthur Schlesinger, Jr., Scholar-Activist in Cold War America: 1946–1956," *Salmagundi* 63–4 (spring-summer 1984).

Yago, Glenn. *The Decline of Transit: Urban Transportation in German and U.S. Cities, 1900–1970.* Cambridge: Cambridge Univ. Press, 1984.

Ziff, Larzer. *Puritanism in America: New Culture in a New World.* New York: Viking, 1973.

Zuckerman, Michael. *Almost Chosen People: Oblique Biographies in the American Grain.* Berkeley: Univ. of Calif. Press, 1993.

Zuckerman, Wolfgang. *End of the Road: The World Car Crisis and How We Can Solve It.* Cambridge: Lutterworth, 1991.

INDEX